CISTERCIAN IDEALS

AND REALITY

edited by JOHN R. SOMMERFELDT

§

CISTERCIAN PUBLICATIONS
Kalamazoo, Michigan
1978

ISBN 0-87907-860-X

Available in the Commonwealth and Europe
through A. R. Mowbray & Co. Ltd.
St Thomas House, Becket Street, Oxford OX1 1SJ

Library of Congress Cataloging in Publication Data
Main entry under title:

Cistercian ideals and reality.

(Cistercian studies series ; 60)
1. Cistercians—History—Addresses, essays, lectures.
I. Sommerfeldt, John R.   II.   Series.
BX3406.2.C57   271'.12'04   78-16615
ISBN 0-87907-860-X

CONTENTS

iv   Contents   page

ABBREVIATIONS

I. General

ASOC	Analecta Sacri Ordinis Cisterciensis; Analecta Cisterciensia. Rome, 1945-.
CC	Corpus christianorum. Turnhout, 1953-.
CCh	Cistercienser Chronik. Bregenz, 1889-.
CF	Cistercian Fathers. Spencer, Massachusetts; Washington, D.C.; Kalamazoo, Michigan, 1970-.
Cîteaux	Cîteaux in de Nederlanden; Cîteaux: Commentarii cisterciensis. Westmalle; Achel, 1950-.
Coll.	Collectanea o. c. r.; Collectania cisterciensia. Rome; Scourmont, 1934-.
CS	Cistercian Studies. Spencer, Massachusetts; Washington, D.C.; Kalamazoo, Michigan, 1966-.
CSEL	Corpus scriptorum ecclesiasticorum latinorum. Vienna, 1866-.
MGH, SS	Monumenta Germaniae historica, Scriptores.
PG	Patrologiae cursus completus, series graeca, 162 vols. Paris, 1857-1866. The volume number proceeds the colon; the column number follows.
PL	Patrologiae cursus completus, series latina, 221 vols. Paris, 1844-1864. Same citation format as PG.
PLS	Patrologiae cursus completus, series latina, Supplementum. Paris, 1958-.
RAM	Revue d'ascetique et de mystique. Toulouse, 1920-.
R Ben.	Revue Bénédictine. Maradsous, 1884-.
RHE	Revue d'histoire ecclésiastique. Louvain, 1900-.
SC	Sources chrétiennes. Rome, 1933-.
Trad.	Traditio. New York, 1943-.
ZKG	Zietschrift für Kirchengeschichte. Innsbruck, 1877-.

II. Bernard of Clairvaux

Op. S. Bern.	S. Bernardi Opera, edd. J. Leclercq et al. Rome: Editiones Cistercienses, 1957-.
Adv	Sermo in adventu domini.

Ann	Sermo in annuntiatione dominica.
Apo	Apologia ad Guillelmum abbatem.
Csi	De consideratione.
Ded	Sermo in dedicatione ecclesiae.
Dil	De diligendo Deo.
Div	Sermones de diversis.
Ep(p)	Epistola(e).
Hum	Liber de gradibus humilitatis et superbiae.
Miss	Homiliae super "Missus est" in laudibus viginis matris.
Nat	Sermo in nativitate domini.
I Nov	Sermo in dominica I novembris.
O Asspt	Sermo in dominica infra octavam assumptionis.
OS	Sermo in festivitate omnium sanctorum.
P Epi	Sermo in dominica I post octavam epiphaniae.
QH	Sermo super psalmum "Qui habitat."
SC	Sermo super Cantica canticorum.
Sept	Sermo in septuagesima.
Tpl	Liber ad milites templi (De laude novae militiae).

III. William of St Thierry

Adv Abl	Disputatio adversus Petrum Abaelardum.
Aenig	Aenigma fidei.
Ep(p)	Epistola(e).
Exp Rom	Expositio in epistolam Pauli ad Romanos.
Sacr altar	De sacramento altaris.
Vita Bern	Sancti Bernardi vita prima.

IV. Aelred of Rievaulx

Inst incl	De institutione inclusarum.
Oner	Sermones de oneribus.
Spir amic	De spirituali amicitia.
Spec car	Speculum caritatis.

V. Issaac of Stella

Ep an	Epistola de anima.
Ep off mis	Epistola ad Joannem episcopum Pictaviensem de officio missa

VI. Guerric of Igny

Ann	Sermo in annuntiatione dominica.
Asspt	Sermon in assumptione.
Nat	Sermo in nativitate domini.

VII. John of Ford

SC   Sermo super Cantica canticorum.

VIII. Geoffry of Auxerre

Vita Bern   Sancti Bernardi vita prima

INTRODUCTION

The papers in this volume were originally presented at the Third and Fourth Cistercian Studies Conferences, sponsored by the Institute of Cistercian Studies of Western Michigan University in 1973 and 1974. The papers were on a wide variety of Cistercian topics, viewed from the insights of many disciplines and covering some four centuries of Cistercian life.

Yet, in assembling the papers submitted for publication, a theme did emerge which makes this collection more than haphazard. That theme was supplied by Father Louis Lekai whose paper stands first in this volume. Ideals and reality are constantly at war in Cistercian--and, indeed, human--life. Father Lekai presents a revisionist view of the 'decline' of Cistercian ideals, postponing that decline until 1348. This is a view which not all will accept, but it is presented with the calm detachment, thoroughgoing knowledge of the sources, and logic which have characterized Father Lekai's many books and articles over the years.

In gratitude, we dedicate this volume to Louis J. Lekai, O Cist, a good monk, an erudite scholar and a true Christian gentleman.

The articles which follow, by Father Chrysogonus Waddell, OCSO, and Father Bede Lackner, O Cist, explore the Cistercian ideal as outlined in early documents of the Order. Then follow a series of articles on the thought of the Cistercian Fathers, also ably illustrating the Cistercian ideal. These authors of these articles represent a sort of 'who's who' of Cistercian scholarship, and we are proud to include examples of their work. The theme of this part of the volume is admirably summarized in the article by Father John Morson, OCSO, who explores a topic common to all the Cistercian Fathers.

Richard Spence's article on Gunther of Pairis is a good transition from the profound spirituality of the Fathers to the popular religiosity inspired by it, but also deviating from it. Constance Berman then shows how the economic realities of early Cistercian life often forced compromises with the ideal of Cîteaux and her daughters. But institutional history can also show a striving for an ideal, as John Nichol's paper on the physical features a Cistercian nunnery shows.

The final two papers, by Charles Stinger and Sister Jane Patricia, CSJB, show how the Cistercian ideal continued to influence life within and outside the cloister, north and south of the Alps, during the fifteenth century. Both papers also show a profound shift from the ideals

of the twelfth century. The Realpolitik of Renaissance Italy provided
a hostile environment to the goals of Saint Bernard. And the dying prayers
of the fifteenth-century Cistercian nun--however appealing--show how far
Cistercian spirituality had come from the optimistic humanism of Bernard
and his contemporaries.

Since this volume was prepared, we have had word of the happy death
of one of the contributors, Father John Morson. Although another volume
published by Cistercian Publications will be dedicated to him, we wish
to celebrate here too the memory of this great scholar and dedicated monk.
It is hard to lose a friend like "Father Christmas," as Father John was
known, but we rejoice that he has been given to us.

                                                                                    J.R.S.

IDEALS AND REALITY

IN EARLY CISTERCIAN LIFE AND LEGISLATION

Louis J. Lekai, O Cist
University of Dallas

It has been stated innumberable times, both by scholars and amateur historians, that the Cistercian Order flourished only as long as it held fast to its original ideals and principles, clearly formulated in the earliest documents of Cîteaux as well as in the first statutes passed by the General Chapter. As to the duration of the 'golden age' or the beginning of decline, however, the same authorities disagree, some stating flatly that the downward slide is noticeable as early as the death of Saint Bernard. The principles and laws, supposedly broken so soon, refer to the meticulous observance of the Rule of Saint Benedict, strict seclusion from the world, poverty and simplicity, but more specifically to the refusal of customary feudal and ecclesiastical revenues coupled with the demand that the monks survive from the fruits of their own labor.

The fact that the first Cistercians indeed cherished such ideals is so evident that it needs no further proof. Hosts of other problems, however, must be examined before a balanced judgment can be formed on the validity of the above quoted and widely accepted relationship between broken laws and decline. Were those laws and principles indeed unbroken before 1153? Could occasional defaults be justified? Were those 'laws' passed and accepted as universally binding regulations? Did the General

Chapter 'legislate' as modern legislative bodies do? Was Cistercian

lawmaking sufficiently orderly and efficient to demand prompt obedience?

Even if someone would be willing to answer with a resounding 'yes' to

most such questions, there remains to be explained the curious fact that

nearly 400 abbeys were founded in rapid succession after 1153, a period

of supposed decline; moreover, some of the greatest and most successful

communities of Cistercian history originated only in the second half of

the thirteenth century (Rauden, Pelplin, Chorin, Goldenkron, Neuzelle,

Königssaal, Grüssau, etc.).

I do not pretend that here and now I am to solve all these problems

with definitive results, but I would like to turn attention to certain

facts and circumstances that may point to a path leading to more realistic

conclusions than those of our predecessors grappling with the same elusive

issues.

I have had the opportunity on a previous occasion to show that the

founders of Cîteaux assumed a peculiarly ambivalent attitude toward the

Rule of Saint Benedict.[1] They declared their utter devotion to it, but

in fact they used that venerable document with remarkable liberality.

They invoked and applied it when it suited their purpose, ignored or even

contradicted it when they thought that they had better ideas. In the

latter category are the exclusion of children and introduction of lay-

brotherhood, liturgical uniformity, restriction of the power of abbots
while emphasizing central authority and control by visitors, together
with many other features of the Charter of Charity, totally beyond the
scope of the Rule. If the founders of Cîteaux were indeed as much devoted to the Rule as they proclaimed to be, their adherence to it was certainly due more to its spirit than to its letter.

Another supposedly firmly established principle demanded that new
abbeys of the Order be established far away from populated regions.
Cistercian authors habitually described such monastic sites by borrowing
the colorful words of Deuteronomy (32:10): locus horroris et vastae
solitudinis. Here we may ask again: was this indeed a 'principle,' and
if so, how firm? For the ambiguity begins with Cîteaux. In spite of the
Exordium parvum's best efforts to assure us that it was an impenetrable
wilderness inhabited only by wild beasts, the site of Cîteaux included
an ancient chapel and some peasant dwellings, and after the first years
of expansion the granges of the abbey became immediate neighbors of well
settled villages.[2] Moreover, there are clear indications that solitude
was not the uppermost condition in the minds of those responsible for
the earliest foundations. If the first site of a new abbey resembled
closely the cherished landscape of a 'place of horror and vast solitude,'
but offered no adequate means of safe survival, the monks did not hesitate
to move to a location far less secluded, but economically more rewarding.

According to Donkin, in England alone there were at least twenty-nine such moves, away from an uninviting wilderness and closer to more fertile lands, even though the new location happened to be near to populated areas.[3]

The rejection of all feudal or ecclesiastical revenues remains one of the most characteristic features of early Cîteaux, firmly established in the first Capitula emanating from the annual sessions of the General Chapter. No doubt, if there was ever a basic law in Cîteaux, the repudiation of 'churches, altaria, oblations and burials, tithes of other people, ovens or mills, vills and serfs,' was such a cornerstone of Cistercian legislation. Nevertheless, the examination of a random selection of cartularies left behind by the earliest foundations must convince anybody that infractions of even such rules were no rare exceptions well before the death of Saint Bernard.

Between 1116 and 1119 Cîteaux herself acquired tithes in Moisey, originally belonging to two priests who, however, transferred their claims to the abbey.[4] The foundation document of Bonnefont (1136-1137) included the donation of tithes, although, as in the case of Cîteaux, there is no clear proof for the actual collection of such revenues by the monks.[5] The same was the case at the foundation of Otterberg in 1144.[6] Elsewhere in Germany similar incidents must have been wide-spread. Thus, Camp received tithes in 1130 from the archdeacon of Cologne;[7] Walkenried accepted at its foundation (1129) three villages; Volkerode, founded in 1131,

experienced grave hardships, soon relieved by the welcome revenues of a
mill. A son of the foundress of the same house was buried in the abbey
church in 1149. At about the same time, life at Sittichenbach was so
hard that Count Friedrich von Beichlingen donated to the monks the village of Ober-Heilingen with an income of 36 marks in tithes. The Polish
abbey of Lekno, founded about 1147, received at its beginning the town
of the same name with the revenues of the local market. Andreow, another
Polish house, possessed since 1149 the town in which the abbey was founded
together with seven villages.[8] According to an undated document (before
1139) Preuilly, the sixth 'daughter' of Cîteaux, received a mill under
the condition that the monks furnish to the donor half a bushel of rye
and the same quantity of wheat each year on the feast of Saint Luke.[9]

What was the reaction of the General Chapter to such manifest infractions of supposedly fundamental rules? I know the answer in only one
case, involving the Roman abbey of Trefontane, an ancient house incorporate
with the blessing of Saint Bernard in 1140, in spite of the fact that it
possessed a village, churches and all kinds of other customary eccesiasti-
cal revenues. There is no indication of subsequent efforts to unload the
'illegal' possessions. Moreover, to make sure that all was in fact per-
missible, Pope Eugene III turned to the General Chapter of 1152 with the
request that the abbey be permitted to retain these sources of income
arguing: licet enim id ordinis rigor inhibeat, loci tamen necessitas

retineri compellit. The Pope then assured the Chapter that he would try to work out some other solution, but, for the time being, the monks could not forgo their usual sources of livelihood, or else they would be forced to go about begging for their food. The General Chapter of 1153 found the exception justifiable and readily consented.[10]

This concession was by no means an isolated incident granted only under the pressure of papal authority. A veritable floodgate to all such illegalities was opened in 1147 by the incorporation advocated by Saint Bernard himself of the Congregation of Savigny (twenty-nine abbeys and three convents for nuns). In the same year the small congregations of Cadouin and Obazine followed Savigny's example, all admitted with their formerly acquired churches, tithes and serfs, without the immediate obligation to conform to Cistercian restrictions. One can hardly suppose that someone with Saint Bernard's intelligence could overlook the discrepancies between the economic basis of the newly admitted abbeys and that of the original Cistercian foundations; neither could he fail to realize the potential effects of wholesale concessions over the rest of the Order. Why then did he promote the fusion? As I see it, the only logical answer is that, in the judgment of Saint Bernard, the spiritual benefits of the union outweighed the drawbacks of the compromise.[11] But it would be unfair to blame Saint Bernard for what followed; the General Chapter took the same lenient attitude even after his death. In 1157, for example, the

Chapter permitted the newly joined abbeys to hold their mills, until
they received other instructions. Meanwhile, as it could be easily
anticipated, the well-publicized concessions encouraged other communities to reach out for hitherto forbidden possessions. By 1169 the
abuse was so widespread that Pope Alexander III addressed a strongly
worded bull to the Order, calling attention to the alarming deviations
from the 'holy institutions' of the founding fathers.[12]

Uniformity in daily life and discipline did not fare much better
either. In such matters the Irish communities posed the greatest
difficulties, in spite of the great care with which the foundation of
Mellifont was undertaken in 1142, under the direct supervision of
Saint Malachy and Saint Bernard. The Clairvaux-trained monks found
so much resistance to Cistercian customs among the Irish that they were
forced to return, among them Robert, the architect of Clairvaux. Saint
Bernard refused to be discouraged, although he must have realized that
no foundation could take root on the island without compromise with the
ancient forms of Irish monasticism. After renewed efforts some abbeys
were constructed according to Cistercian requirements, but the native
monks continued to live in small huts around the cloister, in the
immediate vicinity of nuns. By 1190 the situation had become critical,
but, instead of taking radical measures, the General Chapter merely
ordered ineffectual visitations. In 1228, Abbot Stephen Lexington of

Stanley, who visited the delinquent houses at the risk of his life, no longer could find even the vestiges of Cistercian observances among the constantly rebellious Irish. Yet, all that the General Chapter did was the temporary break-up of local lines of affiliation.[13]

The strange phenomenon of peremptory legislation and indulgent execution can be better understood if considered in the context of contemporaneous legal developments, lumped together with related features as the Gregorian Reform. It witnessed the rebirth of Roman Law, the first systematic collections of canon law, together with papal claims of universal authority, supported by the ever expanding curia as the organ of centralized, bureaucratic administration. These revolutionary novelties ran into the resolute opposition of those who kept faith with the old, traditional concepts of feudal relations based on immemorial customs, local autonomy and extensive privileges. In the ensuing controversy the papacy fought under the banner of divine truth and freedom from secular entanglements, while the emperor defended his position by invoking the power of unbroken traditions and feudal contracts. The outcome could only be a compromise, but from a papal point of view the Concordat of Worms was certainly a far cry from the categorical statements of the Dictatus papae.

The reform program of Cîteaux can justly be conceived as the application of Gregorian ideals to monastic renewal, as opposed to traditional

ways symbolized by Cluny. In the early Cistercian documents, fidelity
to the Gospel was replaced by the purity of the Rule, but the rejection
of long standing customs and the demand of complete freedom from feudal
ties were the same issues as those of the investiture conflict. The
parallel goes even further: just as the papacy was forced to recognize
that the rigid application of Gregorian principles was impossible, the
rapid territorial expansion of the Order forced the General Chapter to
admit that the tenets of Cistercian reform were not always and everywhere
applicable. Cîteaux, of course, did not sign a formal concordat with
local opposition, but in the career of Saint Bernard one may discover
at least the disposition for a tacit compromise.

The great Abbot of Clairvaux cannot be characterized as a protagonist
of the Gregorian Reform without qualifications. When he came to prominence
the long strife had already been terminated and he had no ambition to
renew it. He was, obviously, an intrepid champion of moral reform, but
he had no taste for power politics and the intricacies of canon law.
In his famous De consideratione he wrote about the papacy not in juridical
terms but as a moral power, and about the Church not as a legal entity but
as the mystical bride of Christ. In a much quoted passage he berated the
Curia where 'daily the laws resound in the palace, but they are laws of
Justinian, not of the Lord.' In his mind papal jurisdiction ought to be
motivated by spiritual and pastoral considerations rather than by the

provocative display of force. When Saint Bernard interfered in the
disputed papal election of 1130, he preferred Innocent over Anaclet
not because of canonical formalities, but because he was convinced that
the character of the former was better suited to be the Vicar of Christ.[14]
It was entirely logical, then, that when Saint Bernard spoke up in the
General Chapter, it was not in behalf of the rigid enforcement of laws
and regulations, but in favor of the spiritual welfare of monastic
communities. In case of conflict between the two, as it certainly
happened in 1147, he was willing to bend the law in order to accomodate
the large number of worthy monks for their own good and for the glory
and spiritual benefit of his beloved Order.

That such was, indeed, the frame of mind of Saint Bernard can also
be inferred from his attitude toward the Rule of Saint Benedict. Using
the words of Jean Leclercq, Bernard 'considered it not as a code of
observances but as the expression of an idea; not as a collection of
usages to be followed but as a work of doctrine conveying a spirit and
establishing certain fundamental structures; he did not, in fact, attribute
to it legislative value.'[15]

Saint Bernard's basic position was a source of inspiration, among
many others, to the famed author of the most important canonical work of
the twelfth century, Gratian. His Concordia discordantium canonum,
published about 1140, attempted, as its title indicated, to reconcile

the old with the new, traditional concepts with the Gregorian theories
of law, incorporating much of Saint Bernard's teaching on the Church
and papal jurisdiction. This was the work that dominated legal thinking at the time of the most vigorous Cistercian expansion and certainly
had a decisive influence on the attitude of the more erudite members of
the General Chapter. From our present point of view the most important
is the introductory part of this great work, the Tractatus de legibus,
on the nature and origin of laws, including the relationship between
customs and other forms of human laws. After making the distinction
between divine and human laws, he defined the latter as mores jure
conscripti et traditi. Since 'human laws consist of customs, for the
same reason they are different according to the likes and dislikes
of nations.' Gratian recognized written and statutory laws as well,
but listing the attributes of all valid laws he insisted that they must
be 'honest, just, possible, corresponding to nature, in harmony with
the customs of the country, adapted to place and time, necessary, useful
and manifest.' Furthermore, 'laws are instituted when they are promul-
gated; they are confirmed when approved by the customs of the users.
Namely, just as in our days many laws have been abrogated by the contrary
customs of the users, [other valid] laws have been confirmed by the users'
customs.'[16] In a subsequent discourse he carefully delineated the
necessary attributes of customs of such force, but in conclusion Gratian

still maintained that 'customs should not be resisted as long as they
are not contrary to canonical authority;...traditions instituted by
the fathers should not be broken' and 'daily practices should be taken
as laws.'[17]

It is obvious from these quotations that Gratian shared his
contemporaries' deep-seated suspicion toward novelties, and held that
law-making was conceivable only if and when related to long-established
and living social realities. Medieval rulers, of course, passed new
laws long before the emergence of statutory legislation, but, at least
during the course of the twelfth century, they were anxious to disguise
patent novelties as forgotten and rediscovered customs.[18] That the
fathers of Cîteaux were very sensitive to charges of introducing undue
novelties and vigorously disclaimed any such intentions, is one of the
striking features of virtually all sources dealing with Cistercian beginnings.

We may go, however, one step further and state that what may come
under the term 'legislation,' such as the formulation of the basic principles and norms of life at Cîteaux and the nucleus of the Charter of
Charity, preceded the existence of the General Chapter, and that this
annual convention of abbots did not claim legislative authority and in
fact, until about 1180, passed no new laws. The sessions of the Chapter,
as described in the Charter of Charity, were merely conventions where

'the abbots should consult upon matters that pertain to the salvation of
souls and see to the observance of the Holy Rule and the [usages] of the
Order....'[19] In 1151 Pope Eugene III in his letter to the General Chapter
echoed the same idea referring to the assembly as 'dealing presently in
unison about the rekindling of the holy spirit and the progress of souls,'
adding that 'whenever you, most beloved sons, come together, you must be
concerned with corrections of things to be corrected and ordinations that
need to be ordained for the salvation of souls and the advancement of the
Order...therefore you should carefully consider what can be done to prevent
deviations from the virtues you have planted, [virtues] that you must bring
to fruition.'[20]

As these quotations seem to indicate, the primary goal of the General
Chapter was not legislation but spiritual guidance, watching over the
observance of the Rule, the Charter of Charity and other initial usages of
the Order. This may explain the curious fact that, with the exception
of a few undated and disjointed fragments, until about 1180 there is no
documentary evidence for the annual legislative activity of the General
Chapter. The collection of rules and regulations published under the
auspices of the Chapter in or somewhat before 1152 featuring the Ecclesiastica officia, the Usus conversorum and particularly the Instituta Generalis
Capituli, can be more properly described as adaptations, amplifications
and explanations of already established usages and customs than new

legislation.

If, by exception, there was something definitely new among these early
statutes, it was proposed on a tentative basis, to be approved or rejected
by the membership and in the latter case it was quietly discarded. A
striking example of this attitude is the first statute of 1152, prohibiting
new foundations or incorporations.[21] To us this measure sounds perfectly
reasonable and perhaps we wish it had been heeded. But to contemporaries
it was so blatantly new and so manifestly in contradition to existing
customs and trends that it had no chance to be taken seriously. In the
face of adverse reaction this 'law' was never repeated and no effort was
made for its enforcement.

A further proof of both the tentative nature of new regulations and
the broad-minded, always compromising disposition of the Chapter fathers is
the wording of virtually countless statutes before as well as after 1180.
The beginning of such a paragraph is always a firm command or rigid prohibition, but the end lists the exceptions, often enfeebling the text to
such an extent that it can hardly qualify for more than a fatherly advice.
Thus, for example, the Chapter of 1152 prohibited the use of silk copes,
but authorized the same for abbatial benedictions; forbade abbots to employ
secular servants in the guests' quarters, 'unless there should be many
guests'; excluded meat courses on Saturdays in the infirmary, 'unless there
should be someone so sick that he could take nothing else.'[22] Even far
more significant statutes contain built-in loopholes, placing local considera-

tions above general rules. Thus, when the Chapter of 1182 was informed

about the heavy indebtedness of many houses, it ruled that an abbey

owing more than 50 marks was not to buy new land or construct anything,

'unless there should be a real necessity for such things, ascertained

by the father abbots.'[23] The records of the Chapter of 1184 featured

an explicit admission that local customs might override previously passed

statutes, such as the prohibition to serve wine in the granges.[24] Similar

examples could be multiplied at will, let alone incidents when deviations

were encouraged by the soothing connective: nisi. Thus, the busy

scriptorium of Pontigny paid no attention to the prohibition of multi-

colored illuminations and produced with impunity ornate manuscripts

throughout the twelfth century.[25] The experimental nature of all statutes

was confirmed as late as 1265 in the bull Parvus fons of Clement IV, re-

stating the well-established custom to the effect that no law passed by

the General Chapter was to be considered binding, unless confirmed by the

subsequent session of the Chapter.[26]

One thing seems to be certain, however: after 1180 the annual session

of the General Chapter were better recorded, the statutes became ever more

numerous, less concerned with spiritual guidance and more emphatic on purel

administrative and financial matters, reflecting on the new posture of self

conscious legislators. The time of this rather conspicuous change seems to

support the often debated thesis of Rudolph Sohm, who argued that with the

triumph of Pope Alexander III at the Third Lateran Council (1179) a break

took place in the traditionally 'sacramental' interpretation of canon law,
an interpretation firmly upheld by Gratian. Henceforth a new juridical
concept took hold of the minds of professional lawyers, chiefly concerned
with the powers of ecclesiastical office-holders, constitutional structures
and the intricacies of papal administration. Indeed, it is not unlikely
that when the General Chapter of 1188 ordered to keep all works on canon
law under lock and key and out of circulation among monks, the abbots
acted instinctively, sensing the changing legal climate as it moved away
from the theologically oriented patristic traditions and drifted toward
a utilitarian exploitation of canons as legal weaponry in jurisdictional
disputes.[27]

A final point of our present investigation should be the actual or
potential efficiency of the General Chapter from a purely technical point
of view, quite apart from the question of the true nature of its activity.

The annual Chapter was supposed to bring together all abbots of the
Order. The early regulations accepted only one excuse for absence: illness
The speedy geographical expansion of the Order, however, made regular attendance problematic to those in far-away lands. For reasons of great distance
expenses and danger of travel, exceptions were soon granted. Thus, abbots
of houses in Syria were required to attend the Chapter only in every seventh
year and others received similar concessions in proportion to their distance
from Cîteaux. On the number of abbots participating in the deliberations of
the Chapter during the twelfth and thirteenth centuries no figures have

survived. From the constant complaints about unauthorized absences, however, one may conclude that the ordeals of travel were powerful deterrents.
At any rate, the physical facilities of Cîteaux for the accomodation of
the members of the Chapter were very modest. Even after the completion
of the final Gothic cloister in 1193 ('Cîteaux III') the regular meeting
place, the chapter hall, was a room of 17 x 18 meters, with a double or
perhaps triple row of benches around the walls. It was estimated to hold
about three hundred persons,[28] but it remains highly doubtful that the hall
was ever so well packed. A session with about a third of the abbots in
attendance (250) is perhaps a better estimate.

How was the absent two-third notified about the resolutions of the
Chapter? On record keeping and promulgation of statutes the twelfth-century
documents are silent. The fact that until about 1180 the extant manuscripts
give no information about the proceedings of single sessions seems to indicate
that the consultations remained unrecorded and the resolutions of the Chapter,
if there were any, were passed on orally. The matter was further complicated
by the assembly's continually changing personnel from year to year, so
that a considerable portion of the abbots at any given occasion was un-
acquainted with the discussions conducted in previous years. The often
result was the passage of incongruous or contradictory regulations, leading
to confusion and a skeptical attitude toward the validity of individual
statutes. The reason for repeating important decisions year after year,
was the periodic collection and publication of statutes, such as the

earliest <u>Capitula</u> about 1119, then the <u>Instituta</u> of 1152, and the <u>Libellus</u>

<u>definitionum</u> edited by Arnaud Amaury about 1202. It was in reference to

this latter collection that the General Chapter of 1204 issued for the first

time an order obliging every abbot to obtain a copy of it, 'so that no abbot

could excuse himself in the future under the pretext of ignorance.'[29]

Nevertheless, the method of promulgation continued to be a vexing issue.

The Chapter of 1212 scolded certain 'less solicitous abbots' who neglected

to take home the texts of definitions to be read in the chapter. To make

it sure that each abbey was provided with the latest edition of definitions,

visitors were enjoined to check on the matter. Abbots who for any reason

failed to attend Chapters were obliged to collect the records of the missed

session from their neighbors, from father abbots or from visitors.[30]

But all such measures fell short of the target if the General Chapter

was <u>unable to make up its collective mind</u> on a crucial issue, and this

resulted year after year in a flow of <u>conflicting regulatio</u>ns. Such was

the subject of <u>leasing or renting monastic</u> land to lay tenants, strictly

prohibited by the <u>Instituta</u> of 1152, but becoming inevitable as lay-brother

vocations began to decline. Thus, the Chapter of 1208 permitted the leasing

of 'less useful land,' but the session of 1214 revoked the concession. In

1215 the Chapter not only permitted but ordered the leasing of newly acquired

land. In 1220 the fathers returned to the permission of 1208, and in 1224

the Chapter no longer objected to the leasing of any land if such a move

seemed desirable.[31]

In other cases the careful reader of the records may come under the impression that the wording of important statutes was made deliberately so vague or complicated that it left open a number of possible interpretations. Such an obvious 'hot potato' was the much criticised tendency to acquire more and more land, discussed at length at the Chapter of 1190. The result was a long paragraph composed 'in order to curb cupidity' and in fact prohibited 'forever' the acquisition of any real estate. But the new law was to take effect only upon its confirmation by the session of the following year and the text exempted pastures and lands held for usufruct donations in puram eleenosynam, lands from which pensions or tithes were due and finally dispensed all abbeys where the existing estates were insufficient for the support of thirty monks, a proportionate number of lay-brothers and the usual number of guests.[32] The ruling was repeated in 1191 and thus became an eloquent testimony to the fathers' concern about this important matter, but was also conveniently innocuous and without practical consequences.

To attribute to the General Chapter a high degree of efficiency in at least discplinary matters would be another mistake. Here I wish to refer to only one incident which dragged on from 1190 to 1222 without conclusive results. In 1190 the abbey of Bonlieu in the diocese of Bordeaux experienced grave hardships, whereupon the Chapter ordered an investigation by the abbot of Bonlieu's 'mother,' Jouy. In case the visitation failed to insure the secure support of at least 'twelve regularly living monks' at Bonlieu, the abbey was to be suppressed. But by 1192 no

visitation had taken place, and the abbot of Jouy was told that if he ne-

glected to act, the maternity over Bonlieu would be transferred to Pontig-

ny. However, as late as 1207 nothing still had been done; the order of

1190 was merely repeated. In 1208 the Chapter added a new threat: if the

abbot of Jouy remained negligent in the matter, Bonlieu would be reduced

to a grange. In 1212 the exasperated Chapter entrusted the visitation of

Bonlieu to two other abbots, who turned out to be equally reluctant. In

1213 the Chapter rebuked again the stubborn abbot of Jouy and renewed the

prospect of changing Bonlieu's filiation. Finally, in 1222, the abbot of

Pontigny was charged to assume the role of father abbot over Bonlieu, al-

though there is no evidence of further action in the matter.[33]

In conclusion I wish to make the following observations. Those who

believe that the linking of the non-observance of certain original statutes

with the decline of the Order is logical, identify, at least implicitly,

the Cistercian reform with a set or regulations; accordingly, broken rules

broke the Order itself. Both the presupposition and the conclusion,

however, seem to be unjustifiable. The Cistercian reform was a movement

of spiritual renewal and the initial regulations were merely instrumental

toward a new height of monastic perfection. Cistercian ideals certainly

included a greater degree of poverty, simplicity and detachment from the

world than practiced elsewhere; but preconceived principles and rigid

adherence to a dogmatic position that admitted no exceptions were far

from Cistercian mentality. Rhetorical flourishes employed by the defende
of Cîteaux in their debates with the Cluniacs should not mislead us.
Cistercian regulations sounded peremptory, but in their application indiv
ual abbots as well as the General Chapter were always circumspect and con
promising whenever the welfare of a community demanded concessions. In t
minds of the founders of Cîteaux, just laws were closely associated with
the customs and living realities of a given environment, and in case of
conflicts local needs and considerations prevailed. Without such a flexi
ble and tolerant mentality the Order could never have grown beyond the co
fines of Burgundy, and conversely, the very fact of the speed and extent
growth attest to the universal appeal, not of rules, but of spiritual val
This is why, during most of the twelfth-century, the General Chapter neit
claimed nor exercised legislative powers in a modern sense of the term.
Instead, the annual assemblies of abbots served as occasions for a collec
tive examination of conscience, watching primarily over the spiritual wel
fare of communities. New regulations, if indeed such was the case, were
passed on a tentative basis and gained validity only after the approval o
a broad segment of the membership. Even when the Chapter did eventually
assume legislative functions, its effiency was seriously hampered by in-
soluble problems of attendance, record-keeping, promulgation and enforcem
A tolerant and flexible attitude, then, far from being a sign of decay, w
in fact a necessity, and its judicious practice should be taken for evide
of health and vitality. IMP.

This is why I cannot find indications of a universal Cistercian decline until at least the fourteenth century. The growing number of disciplinary cases dealt with in the General Chapter is no reliable gauge for declining standards of morality. By the end of the thirteenth century the Order might easily have had ten thousand members, and with such a growth the number of delinquents was bound to grow too. Neither was the much castigated greed and land-grabbing an unfailing symptom of spreading materialism at the expense of spiritual values. A largely agrarian economy was always full of hazards. Failing crops or pestilence among farm animals often brought otherwise prosperous communities to starvation, forcing the temporary dispersal of the monks. If, after such a disaster, the abbot attempted to broaden the economic basis of his house by new acquisitions, it was a proof of his foresight and solicitude for the welfare of his subjects. The abandonment of direct cultivation and the leasing of large tracts of monastic land to lay tenants was simply imposed on the Order by drastically changing social and economic factors and cannot be construed as a deliberate breach with early Cistercian practices. Similarly, the progressive commercialization of monastic economy was part of a universal trend that monks could not ignore if they wished to provide for themselves.

What should be then the first signs of decay? The sudden arrest of Cistercian expansion after 1300 (the number of new foundations was between 1250 and 1300: 50; 1300 and 1350: 10; 1350 and 1400: 5), the precipitate drop in membership, the inability to recover from a physical or financial disaster, all point to the period between 1300 and 1350. For the fragmentation, all point to the period between 1300 and 1350. For the sake of convenience I suggest as divider 1348, the terrible year of the great plague, a fatal calamity that struck even contemporaries as a portent of impending doom. Among other external causes one may refer to the fall of both the Empire and Papacy, political chaos in Germany and Italy, the disappearance of the Crusader states, the menace of Turkish expansion and the outbreak of the Hundred Years' War. All these, of course, were merely symptoms of a fast changing civilization that had lost faith in its old institutions, but was yet unable to find acceptable alternatives. Western monasticism, and in it the Cistercian Order, shared the fate of other medieval organizations. It grew and flourished as long as it enjoyed the enthusiastic support of society, but was forced to contract when appreciation changed to suspicion and resentment. No religious order can possibly thrive in uncongenial surroundings.

NOTES

1. L. J. Lekai, "The Rule and the Early Cistercians," _Cistercian Studies_
   5 (1970) 243-51.

2. J. Marilier, _Chartes et documents concernant l'abbaye de Cîteaux, 1098-_
   _1182_ (Rome, 1961) p. 50.

3. R. A. Donkin, "The Site Changes of Medieval Cistercian Monasteries,"
   Geography 44 (1959) 251-58.

4. Marilier, _Chartes_, pp. 76-77.

5. Charles Samaran and Charles Higounet, _Recueil des actes de l'abbaye_
   cistercienne de Bonnefont en Comminges (Paris, 1970) p. 50.

6. G. Kaller, _Wirtschafts- und Besitzgeschichte des Zisterzienser-_
   klosters Otterberg (Heidelberg, 1961) p. 82.

7. Giles Constable, _Monastic Tithes from their Origins to the Twelfth_
   Century (Cambridge, 1964) p. 191.

8. Franz Winter, _Die Zisterzienser des nordöstlichen Deutschlands_ (Gotha,
   1867-1871) I, 32-81.

9. Albert Catel and Maurice Lecomte, _Chartes et documents de l'abbaye_
   cistercienne de Preuilly (Paris, 1927) p. 14.

10. J. Canivez, _Statuta Capitulorum Generalium Ordinis Cisterciensis_
    (Louvain, 1933-1941) I, 43-45, 51-52. Henceforth: _Statuta_.

11. 'Cum Savigniacenses in nostri Ordinis societatem transire decreverunt,
    dispensatione in hac parte habita ecclesias et earum beneficia permissi
    sunt habere. Durum numque visum est loci cognita infecunditate ab

huiusmodi eos prohibere beneficiis. Si quis ergo de perceptione
talium beneficiorum adversus eos obloquitur, noverit sinceritas ves
huius Ordinis patres misericorditer hoc eis indulsisse.' Letter
of Guillaume, abbot of Clairvaux, to Achard, bishop of Avranches (a
1161), quoted by B. Griesser, "Registrum Epistolarum Stephani de
Lexington," ASOC 8 (1952) 189.

12. J. Leclercq, "Passage supprimé dans une épitre d'Alexandre III,"
     R Ben. 62 (1952) 151.

13. J. A. Watt, The Church and the Two Nations in Medieval Ireland
     (Cambridge, 1970) pp. 85-107.

14. See this interpretation of the role of Saint Bernard in Hayden V.
     White, "The Gregorian Ideal and Saint Bernard of Clairvaux," Journa
     of the History of Ideas 21 (1960) 321-48. See the problem of
     "Saint Bernard and the Law" discussed in Stanley Chodorow in Christ
     Political Theory and Church Politics in the Mid-Twelfth Century
     (Berkeley, Los Angeles, 1972) pp. 260-65. See a most recent attemp
     to reconcile the legal and purely moral considerations in Saint
     Bernard's approach by John R. Sommerfeldt, "Charismatic and
     Gregorian Leadership in the Thought of Bernard of Clairvaux," in
     Bernard of Clairvaux: Studies Presented to Dom Jean Leclercq,
     CS 23 (Washington, D.C., 1973) pp. 73-90.

15. J. Leclercq, "S. Bernard et la Règle de S. Benoît," Coll. 25 (1973)
     183.

16. PL 187:35.

17. PL 187:63.

18. See on the prevailing legal conservatism, M.-D. Chenu, Nature, Man and
    and Society in the Twelfth Century (Chicago, 1968) pp. 310-30.

19. J.-B. Van Damme, Documenta pro Cisterciensis Ordinis historiae ac
    juris studio collecta (Westmalle, 1959) p. 17.

20. Statuta, I, 40-41.

21. Ibid., p. 45.

22. Ibid., 1152: 16, 17, 19.

23. Ibid., 1182; 9.

24. Ibid., 1184: 15.

25. C. H. Talbot, "Notes on the Library of Pontigny," ASOC 10 (1954)
    107.

26. Statuta, III, 27.

27. See the Sohm thesis discussed in Chodorow, Christian Political Theory,
    pp. 7-11.

28. G. Müller, "Studien über das Generalkapitel," C Ch 12 (1900) 248.

29. Statuta, I, 1204: 8.

30. Ibid., 1212: 6, 7.

31. Ibid., 1208: 5; 1214: 58; 1215: 65; 1220: 5; II, 1224: 10.

32. Ibid., I, 1190: 1; 1191: 42, 43.

33. Ibid., I, 1190: 22; 1192: 25; 1207: 13; 1208: 24; 1212: 33;
    1213: 39; II, 1222: 28.

THE EXORDIUM CISTERCII AND THE SUMMA CARTAE CARITATIS:

A DISCUSSION CONTINUED

Chrysogonus Waddell, OCSO
Abbey of Gethsemani

Almost exactly a decade ago, Fr Polykarp Zakar, O Cist, released for publication a study which came none too soon for many of us. It was a survey of the more important contributions made during the preceding decade by scholars deeply interested in the question of the beginnings of the Cistercian Order and its early evolution.[1] The problems under discussion were many and intricate; the documentation lent itself to conflicting interpretations; and the principal scholars engaged in the discussion frequently failed to see eye to eye. If proof of the complexity of the discussion is needed, consider the discouraging fact that even so impeccable and admired a scholar as David Knowles was unable to summarize with tolerable accuracy the main positions defended by just one of the authors concerned--J.-A. Lefèvre.[2] When even a David Knowles falters, it can be understood that we of a lesser breed were justified in feeling a bit lost in the maze of interesting, important, but terribly confusing discussions. Fr Zakar's survey came as a God-send, providing us with something of a street-map useful for helping us through the turns and twists of the labyrinthine debate.

In point of fact, Fr Zakar's survey was more than a simple report of who said what; for he included in his presentation a personal evaluation of much that he reported.[3] This was particularly true with regard

to the many contributions by Fr Jean Baptiste Van Damme, OSCO,[4] whose ar-
ticles--unlike those by J.-A. Lefèvre--had never been the object of a systematic critical recension. The reserves expressed by Fr Zakar were coun-
tered by Fr Van Damme in a ten-page reply printed the very next year (1965)
in Analecta Cisterciensia;[5] and since the same issue also included an article by Edith Pasztor, critical of the methodology heretofore employed by
the scholars involved in the discussion,[6] as well as a reply by Fr Zakar to
Fr Van Damme's reply,[7] it looked for a moment as if a new decade of fruitful
exchange was being inaugurated. This was not to be. Apart from an important article by Fr Van Damme, on the Summa Cartae caritatis as a source of
legislation for various groups of canons,[8] nothing very much was printed
by way of furthering the earlier discussions.

But surely the relatively fallow period is now at an end, and fruitful discussions will once more be resumed, thanks to the publication, in
the spring of 1974, of a book which promises to become a standard reference work for students of monastic history. Under the title Les plus
anciens textes de Cîteaux: Sources, textes et notes historiques,[9] Fr
Jean de la Croix Bouton, OSCO, and Fr Jean Baptiste Van Damme, edited
and commented on a series of documents which figure massively in any
historian's dossier on early Cîteaux--the Exordium parvum, the Carta
caritatis prior, and the Exordium Cistercii et Summa Cartae caritatis.[10]

A succinct historical introduction by Fr Van Damme serves to introduce the various documents and to provide their Sitz im Leben.[11] It is

fairly safe to predict, however, that, enthusiastic as all scholars are bound to be over the idea of a critical edition of these important texts, at least some historians will hesitate over the question of the historical introduction. Their hesitation will be based simply on their persuasion that, at the present moment, the number of solidly established facts are too few to allow of a synthesis such as will one day hopefully be possible, thanks to the pioneering efforts of scholars such as Fr Van Damme and Fr Bouton. As things stand now, however, the solidly established facts are disproportionately few in comparison with the working hypotheses and informed guesswork needed to round out any survey of the genetic evolution of the Order's early legislation and related documents.

For the purpose of this paper, my own area of interest is delimited by the Exordium Cistercii et Summa Cartae caritatis. Since what I have to offer is chiefly working hypotheses and (hopefully) informed guesswork, the following remarks are made chiefly with a view to providing stimulus for further scholarly discussion, rather than with a view to providing clear answers to disputed questions.

For those unfamiliar with the terms of the discussion, the briefest of summaries will have to do. Until recent times, scholars have assumed that the Cistercian Order's Carta caritatis—a sort of monastic constitution providing the framework for the organization of the Order—had always existed as something of a ne varietur text. Apart from minor variants, the known manuscripts and numerous printed editions all tended to agree with the version published by the Dijon librarian and scholar, Philippe Guignard, in his important collection of Cisterciana edited in 1878, Les monuments primitifs de la règle cistercienne.[12] True, as early as 1927, the patriarch of Cistercian scholarship, Fr Gregor Müller, had drawn attention[13] to a manuscript discovery made by Auguste Trihle[14] --an apparently abridged version of some earlier and no longer extant form of the Carta caritatis, such as might suggest to the alert scholar that the textus receptus, as published by Guignard and others, was far from being the primitive one. After a series of editorial vicissitudes, the text was finally published in 1932 by a scholar of the Hungarian Cistercian Abbey of Zirc, Fr Tiburtius Hümpfner,[15] who gave this mini-version the name Summa Cartare caritatis, claiming that this document was a summary of a yet to be discovered earlier version of the Carta caritatis. Within a few years, Monsignor Josef Turk, of the University of Laibach (Ljubljana, Yugoslavia) had the great good fortune of discovering what he insisted was this earlier version, which he found in, not one, but two different manuscripts.[16] This new version of the text he dubbed Carta caritatis prior, which automatically made the textus receptus into the Carta caritatis posterior. So now there were three versions of the Carta caritatis: Posterior, Prior, and Summa.

Scholars were already attempting to sort out the relationship between these several versions when, in 1952, Fr Jean Leclercq, OSB, provided important new material by discovering, in the Biblioteca Comunale

of Trent, a manuscript of the Cistercian <u>consuetudines</u> much earlier
than anything yet exploited by historians of Cistercian origins.[17]

In point of fact, no matter which form of <u>Carta caritatis</u> we are
dealing with, manuscripts inevitably present it, not as an isolated
text, but as part of a much larger <u>corpus</u> of related texts. In general,
and with due allowance made for lacunose manuscripts, the "normal" compilation of the Cistercian customary or <u>consuetudines</u> begins with (a)
a historical <u>NARRATIVE</u> touching on the beginnings and early evolution
of the Order; and of this historical narrative there are two totally
different versions:

1. The <u>EXORDIUM CISTERCII</u> (<u>Ex Cist</u>), so called from its incipit,
    is a straightforward narrative.

2. The so-called <u>EXORDIUM PARVUM</u> (<u>Ex P</u>) is a complex document
    featuring official documents set in the context of a running
    commentary and historical narrative.

This narrative leads up to a presentation of (b) the <u>Carta caritatis</u>
in one of its three known forms: <u>Posterior</u> (<u>CC</u>²), <u>Prior</u> (<u>CC</u>¹) or <u>Summa</u>
(<u>SCC</u>).

Next, (c) a series of statutes or <u>Instituta</u> (<u>Inst</u>), of which we can
distinguish two types:

1. a series of statute-texts arranged in <u>logical order</u>;

2. a longer series subject to on-going revision, and apparently
    based on some sort of <u>chronological principle</u>.

Then comes (d) the bulkiest part of the manuscript, which contains the Ecclesiastica officia (EO), that is to say, the Cistercian customary proper; and of this we can distinguish three major recensions: EO^1, EO^2 and EO^3. Many of these manuscripts end with one or another form of the ever-evolving lay brother usages, the Usus conversorum (UC), which, however, need not enter into the present discussion.

In summary:

Customary manuscript

(a)	Historical Narrative:	Ex Cist or Ex P
(b)	Carta caritatis:	CC^2 or CC^1 or SCC
(c)	Statues:	"logical" arrangement or "chronological" arrangement
(d)	Customary proper:	EO^1 or EO^2 or EO^3

For a number of years, scholars have been busy attempting to date and study the relationships between these various items, with a view to reconstructing a history of the genetic evolution of the Order on the basis of this material. But, as Fr Zakar's survey amply demonstrates, informed opinions are bewilderingly varied. To cite a few instances:

For J.-A. Lefèvre, SCC dates from the year 1119, and is really the form of the CC confirmed by Pope Callistus II in 1119;[18] CC^1 is a much evolved version prepared for confirmation by Eugenius III in 1152.[19] Ex P is, in the main, a tendentious bit of pamphleteering propaganda,

dating, in its present extant form, from 1151;[20] while Ex Cist is a
sober, objective historical account prepared with a view to the confirmation of SCC in 1119.[21]

In an earlier stage of the discussion, Fr Jean de la Croix Bouton
suggested sometime between 1119 and 1123 as the date for SCC, which was
probably redacted for the information of novices.[22] CC^1 marked the
term of an evolution beginning in 1114, and ending with the borrowing
of Chapter X from SCC at some unspecified date.[23] And Ex P dated in
its present form from sometime between October of 1119 and October of
the following year, 1120.[24]

For Fr Jean Baptiste Van Damme, also writing prior to the recent
publication of Les plus anciens textes de Cîteaux, SCC would date from
1123 or 1124,[25] and, as Fr Bouton, following Mgr Turk, had suggested,
might well have been destined for the use of novices.[26] Ex Cist and
SCC would both have come from the same period, that is, 1123-1124.[27]
And Ex P as we know it today would be the fruit of an evolution termi-
nating in 1119.[28]

Collaboration on Les plus anciens textes de Cîteaux brought Fr
Bouton and Fr Van Damme into mutual agreement.[29] For Ex P, the ultimate
date of redaction would still be in the area of 1119.[30] Ex Cist and SCC
would be a non-official compilation, representing a resumé or brief
redaction of Ex P and CC^1.[31] CC^1 would date in its particular redaction
from the year 1119, but would represent a re-working of an early version

of CC.[32] The date of the later collection, Ex Cist and SCC, would be
sometime between the end of 1123 and the early part of 1124, with a
year added on either side to provide a margin of error.[33] Fr Van Damme
thinks it likely that this document is of Clairvaux provenance,[34] and
re-affirms his and Fr Bouton's earlier hypothesis that these texts did
service as a manual of instruction for novices,[35] even though it was
also used for other purposes, that is to say, as a source of material
for the legislation of several different groups of canons.[36]

A NEW WORKING HYPOTHESIS

My own first hand contact with manuscripts of this material came
about several years ago, when I had occasion to leaf through numerous
manuscripts of EO in all three redactions. Uninterested as I was at the
time in the introductory documents which almost inevitably preceded EO,
I was frequently puzzled that so many scribes had placed the rubric
Incipit usus cisterciensium monachorum (as in the very earliest known
redaction of EO, in Trent, MS 1711) or Incipiunt consuetudines cisterciensium (as in the second redaction, in Laibach, MS 31), not immediately
before the first chapter of the actual usages, but curiously enough, at
the very beginning of the compilation, as the rubric which began the
historical narrative. So frequently did this happen that it gradually
was borne in upon me that, in the mind of the compilers, the historical
narrative had an intrinsic connection with the usages proper, which followed later in the manuscript--very much along the lines of other similar

historical introductions, prefaces or introductory letters which one
frequently finds at the beginning of so many monastic customaries--
documents intended to explain how this particular customary came to
be.[37] Indeed, we find precisely such introductions in the case of the
reformed Cistercian antiphonary of around 1147,[38] the gradual which was
the fruit of the same reform,[39] the lay brother usages,[40] and the pre-
1147 Cistercian hymnal.[41]

Now, _EO_ represents nothing less than a concrete expression of the
Cistercian programme of monastic life in all its details of day to day
living. Granted the importance of such a customary for the concrete
living out of the Cistercian interpretation of the Rule of Saint Benedict,
it seems hardly a matter of surprise that the Cistercian customary should
have been introduced by a historical document purporting to provide the
Sitz im Leben for the customary which follows.

The two manuscripts which first claimed my attention were the two
most studied by scholars in recent years--Trent, Biblioteca Comunale,
MS 1711, with its first extant redaction of EO,[42] and Laibach, University
Library, MS 31, with _EO_ in a somewhat later, quite distinct redaction.[43]
As regards structure, the two manuscripts are perfectly parallel; as re-
gards content, they represent two very distinct redactions.

I		II
TRENT, MS 1711		LAIBACH, MS 31
(before 1147)		(before 1152)
Ex Cist	-1-	Ex P

I		II
$\underline{SCC}$	-2-	$\underline{CC^1}$
$\underline{Inst}$ (logical series)	-3-	$\underline{Inst}$ (chronological series)
$\underline{EO^1}$	-4-	$\underline{EO^2}$
$\underline{UC^1}$	-5-	[$\underline{UC^2}$?: MS lacunose at end]

In the light of my own earlier research into questions touching on the evolution of the Order's liturgy, things now began falling into place--at least for me. It was abundantly clear that, sometime around, and probably before 1147, a sweeping liturgical reform had taken place.[44] This reform was drastic enough to render obsolete many of the earlier Cistercian liturgical books, such as the hymnal, antiphonary and gradual --all of which survive, in the earliest redaction, only in fragmentary form. It was also drastic enough to necessitate an up-dated version of the Cistercian customary, which dealt with so many particular points connected with the liturgy. In brief, the archaic Trent manuscript would offer us the pre-1147 Cistercian customary in all its integrity; the somewhat later Laibach manuscript would offer us the up-dated revision of the same, in the form it assumed as the result of the liturgical reform of around 1147. In Recension I, the author responsible for the introductory matter provided a straightforward, rather brief account of the Order's origins and early spread. This historical introduction led up to a summary version of $\underline{CC}$--since it was in virture of this monastic "constitution" that all houses of the Order had to follow the usages of Cîteaux. Next came a series of capitular decisions which represent something of an abridgement and logical arrangement of pre-existing series of General Chapter statutes. And, finally, the text of the customary proper, EO^1. In Recension II, represented by the Laibach manuscript, all that had been presented summarily in Recension I was now given _in extenso_: no longer a brief historical account, but a detailed narrative accompanied by every possible justificatory act and legal document; no longer a mere summary of CC, but the integral (and up-dated) text; not just an abridged synthesis of the summa capitula of earlier General Chapter legislation, but an up-dated series of statutes such as resulted, apparently, from the stringing together of earlier series in roughly chronological order.[45]

Possibly provision should be made for yet another later Recension --Recension III. It seems quite certain that, sometime around the early 1180s, a relatively modest revision of many of the Order's liturgical book took place.[46] It was in this context that EO underwent yet another systematic revision, resulting in EO^3--the version contained in the famous manuscript-type, Dijon, MS 114. But by this time, scribes were juggling the various constitutive elements of the complete Cistercian customary with wild abandon.[47] Sometimes the usages appeared without historical introduction; or sometimes with only CC; or again, the place of CC or Inst would shift from before to after the usages. Occasionally a lazy scribe combined the stream-lined SCC and Ex Cist with the revised EO of a much later period, in order, apparently, to escape having to write out the lengthier texts of Ex P and CC^2. Accordingly, any hypothetical

'Recension III' would have to be flexible enough to provide many different arrangements of the material included in the compilation.

As regards SCC in particular, the hypothesis that it was composed
simply as part of the introductory matter to the usages seems rather
more plausible than hypotheses formulated to date. We have seen that
J.-A. Lefèvre holds the text to be what Pope Callistus II had approved
in 1119; but it seems rather unlikely that any pope would in conscience
dare approve a mere summary, when he could have asked to see the integral
text with all its foot-notes and points of detail.[48] Both Fr Bouton and
Fr Van Damme have been consistent in rallying to the idea that the text
was prepared as something of a study-aid for novices.[49] Perhaps--but
the integral text is no more "difficult" than the original version, and
the Summa is not all that shorter than CC^1. Why give the novices SCC
to pore over, when CC^1 or CC^2 would have done as well? A much more unlikely hypothesis has also been advanced by Mgr Turk[50] and Fr Paschalis
Vermeer, O Cist.[51] They suggest that the early Cistercians were convinced that their success was due to their admirable CC. So possessive
were they when it came to this thesaurus absconditus, that they refused
to let other groups of religious have access to the authentic version.
When the Canons of Arrouaise and the Premonstratensians came to the
Cistercians looking for material to borrow for their own legislation,
the wily Cistercians would have let them have, not the genuine CC, but
the ersatz SCC. I frankly find it a bit more likely that, when these

and other groups of canons were shaping up their own customaries, and
wanted to benefit from the experience of the highly successful Cistercians, the White Monks simply handed them copies of the then current
version of the Cistercian customary, which, before 1147, would have been
Redaction I, with $\underline{SCC}$ rather than the integral text of $\underline{CC}$.

And now for a few further clarifications and answers to possible
objections.

In the preceding Table showing the contents of Trent, MS 1711,
and of Laibach, MS 31, $\underline{Ex}$ $\underline{P}$ and $\underline{CC}^1$ seem to be provided with a rather
late chronology, since they are in a manuscript which can be dated
before 1152, but after 1147. It is true that the Laibach manuscript
is the very earliest known extant manuscript with these two texts; but
this does not exclude the possibility, or even the probability, that both
documents had enjoyed a previous existence. In its present form, $\underline{CC}^1$
has clearly had a long history. Fr Bouton has studied the relationship
between $\underline{CC}^1$ and $\underline{SCC}$[52] and, on the basis of a careful linguistic comparison, suggested that the redactor of $\underline{SCC}$ had his eye on a version of $\underline{CC}$
rather more modern than $\underline{CC}^1$. I am not so sure. Just recently I had
occasion to write a brief historical sketch about an incident touching
on the origins of Gethsemani Abbey. In summarizing a number of official
memoranda dated 1847 and 1848, I modernized vocabulary and used current
expressions. It would be a methodological error, however, were some
future historian to conclude. centuries from now, that, on the basis of

my more "modern" terminology, I must have been using documentation later than my sources of 1847 and 1848. Moreover, were I to do a more detailed treatment of the same subject at some later date, I would doubtless give _in extenso_ much of the material summarized and modernized in my earlier sketch. But the more "archaic" vocabulary of this longer study would not mean that the more ample version preceded the version with the updated terminology. I do not know whether, in the light of subsequent research, Fr Bouton has shifted his earlier position concerning the existence of several different versions of SCC.[53] If I follow the thread of his argumentation correctly, he infers a plurality of versions of SCC from variations in the parallel texts used by Arrouaisians and Premonstratensians and late medieval scribes. But this inference seems a bit risky, inasmuch as it cannot be expected that those who cribbed our Cistercian texts did so without modifying the originals. Like any medieval text, SCC suffered at the hands of careless scribes, but the variants in no way postulate the existence of more than one authentic version of the text, such as we find in Trent, MS 1711.

As regards Ex P, there is no doubt that the document is a complex one. Most scholars are in substantial agreement as to the authenticity of the various official documents which make up the dossier imbedded in the narrative sections.[54] J.-A. Lefèvre attempts to make out a case against the reliability of precisely these narrative sections.[55] My own impression is that most of the apparent inconsistencies are usually no more than indications that the text has gone through several stages

of evolution. With regard to a few concrete cases—Fr Zakar has sug-

gested that the prologue to Ex P, which begins 'We Cistercians, the

first founders of this church,' is redacted in the form of a literary

fiction familiar to pseudoepigraphic writers of antiquity.[56] Whatever

the literary genre adopted for the prologue, however, one would expect

it be in harmony with the integral document it introduces; which is not

wholly the case. In point of fact, the prologue is addressed exclusively

to the successors of this first generation ('We. . .the founders of this

church'), and in that particular monastery, without the slightest hint

of filiations or an Order-wide organization. Again, the prologue claims

to introduce an account about the circumstances of time, person and

place relevant to the beginnings of the monastery (rather than the be-

ginnings of the Order) and of the way of life followed there. Logically,

the compilation could have ended with the text of the Privilegium Romanum

(or Romanorum) or perhaps with the Instituta monachorum cisterciensium

de Molismo venientium, and, in this case, the prologue would have fitted

well. But the compilation goes on to include a mass of material not

taken into account by the prologue. Or consider the third person refer-

ences to Stephen Harding in Chapter XVI, which read most naturally under

the hypothesis that Saint Stephen was no longer alive. Again, the chap-

ter-headings and preliminary index of chapters consistently refer to

Cîteaux under some form of the word Cistercium, which suggests a period

after 1119, when the name _Cistercium_ superseded the name _Novum monas-_
terium characteristic of the older, pre-1119 documentation.[57] In
brief, I think that a careful _formgeschichtliche_ analysis of Ex P by
scholars not given to flights of fancy would tend to suggest that Ex P
began as an _apologia_ for _Novum monasterium_; that this compilation began
as a file of documents with literary prologue and commentary, and that
it dated from a time prior to the population explosion which began with
the birth of La Ferté in 1112; that this original material was then
subject to later additions, so as to take into account the Order's
growth and rapid expansion and organization based on CC; and that the
index and chapter-headings, with their "modern" terminology (_Cistercium_
for _Novum monasterium_) would simply be editorial additions of a relatively late date. Thus, Ex P as we find it in the Laibach manuscript
could well be an up-dated version of a much earlier compilation, and,
in this hypothesis, the up-dating and editorial revisions would have
been in function of providing a more ample, more detailed introduction
to the Cistercian customary of around 1147. (Possibly the desire for a
more abundant documentation of Cistercian beginnings could be explained
by the fact that, in 1147, literally dozens of non-Cistercian communities
were affiliated with the Order in one fell swoop--the monasteries of the
Obazine and Savigny filiations. Certainly the more detailed Ex P and
CC[1] would have been even more helpful as an introduction to EO[2] than the
more stream-lined Ex Cist and SCC.)

What about the date of Ex Cist and SCC? Since they appear in the pre-1147 Cistercian customary, obviously they date from a period prior to 1147. But I personally have difficulty postulating a date much earlier than around 1134.

Several scholars have made out an excellent case for an earlier date by appealing to the fact that the Canons of Arrouaise and the Praemonstratensians had cribbed massively from SCC and EO[1] already by the early 1130s.[58] Unfortunately, the recent editor of the Constitutiones Canonicorum Regularium Ordinis Arroasiensis[59] has had to conclude, on the basis of his painstaking collation of source material, that any date prior to 1135 is out of the question.[60] Studies dealing with the Premonstratensian customary have abounded in recent times,[61] but the only really safe conclusion we can draw on the basis of the present state of research is this: Cistercian influence on Prémontré was certainly present; but influence (via SCC and EO[1]) was subsequent to the compilation of the first books of the Premonstratensian Order, and we do not know when this influence made itself felt.[62] Surely the best and most detailed explicit study of this question is the fairly recent (1972) study by Fr Van Damme, "La 'Summa Cartae caritatis' source de constitutions canoniales."[63] But even though the author accepts an early date (1123/1124) for SCC, none of the facts he musters suggests any borrowing of Cistercian material much before 1134.

Objection! Fr Bruno Griesser, O Cist, editor of Trent, MS 1711,[64] dated the manuscript between 1130 and 1134.[65] Since our two texts are

contained in this manuscript, they obviously existed before 1134. An-

swer: the only real argument formulated by Fr Griesser in favor of a

date as early as 1130 was the argument based on early Cistercian influ-

ence on Prémontré--in the light of current research, an unverifiable

hypothesis. The other arguments brought forward by Fr Griesser are

excellent, but only prove that the Trent manuscript is earlier than 1147,

the approximate date for the conclusion of the liturgical reform which

resulted in a new version of EO.[66]

Again, Fr Van Damme argues for 1123/1124 on the basis of a much

discussed passage in Ex Cist--a passage which Fr Van Damme understands

to refer to the state of the Order in 1123 or 1124.[67] But granted that

Fr Van Damme is correct in assigning 1123/1124 as the last datable ref-

erence in the text of Ex Cist, it seems (to me) a bit risky to conclude

that the entire document dates from around the time of the last histori-

cal reference mentioned in the text.[68]

And what is my own reason for feeling uncomfortable about a date

earlier than 1134? Simply this: the author refers to Stephen Harding

in honorific terms such as could hardly have been used by Stephen him-

self had he authored the text or even simply approved it;[69] and if the

text, used in official compilations of the Order, really did pre-date

1134 (Stephen resigned as abbot of Cîteaux in 1133, and died the following

year),[70] then Stephen himself must have written it, or at least authorized

it. Fr Van Damme refers to <u>Ex Cist</u> and <u>SCC</u> as non-official texts,[71]
but this surely fails to meet the objection that they formed the
official introduction to the early Cistercian customary and were an
integral part of the <u>consuetudines</u>. Cistercian abbots often styled
themselves <u>humilis abbas</u>, but never <u>venerabilis</u>, and, so far as I know,
even the worst prigs of the lot never wrote about their own <u>sagacitas
pervigilis</u>.[72] Besides, when Stephen wanted to refer to himself, he knew
how to do it in the first person, as we know from several texts certainly authored by himself.[73]

     Accordingly, I would prefer to opine (but only tentatively) that
the introductory matter to EO^1 was put together either by, or under
the aegis of Renard de Bar, who early in 1134 became abbot of Cîteaux
in succession to the deplorable Gui I of most unhappy memory.[74] I feel
confident that EO existed in some form long before 1134, and I also
consider it likely that Stephen, its author or compiler, would have
provided it with an introductory preface. However, on the basis of the
manuscript evidence here and now at our disposal, I cannot see that the
controllable facts allow us to situate <u>Ex Cist</u> and <u>SCC</u> in their present
form much earlier than 1134.

     In concluding, I should like to insist on the hypothetical nature
of most of my foregoing remarks. However, it seems to me that the
evidence we have to go on does not allow us to advance much farther
than the formulation of working hypotheses. At the same time, of all

the hypotheses proposed to explain the existence and shape of Ex Cist and SCC, I believe that the most satisfactory by far is this quite new hypothesis: namely, that Ex Cist and SCC were redacted simply as part of the prefatory matter to the ever-evolving Cistercian customary. However, my real intention is less to propose yet another hypothesis, than to provide the possible occasion for a renewed study of the documentary sources made available in so convenient a form by the scholarly collaboration of Fr Bouton and Fr Van Damme.

50   Ideals and Reality

NOTES

1. P. Dr. Polykarp Zakar, O Cist, "Die Anfänge des Zisterzienserordens: Kurze Bemerkungen zu den Studien der letzen zehn Jahre," ASOC 20 (1964) 103-138 (= Zakar, "Anfänge").

2. See David Knowles, "The Primitive Cistercian Documents," in <u>Great Historical Enterprises: Problems in Monastic History</u> (London, Edinburgh, Paris, Melbourne, Johannesburg, Toronto, New York, 1963) pp. 197-222; and Zakar, "Anfänge," pp. 134-37.

3. Zakar, "Anfänge," p. 107.

4. The bibliographical listings under Fr Van Damme's name, in Zakar, "Anfänge," p. 104, give only those studies of immediate interest to the subject at hand. A full listing of Fr Van Damme's studies on things Cistercian would be much more ample.

5. "Autour des origines cisterciennes: Quelques à-propos," ASOC 21 (1965) 128-37.

6. "Le origini dell'Ordine Cisterciense e la riforma monastica," ASOC 21 (1965) 112-27.

7. "Réponse aux <u>Quelques à-propos</u> du Père Van Damme sur les origines cistercienne: Quelques conclusions," ASOC 21 (1965) 138-66.

8. "La <u>Summa Cartae caritatis</u> source de Constitutions canoniales," Cîteaux 23 (1972) 5-54.

9. In <u>Cîteaux: Commentarii Cistercienses, Studia et Documenta,</u> II (Achel, 1974). Hereafter abbreviated: <u>PATC</u>.

10. A few other related early documents are edited in Part IV. Annexes,
    p. 129 ff.

11. <u>PATC</u>, pp. 9-23.

12. The full title rees on to read: ...publiés d'après les manuscrits
    de l'Abbaye de Cîteaux (Dijon, 1878).

13. In <u>Vom Cistercienser Orden</u> (Bregenz, 1927) p. 258. This volume brings
    together under one cover the series of articles published piece-meal
    in C CH 37 (1925)-39 (1927).

14. Perhaps better known by his name in religion, Robert Trihle.

15. T. Hümpfner, <u>Exordium Cistercii cum Summa Cartae Caritatis et
    fundatio primarum quattuor filiarum Cistercii</u> (Vác, 1932).

16. Laibach, University Library, MS 31; Zürich, Zentralbibliothek, MS 75.
    Mgr. Turk presented his discovery and argued his case, first in
    Slovene: <u>Prvotna Charta Caritatis: Akademija znanosti in umetnosti v
    Ljubljani, Filozofvko-filovko-historivni razred, historivna sekcija</u>
    (ljubljana, 1942); then in Latin translation: "Charta Caritatis Prior,"
    in ASOC 1 (1945) 11-61; finally in his edition, <u>Cistercii statuta anti-
    quissima</u> (ASOC 4 [1948--though this issue actually appeared in 1949] 1-159).

17. Jean Leclercq, OSB, "Une ancienne rédaction des coutumes cisterciennes,"
    RHE 47 (1952) 172-76.

18. "La véritable constitution cistercienne de 1119," Coll. 16 (1954) 77-104,
    with special reference to the conclusion, p. 95.

19. Ibid., pp. 93-94.

20. "La vrai récit primitif des origines cisterciennes est-il l'
     Exordium Parvum?,' Le Moyen Age 61 (1955) 79-120 and 329-61. The
     same hypothesis figures massively in the author's article, "Que
     savons-nous du Cîteaux primitif?," RHE 51 (1956) 5-41.

21. First article listed above, note 20, with special reference to
     the summary statement, p. 105.

22. G. De Beaufort (alias Jean de la Croix Bouton, OSCO), "La charte
     de charité cistercienne et son évolution," RHE 49 (1954) 432.

23. Histoire de l'Ordre de Cîteaux. Fiches cisterciennes (Westmalle,
     1959) p. 107.

24. Preface to Autour de la spiritualité cistercienne, III. Pain de
     Cîteaux 15 (Chambarand, 1962) p. 102.

25. Autour des origines cisterciennes [a collection of articles
     published in Coll. 20 (1958)-21 (1959)] p. [94] 156. In the
     body of the text, Fr Van Damme qualifies this date as "probable";
     but in his earlier edition of early Cistercian texts, Documenta
     pro Cisterciensis Ordinis Historia ac Juris Studio (Westmalle, 1959)
     p. 21, he edits the texts of Ex Cist and SCC under the date 1123/1124
     without further qualification.

26. "Autour des origines cisterciennes: Quelques à-propos," ASOC 21
     (1965) 129.

27. In Documenta, Fr Van Damme edited both texts under the same date.

28. Autour des origines, pp. [91] 153-[94] 155.

29. See the prefatory note, PATC, p. 4.

30. PATC, pp. 9-14, with summary of conclusion given, p. 14.

31. PATC, p. 18.

32. PATC, pp. 16-18.

33. PATC, p. 19.

34. PATC, p. 22.

35. Ibid.

36. Ibid.; see also the article which deals explicitly with this topic,
    listed above, note 8.

37. Examples abound. See, for instance, "Prologus in Libro Constitutionum
    Ordinis Arroasiae," edited in L. Milis, Constitutiones Canonicorum
    Regularium Ordinis Arroasiensis. CC. continuatio mediaevalis XX
    (Tournai, 1970) pp. 243-44. This text is a literal adaptation of
    the parallel Premonstratensian text dating from 1171-1175 onwards;
    the edition I have at hand is the one in E. Martène, De antiquis
    Ecclesiae ritibus III (Bassani, 1787) p. 323. Many of these prefaces
    are little more than a modestly expanded rubric; whereas others,
    such as the long introduction to the Concordia Regularis (excellent
    edition by Thomas Symons, OSB, [New York, 1953]), consist of an
    ample historical narrative running to nine printed pages. Quite
    different is the less pretentious preface to the first customary of
    Grandmont, p. 17, of the edition by Jean Becquet, OSB, "L'Institution:

premier coutumier de l'Ordre de Grandmont," <u>Revue Mabillon</u> 46
(1956). The variety of such prefaces can best be seen by thumbing
through the abundant collection of religious rules and constitutions
collected by L. Holstenius, OSB, <u>Codex Regularum</u> (Vienna, 6 tomes,
1759) or by tracking down the material listed in the massive bibliography of monastic customaries in Tome I, pp. lix-lxxiv, of the
series <u>Corpus Consuetudinum Monasticarum</u>.

38. There is a letter-"prologus" by Saint Bernard, edited by Jean
Leclercq, OSB, pp. 515-16 of vol. III of his Op. S. Bern.; in the
manuscripts, this is followed by a long treatise explaining the
theoretical basis of the Cistercian chant reform of around 1147.
The most accessible (though poor) edition is the one by Dom Mabillon
in PL 182:1121-32.

39. PL 182:1151-54.

40. The earliest known manuscripts of these usages are edited in the
"Annexe" to the long study by J.-A. Lefèvre, "L'évolution des <u>Usus
Conversorum</u> de Cîteaux," Coll. 17 (1955) 84-97. Unfortunately the
editor has included among these three manuscripts Montpellier H. 322
which, far from being "early," is actually composed chiefly of
extracts and abridgements of a manuscript basically the same as
Laibach 31.

41. Often re-printed since the first transcription appeared in Pierre
Blanchard, OSB, "Un monument primitif de la règle cistercienne,"

R Ben 31 (1914) 35-44. The last edition was in Chrysogonus

Waddell, OCSO, "The Origin and Early Evolution of the Cistercian

Antiphonary: Reflections on Two Cistercian Chant Reforms," in

The Cistercian Spirit. CS 3 (Spencer, 1970) p. 206, where the text

appears with brief commentary.

42. Edited by the late Cistercian scholar to whom Cistercian studies

owe so much: Fr Bruno Griesser, O Cist, "Die Ecclesiastica Officia

Cisterciensis Ordinis des Cod. 1711 von Trient," ASOC 12 (1956)

153-288.

43. Edited by Fr Canisius Noschitzka, O Cist, in ASOC 6 (1950) 1-124:

Codex manuscriptus 31 Bibliothecae Universitatis Labacensis.

44. Justification for the date 1147 is based chiefly on the fact that

the Cistercian books in use at the then non-Cistercian abbey of

Obazine had to be revised when this monastery with its affiliated

communities was incorporated into the Cistercian Order in 1147. For

more ample details, see pp. 192-93 of the article by C. Waddell,

referred to above, note 41. The approximative nature of the date

1147 should be insisted on.

45. Abundant material and manuscript references in Fr Van Damme's

study, "Genèse des Instituta Generalis Capituli," in Cîteaux 12

(1961) 28-60.

46. For a brief treatment of the dating and content of this revision,

see Chrysogonus Waddell, "The Early Cistercian Experience of

Liturgy," in <u>Rule and Life</u>.   CS 12 (Spencer, 1971) p. 80, note 6,
and pp. 99-100.

47. Obviously, scribes intent upon providing copies of the Cistercian
usages would have been less interested in the ample prefatory
material, which is perhaps why even relatively late manuscripts
continue to use for the narrative section <u>Ex Cist</u> rather than the
prolix <u>Ex P</u>. The fact that <u>Ex Cist</u> introduces <u>SCC</u> with an explicit
rubric apparently caused the scribes no embarrassment: having
stated that they were about to transcribe a summary of <u>CC</u>, they either omitted it or substituted a later version of the integral text
of <u>CC</u>. Certain manuscripts retain, by way of introductory matter,
only <u>CC</u>. And the statutes found in earlier manuscripts before the
first chapter of the customary proper, are usually transferred to
the end of the customary, where scribes habitually tacked on additional material with a view to keeping the usages up-dated according
to the successive legislation of the annual General Chapters.

48. For a brief rebuttal of J.-A. Lefèvre's position with respect to
this one point, see Zakar, "Anfänge," pp. 109-110.

49. <u>PATC</u>, p. 22, with special attention to note 65.

50. In the final pages of <u>Cistercii statuta antiquissima</u> (Rome, 1949)
157-59.

51. P. Dr. Paschalis Vermeer, O Cist, "St Bernardus en de Orden der
Reguliere Kannunniken van Prémontré, St Victor en Arrouaise," in

Sint Bernardus van Clairvaux: Gedenkboek (Achel, 1953) 55-64, with special reference to p. 61.

52. "La charte," p. 395ff.

53. _Ibid._, p. 402.

54. A glaring exception is the Dijon archivist, Jean Marilier, in his _Chartes et documents concernant l'Abbaye de Cîteaux 1098-1182._ Bibliotheca cisterciensis I (Rome, 1961). Nowhere does he state his norms for identifying several (unimportant) items of the dossier as falsifications. His overly frequent errors, however, suggest a certain reserve in accepting his highly personal, unsubstantiated judgments about particular points, without further verification of the facts.

55. This seems to be one of the main points in his long study, "Le vrai récit," and in his later synthesis, "Que savons-nous," indicated above, note 20.

56. Zakar, "Anfänge," p. 129; re-iterated with detailed argumentation in "Reponse aux Quelques à-propos," ASOC 21 (1965) 150-51.

57. See J. Marilier, "Le vocable Novum Monasterium dans les premiers documents cisterciens," C Ch 57 (1950) 81-84, of which the essential is repeated in the author's edition referred to above, note 54 (pp. 24-26).

58. Among them, J.-A. Lefèvre, "Le véritable constitution cistercienne de 1119," Coll. 16 (1954), with special reference to pp. 90-93;

Mgr Turk, in his conclusions, p. 157 of his <u>Cistercii statuta</u>

<u>antiquissima</u>, based on his analysis of material presented p. 142 ff.;

Fr Bouton, "La charte," pp. 404-405; Fr Van Damme, <u>Autour des origines</u>

<u>cisterciennes</u>, p. (23) 59; Fr Griesser, in his introduction to his

edition of Trent 1711, in ASOC 12 (1956) 162.

59. L. Milis, in the edition referred to above, note 37.

60. Starting with 1121 and 1139 as the extreme limits, the author narrows

the date to "1135 or thereabouts," <u>ibid.</u>, p. lii. The problem of

the dating of this compilation, based on an analysis of the sources,

is treated systematically, pp. xlix-lii.

61. For a bibliography of studies touching on the early Premonstratensian

liturgical books and their sources—a bibliography of material prior

to 1957—see Placide F. Lefèvre, O Praem, <u>La liturgie de Prémontré</u>.

Bibliotheca Analectorum Praemonstratensium 1 (Louvain, 1957) pp. viii-

xvii. For bibliographical references to the literature for the fol-

lowing decade, see the study by L. Milis, "De Premonstratenzer-

Wetgeving in de xiie eeuw: Een nieuwe getuige," <u>Analecta Praemon-</u>

<u>stratensia</u> 44 (1968) 181-214 and 45 (1969) 5-23. Also extremely

helpful are the references in Fr Van Damme's study referred to above,

note 8.

62. The summary-statement formulated by Fr Zakar, "Anfänge," p. 128, retains

its full force a decade after it was written: "Ausserdem sind die

Forschungen über das ursprüngliche Ordensrecht der Prämonstratenser

und der Kanoniker von Arrouaise noch im Fluss und mit sehr vielen

Hypothesen belastet." Thanks, however, to the studies by L. Milis, preparatory to his edition of the customary from Arrouaise, the situation with regards to the Canons of Arrouaise is much clearer than is the case of the Norbertines.

63. See above, note 8.

64. In ASOC 12 (1956) 153-288.

65. _Ibid._, with special attention to the Summary, pp. 174-75.

66. Fr Griesser shows that Trent 1711 agrees with the readings of the so-called "Stephen Harding Breviary," the sole manuscript of which can be dated around 1132 (on the basis of calendar indications and computation tables). But since this particular recension of the Cistercian breviary was superseded by a revised version around 1147, Fr Griesser's argument shows simply that Trent 1711, with its Ex Cist and SCC, is earlier than 1147. His second argument, based on the reform of the Order's chant, is bound up with the same liturgical revision of around 1147, and leads to the same ante quem date. (In this section, Fr Griesser reproduces a number of inaccuracies found in the material from which he drew his information.) The third element to establish the date of EO^1 is the alleged fact that the Premonstratensians had already borrowed from EO^1 as early as around 1131--an argument already demolished earlier in the course of the present study. In point of fact, Fr Griesser himself was more cautious when he returned to the question in the final paragraph of his summary, ibid., p. 175. The fourth element--the

introduction of the ferial day Office for the Dead--simply suggests

that Trent 1711 would be after 1127/1128, the date of a Benedictine

"response" to Saint Bernard's Apologia, in which the author complains

of the White Monks: "vigiliae pro defunctis. . .minime decantantur."

The introduction of the Ascension procession (absent from the Trent

MS) would certainly place the manuscript before 1151; and the refer-

ence to albis induti in choir--a reference modified in EO^2--simply

indicates that EO^1 came before EO^2. In brief, the elements for

establishing the date of the Trent redaction point to sometime be-

tween the early 1130s and around 1147. The period 1130-1134 is much

too restrictive, if based on the clues for dating put forward by

Fr Griesser.

67. Details relative to this text can be found in Fr Van Damme's Autour

    des origines cisterciennes, p. [15] 51, with particular attention

    to pp. [22] 58 - [24] 60; and Zakar, "Anfänge," pp. 109-110, note 7.

68. The principle on which Fr Van Damme bases his case is clearly ex-

    plained on p. [24] 60 of Autour des origines cisterciennes: unless

    there are positive reasons to the contrary, a historical narrative

    is generally dated by the event which brings it to a close. But in

    this present instance, there just might be a positive reason to the

    contrary. If it is a tenable hypothesis that Ex Cist and SCC were

    redacted to provide the introduction to an early form of EO, it would

    be perfectly understandable were the author to limit his material to

the essentials of his narrative. Having written about the beginnings of New Monastery and the growth of the community into an
Order organized along the lines stipulated by CC, there was no
reason why he should pursue the narrative after the confirmation
of CC by twenty abbots and the pope. Thus, the possibility of a
period between the last event mentioned and the redaction should
not be excluded.

69. "Venerabilis pater Stephanus sagacitate pervigili mirae providerat
     discretionis scriptum...." PATC, p. 113.

70. J. Marilier, "Catalogue des abbés de Cîteaux pour le XIIe siecle,"
     C Ch 55 (1948) 5.

71. PATC, pp. 18 and 22-23.

72. Note 69, above.

73. It would take a fairly inventive mind to make out a case against
     Stephen's authorship of the Prologue to the Usus Conversorum. See
     pp. 85-86 of J.-A. Lefèvre's study referred to above, note 40. See,
     too, Stephen's Monitum to the recension of the Vulgate made at
     Cîteaux; the brief text has been edited in Marilier, Chartres et
     documents, p. 56. Or the frequently edited Monitum to the pre-1147
     Cistercian hymnal.

74. Chronological details based on J. Marilier, "Catalogue des abbés."

EARLY CISTERCIAN LIFE AS DESCRIBED BY THE

ECCLESIASTICA OFFICIA

Bede K. Lacker, O Cist
University of Texas in Arlington

The study of the early Cistercian ideals has made great progress in recent years; yet the task is far from accomplished. This paper seeks to make a modest contribution to the project by examining the life and the daily routine of the first Cistercians on the basis of the earliest extant draft of the Ecclesiastica officia, the customary of Cîteaux, probably dating in part from the third decade of the twelfth century.[1] Such an undertaking, not as yet attempted in a comprehensive fashion, has its advantages and its rewards, since the other early sources, the Exordium parvum or even the decisions of the first general chapters-- to mention only the most obvious--treat but particular aspects of the Cistercian life and remain unsettled in their chronology. Nor does Saint Bernard provide an extensive or systematic overview of the subject for, pursuing loftier goals bordering on the sublime, he was less con- cerned with matters of ordinary routine.[2] The Ecclesiastica officia, on the other hand, describes the early Cistercian ways in a rather exhaustive manner, yielding authentic and vital information about the Order in its fervor novitius and thus furnishing the tools for greatly needed further investigations.[3] But, first, a look at the fundamentals is in order.

Early Cîteaux has often been described as a locus horroris et vastae solitudinis and its reform called a retrogression to more

primitive, that is, inferior, monastic forms,[4] but such a characteriza-
tion, contradicted by unassailable historical evidence, must not be
taken literally as this investigation will seek to demonstrate.

The physical plant of the monastery, with its diverse localities
and quarters, gave early evidence of a rich and vibrant monastic life.
To list some particulars: there was the chapel and the adjoining
sacristy for the divine office and the liturgy. In the chapter room
the monks assembled for prayers, spiritual instruction and community
matters (profession, discipline, information, obligations, etc.). In
the auditorium or parlor they could speak about necessary matters. The
kitchen, the cellar, the two refectories--of the community and the abbot,
respectively--the dormitory and the infirmary served their obvious and
necessary purpose. In the calefactorium or heated room all could warm
themselves, grease their shoes and have the minutio (bleeding). In the
cloister, the wide corridor connecting most of these places, they did
their reading and study, had the weekly maundy and their periodic haircut
and shave. Special quarters housed the novices and the guests, each with
its own refectory, dormitory and infirmary.[5]

Other examples demonstrating our argument may be gathered from the
way the monastic community had been structured. For, it could on no
account be called a primitive society. It consisted of professed monks
--some of them priests--novices and two types of brothers,[6] all of whom
were organized in the proper order of seniority in the choir and the other

regular places.[7]

Within this monastic family additional classifications prevailed, since the monks discharged a great variety of duties and offices, often with substitutes. Thus we know of at least ten different regular offices. The abbot had the overall responsibility in the monastery; in his absence the prior or the subprior carried out some of his routine duties.[8] The sacristan was responsible for the church and the sacristy and for the monastery's clock acting, in a way, as the official timekeeper. The cantor, that is, the chant and choir master, was also the official announcer in the chapter room and was also in charge of the armarium (aumbry) where the books--liturgical and other--and the documents of the monastery were kept. The novice master taught and trained the young. The cellarer looked after the material needs of the brethren, particularly in the kitchen and the refectory, and supervised the lay brothers who did, among other things, the house-cleaning. The infirmarian cared for the sick brethren. The gate-keeper and the guest-master received and accomodated the visitors and guests.[9]

In addition to these regular offices there were numerous other, weekly rotating assignments in the choir (hebdomadary, invitator, reader, etc.), the kitchens and the refectory (for example, the cooks and the servers), again attesting a wide range of activities and occupations within the monastery.[10]

Added to the list must also be the so-called familia, that is, domestics closely associated with the monks, the visitors and guests--

Cistercians and other monks, ecclesiastics, canons and laymen--and,

finally, the neighbors and passersby who were received and given assist-

ance at the gate of the monastery.[11]

Obviously, these activities of the monastery centered around the

three basic occupations assigned to the monks by St Benedict, to whom

the Ecclesiastica officia--significantly--referred as "our holy Father

Benedict."[12] But they involved more than one would think at first sight.

The work of God, or choir, consisted of seven separate canonical hours

made up primarily of psalms, hymns and readings. To this the Cistercians

added, on ordinary weekdays, the Office of the Dead. They also celebrated

a daily community Mass--two such Masses on great feasts and during Lent

--and a daily Mass for the dead, while individual priests were free to

offer Mass privately. They devoted the morning and afternoon hours

(after chapter and None, respectively) to manual labor which involved

all kind of work: officials looked after their duties, scribes kept

busy in the scriptorium and, in the haying and harvesting season, the

whole community went out to the field. Each morning, moreover, the monks

gathered in the chapter room to deal, among other things, with matters

of common interest. Then there was the collatio or daily community

reading which preceded the office of Compline, while the intervals after

Lauds and Vespers and the free periods on days when there was no field

work could be devoted to reading, prayer, chant practice and the prepara-

tion of the readings. To complete the list, mention must finally be
made of the daily community meals which on non-lenten days included
breakfast, the noon and evening meals and the two so-called biberes
('bevers'). All this shows that the daily routine was filled with
numerous, highly productive activities which benefited not only the
monks themselves, but--through their apostolate and hospitality--also
the world at large.[13]

Nor were opportunities for a personal enrichment lacking, for,
contrary to widespread beliefs, the lectio was not restricted to a bare
minimum. Thus, some members of the community could read and write quite
well; among them must have been the scribes[14] who, as we know from other
sources, greatly excelled in their field. Others knew the whole psalter
by heart or else managed to memorize at least fifty psalms, while the
remainder was able to recite only Psalm Fifty or the Lord's Prayer.[15]
Readers uncertain about accents and pronunciation were assisted by the
cantor or another competent brother.[16] The novices studied the Rule of
St Benedict which was read to them several times during their year of
probation; they were tutored by the novice master through instruction
and correction. During the noviciate they must also have learned the
so-called sign language which enabled the necessary communication in an
atmosphere of silence.[17]

But the monks' education continued even after the year of initiation
This first of all through the various scriptural and patristic readings

of the liturgy, the table reading and the collatio.[18] In addition there

was, in the chapter room, the daily explanation (by the abbot or someone

he had appointed) of the Rule of St Benedict which--in view of its in-

debtedness to scriptural, patristic and early monastic sources--contains

not only rules and regulations, but also an impressive amount of in-

structional material.[19] Special sermons, given on great feasts to the

assembled monks, novices and lay brothers in the chapter room, provided

an additional channel of instruction.[20] To this should be added that

visiting churchmen could address the monks in the chapter room, offering

them, one may presume, words of enlightenment and edification.[21] Finally,

the daily schedule left ample time, the various free periods (intervals),

for private reading and study, and many hours on feast days when the

community did not work.[22] The rule was that everyone should hold a book

in his hand during the lectio, while special books were distributed to

all for the season of Lent.[23] Of course, these books were not the libri

communes--the antiphonary, gradual, book of readings, book of collects,

the martyrology, the books used in the refectory or at the collatio--

but works of the Fathers, among them the writings of Augustine, Jerome,

Gregory and, very importantly, Origen. Considering the fact that even

at a much later date the library of Cambridge University numbered but

some 122 volumes, the first Cistercians, quite endowed also in this re-

spect, should be given full credit for their desire to cultivate true

knowledge and learning.[24]

The elements just outlined clearly underscore the communitarian
nature of early Cistercian life. This found its eminent expression in
the weekly maundy, and in numerous other ways. Thus, when meeting each
other, the brethren made a silent bow in salutation. Officials, never
claiming power or a preferential treatment, simply worked for the
brethren's welfare, that is, for the common good. While the atmosphere
of silence was strictly maintained, the brethren could talk in the
parlor about necessary matters or legitimately ask for a book used by
another during the lectio if they needed it, while those practicing or
rehearsing for the office received help from the cantor or a competent
substitute. In the dining room the cellarer could distribute extra
food to individual monks who in turn were allowed to share it with thei
immediate neighbors. Special care, bodily as well as spiritual, was
given to the sick and the ailing, and the whole community assisted when
someone was anointed or lay dying. And, in the chapter room, the senio
had the right to intercede on behalf of those who were to be flogged an
plead for mercy while, after the flogging, the penitent was helped up
by the very brother who administered the blows.[25]

Many-faceted as it was, the life of the early Cistercians remained
one of poverty and simplicity. Mutatis mutandis, this applied to the
chapel, the choir and to the liturgy.[26] In line with this spirit, the
monks' wardrobe numbered but a few items: the tunic, the scapular,
cincture, the cuculla or cowl, stockings, day and night shoes, and a

knife.[27] The brethren wore the traditional tonsure, a narrow hair crown just above the ear, and had their beards shaven and their hair cut only seven times during the year. They used combs, scissors and razors only on these occasions. Equally simple was the daily diet, consisting of bread, salt, cruder herbs, greens and vegetable dishes prepared without fat or lard (a rule they observed even during travel), and, rejecting contemporary ingenuities, they drank only water, milk, wine and ale.[28]

But the rigor ordinis--a condition for admission--made additional demands on the brethren. There was, for instance, no recreation in the modern sense, only the recuperation brought about by the alternation of activities. And sleep, in spite of the midday rest granted during the summer months, was not superfluous, for, unlike most of their contemporaries, the Cistercians did not return to their beds after Lauds. Nor did they make allowances to fatigue: tired brethren were awakened (by the cantor and his substitute) during the night office, and when reading (privately) in the cloister or in the chapter room, they kept their hoods in such a way that it could easily be ascertained if they had fallen asleep.[29] But their life called for still more sacrifices. On regular fast days the (main) meal was deferred until after the office of None (rather than after Sext), while during Lent everyone fasted until after Vespers.[30] They spent the day in total silence, even in the infirmary, and also in the refectory during meals when all listened to the table reading. Travel was, understandably, prohibited. An exception was made

only when the good of the monastery made it necessary, but even then
the rule of silence and the provisions about food and prayer remained
in full force. Work, too, was done in silence--hence the prohibition
against taking along books when going to field work. In case of an
urgent need during field labor or in the infirmary the rule was simply:
speak with the proper official briefly, in a low voice and at a distance
from others. To keep the rule of silence, the gate-keeper would not
speak with a visitor while the brethren were praying the divine office,
but asked him to wait until after the hour, and once the guest-master
had taken the guest, the porter spoke with him only when he left again.
But neither he nor the guest-master communicated with a visiting monk
or lay brother of the Order, for reasons not specified though easy to
imagine.[31]

The government of the monastery rested primarily with the abbot.
He had his special duties in the choir and in the liturgy, he led the
proceedings in the chapter room and presided at the <u>collatio</u>. He tonsured
the novices and received their profession. He appointed the monastic
officials. He made promotions or demotions in seniority, assigned pen-
ances for external transgressions, gave absolution from them, and if
the situation called for it, dismissed novices or monks.

Yet his duties involved more ministrations than prerogatives. For,
in the choir the abbot was among the brethren, not in an ornate stall
of his own. He was hebdomadary like every other priest and made the

prescribed satisfactions for mistakes. He kept the rule of silence,
also in his refectory, took part in manual labor when at home and slept
in the common dormitory. He used no pontificalia, only his pastoral
staff, symbolic of the true nature of his office. On Holy Thursday he
washed the feet of the brethren. The spiritual father of the monastery,
he heard the confession of the brethren in the chapter room, anointed
the sick, assisted the dying and buried the dead. He had no privileged
status that could have set him apart from the community. He even shared
his responsibility with the various officials who had full superinten-
dence in their departments and treated community matters in the chapter
room in a truly collegial fashion—a very modern exercise of government
by consultation and participation.[32]

Determined to be faithful to their ideals, the first Cistercians
found many ways to rectify external disorders. Officials made public
amends if they failed in their duties. Latecomers to the choir or other
community exercises performed similar public satisfactions varying according to places and seasons. The same was done by those who mispro-
nounced texts in the recitation or during the readings, not excluding
the abbot. The monk who confounded another had to prostrate himself
before the prior until the latter told him to rise. While the novices
revealed their (external) faults to the novice master, the monks confessed
them in the chapter room, either of their own accord or else they were
denounced by others, but always with the proper safeguards to exclude

unfairness. Sanctions in these cases could mean degradation from the
seniority, flogging in the chapter room, placement in _gravi_ _culpa_,
and even ejection from the monastery. The fact, however, that the abbot
and in his absence the prior--the latter only in case of necessity--would
give absolution _a_ _criminalibus_ shows that the emphasis was on the remedial
rather than the punitive in these sanctions.[33]

The Cistercian life portrayed thus far may seem rather self-
directed, with no great concern for the outside world; a closer look,
however, reveals an entirely different picture. As is known, visitors
came rather frequently to the monastery and were duly greeted _pedum_
lotione. They included not only members of the Order, but also a great
variety of other people: monks, canons, secular priests, Church digni-
taries--bishops, archbishops, legates--and lay lords. All participated
in the Mass, received Holy Communion with the kiss of peace, and took
part in other liturgical celebrations in the church and the cloister.
The local ordinary, the pope or his representative and prospective lay
benefactors--including those who sought an association with the Order--
were properly welcomed also in the chapter room. Some visitors could
freely enter the monastery; they did not have to be announced to the
abbot since it was not fitting to keep them waiting at the gate. The
passersby and women with infants were given bread at the gate. Women
of the neighborhood even received free food if they suffered from lepro-
sy, or in the case of famine if the abbot ordered the relief. On Holy

Thursday the abbot washed the feet of twelve poor who were later given
a meal and a coin, in imitation of Christ's loving concern for man. In
an equally genuine solicitude for the spiritual well-being of others,
numerous efforts--Masses, prayers, offices, psalters or their equivalent
--were made on behalf of the deceased, particularly deceased confreres,
parents, brothers, sisters and benefactors. And, since the monks' life
revolved around the work of God to which they were summoned by the
church bell, this bell, heard by all in the neighborhood, certainly
elicited prayerful sentiments in them; thus the monastery shared its
goods and blessings with the outside world.[34]

In conclusion, a brief reply is still in order to those who tend
to see in medieval monastic customaries--in this instance, the Ecclesiastica officia--an exercise in ritualism, with all its negative conno-
tations. To begin with, all the provisions in question--minute and
otherwise--were meaningful to, and well understood by, the early Cistercians. Nor were the postulates of the Ecclesiastica officia in any way
confining, restrictive or spiritually, intellectually stifling. They
did not demand a mechanical observance. On the contrary, the purpose
of the regulations was to cultivate ideals, not paragraphs. Thus no
absolute uniformity was insisted upon, nor was spiritual freedom, individual responsibility or personal growth restricted. For, the raison
d'être of the Ecclesiastica officia was not a compartmentalization of
the monastic life--as today's anti-legalist would call it--but the

creation of an _acies bene ordinata_, of a world of peaceful tranquillity and harmony devoid of confusion, disorder and uncertainty. This is the atmosphere in which virtue was to grow. And, finally, a dedication to this kind of life required no small degree of dedication, loyalty and courage, for only heroic souls were able to embrace the _rigor ordinis_. Understandably, then, this was the framework which helped the first Cistercians to reach the lofty heights we still admire today.

NOTES

1. The three twelfth-century drafts of the Ecclesiastica officia have been published by Bruno Griesser, "Die Ecclesiastica Officia Cisterciensis Ordinis des Cod. 1711 von Trient," ASOC 12 (1956) 153-288; Canisius Noschitzka, "Codex manuscriptus 31 Bibliothecae Universitatis Labacensis," ASOC 6 (1950) 38-124; and Philippe Guignard, Les monuments primitifs de la règle cistercienne (Dijon, 1878). Additional information may be gathered from Ursmer Berlière, "Les coutumiers monastiques," R Ben. 23 (1906) 260-67; Watkin Williams, Studies in St Bernard of Clairvaux (New York, 1927) pp. 73-106; Jean Leclercq, "Une ancienne rédaction des coutumes cisterciennes," RHE 47 (1952) 172-76; and Bruno Schneider, "Cîteaux und die benediktinische Tradition: Die Quellenfrage des Liber Usuum im Lichte der Consuetudines monasticae," ASOC 16 (1960) 169-254 and 17 (1961) 73-111.

2. See Bede Lackner, "The Monastic Life According to Saint Bernard of Clairvaux", in John R. Sommerfeldt (ed.), Studies in Medieval Cistercian History, II. CS 24 (Kalamazoo, 1976) pp. 49-62.

3. Such studies will not only have to examine the existing material in a much greater detail, but also compare it with later drafts of the Ecclesiastica officia and with the customaries of other monastic

institutions in order to determine their relationship, dependence

and possible interaction.

4. Exordium Cistercii, 1, ed. Joannes-B. Van-Damme in Documenta pro

    Cisterciensis Ordinis historiae ac juris studio (Westmalle, 1959)

    p. 22. Such views are also reflected in Cuthbert Butler, Benedictine

    Monasticism (New York, 1961) p. 360 and Louis J. Lekai, The White

    Monks (Okauchee, Wisconsin, 1953) p. 147.

5. See Ecclesiastica officia (hereafter cited EO), chaps. 70, 72, 76,

    92, 102, 113 and 120. These regular places were certainly needed

    from the very outset even though one must not think of elaborate or

    fancy structures.

6. EO, chaps. 17, 22 and 47. On the lay brothers see Kassius Hallinger,

    "Woher kommen die Laienbrüder?," ASOC 12 (1956) 25 and 51.

7. EO, chaps. 17, 22 and 102. On parallels in eastern monasticism

    see Georg Schreiber, "Anselm von Havelberg und die Ostkirche," ZKG

    60 (1942) 400.

8. EO, chaps. 110-12. See also below, n. 32.

9. EO, chaps. 113-20.

10. EO, chaps. 103-109.

11. EO, chaps. 86-87, 117-20. See also above, no. 6, and K. Hallinger,

    "Woher kommen die Laienbrüder?," p. 17 f.

12. EO, chaps. 15, 24, 60, 67 and 110. In addition to explicit re-

    ferences, a great many regulations simply repeat the injunctions of

the Rule. On the whole subject see also Bede Lackner, The Eleventh-
Century Background of Cîteaux CS 8 (Washington, 1972) p. 268f.,
and Anselm Le Bail, "La paternité de saint Benoît sur l'Ordre de
Cîteaux," Coll. 9 (1947) 110-30.

13. EO, chaps. 2, 48-50, 53f., 59f., 69-71, 73-76, 78, 80-84. For a
later version of the daily schedule, see Gregor Müller, "Die
Tagesordnung," C Ch 6 (1894) 343-48 and 369-72; and M. Stanislas
Barbey, Vision de Paix (Fribourg, 1951) pp. 115-26.

14. EO, chaps. 72 and 115. On the activities of the early Cistercian
scribes see Wilhelm Koehler, "Byzantine Art in the West," Dumbarton
Oaks Papers 1 (Cambridge, Massachusetts, 1941) p. 72.

15. EO, chaps. 71, 90, 98f. and 113.

16. EO, chap. 71. This concern about accents, spelling and pronunciation is also attested by Lambert of Pothières when replying to St
Alberic's inquiry. See Jean Marilier, Chartes et documents concernant l'abbaye de Cîteaux, 1098-1182 (Rome, 1961) pp. 41-46.

17. EO, chaps. 102, 113 and 67. More on this subject is found in
Vincent Hermans, "De novitiatu in Regula S. Benedicti et in Libro
Consuetudinum Ordinis Cisterciensis," Coll. 9 (1947) 142-52.

18. EO, chaps. 1, 3, 8, 11, 16, 18, 21-23, 27, 39, 41, 76 and 81.
It will still be necessary to compare the readings prescribed by the
EO with those of the so-called Breviary of St Stephen (Harding),
published by Bruno Griesser, "Das Lektionen- und Perikopensystem im

Stephansbrevier," C Ch 71 (1964) 67-92.

19. EO, chap. 70.

20. EO, chap. 67.

21. EO, chap. 86.

22. EO, chaps. 5, 15, 25, 59f., 70f., 74f., 78, 81, 83, 90, 110 and 115.

23. EO, chaps. 5, 15, 25, 40, 60, 71, 74f., 79 and 83.

24. EO, chaps. 1f., 12, 16, 71, 74 and 115. See also Tiburtius Hümpfner
     "Archivum et bibliotheca Cistercii et quatuor primarum filiarum
     eius," ASOC 2 (1946) 119-32; and Kurt F. Bühler, The Fifteenth-
     Century Book (Philadelphia, 1961) p. 19.

25. EO, chaps. 23, 70-72, 77, 89ff. and 106ff.

26. EO, chaps. 21f. and 67. The liturgy showed no traces of Cluniac
     splendor: the EO list only seventeen hymns, twelve canticles,
     thirty-one collects and eight Gospels by name.

27. EO, chaps. 108f., 71f., 75 and 82f. See also W. Williams, Studies
     in St Bernard of Clairvaux, pp. 86 and 89.

28. EO, chaps. 73, 75, 77, 80, 83f., 108-11, 114 and 117. It is in-
     teresting to note that, next to the liturgy, the provisions are the
     most detailed when dealing with this subject.

29. EO, chaps. 71f., 74, 82f. and 115.

30. EO, chaps. 14, 31, 40, 73, 76, 88, 90 and 92.

31. EO, chaps. 71f., 75f., 78, 88, 92, 102, 109f., 113, 115-17 and
     119f.

32. EO, chaps. 21, 54, 68, 71f., 75, 92-94 and 110-12.

33. EO, chaps. 68-70 and 110.

34. G. Müller, "Die Tagesordnung," p. 372.

THE CANONIZATION OF SAINT BERNARD

AND THE REWRITING OF HIS LIFE

Adriaan Hendrik Bredero
Free University, Amsterdam

When writing a biography nowadays, it is customary to place the life of the subject in his historical context. In this way the human qualities of such a person can be better understood and judged. Medieval hagiography had rather the opposite in mind. Someone's Life was told to express something which was not timebound, his holiness. A Life either made clear why someone had been raised to the honor of the altars, an honor which would be his until the end of time, or it tried to show why he deserved to be raised to such an honor. In the latter instance, which occurred frequently, one tried to achieve the canonization of this person through a written Life. This was because a canonization was the declaration by ecclesiastical authorities that someone was allowed to be venerated as a saint. His feast, which celebrated his birth in heaven was then incorporated in the liturgical calendar. His mortal remains were allowed to be exhumed, to be placed in an altar above his tomb or transferred to a shrine elsewhere, so that they could be venerated as relics of the saint.

Moreover, the relation between the Life and canonization extended beyond the importance attached to the Life as a condition for canonization. At a canonization the Life of him whose canonization was requested was judged, among other things, to verify how far this writing was fit to achieve the purpose of canonization: in how far the reader or listener

of this writing, of this 'legend,' could be roused to such a devotion
to this 'saint' that he would be brought to imitate the virtues which
the Church recommended to her faithful as an expression of a Christian
life. Of these virtues this 'saint,' at least in the way his _Life_
described him, must have been an example. As such an example the saint
lived on after his death; therefore, he was not considered an ordinary
mortal, but rather a man visibly favored by God during his lifetime.
This was clear from a heroic practice of virtue, which equalled the
martyrdom of the early Church. His was a miraculous power, granted
both during his life and after death, by which he penetrated beyond the
limits of human power. Thus the saint was for all times an athlete of
God, and his _Life_ had to demonstrate him as especially favored in ac-
cordance with this basic concept.

In this way the saint appeared in hagiography as an ahistorical
being. His earthly life had a purely accidental value. The visions
which preceded his birth and announced his holiness made clear that he
had already been sanctified in his mother's womb. A judgment on his
human qualities and shortcomings was superfluous, because these had to
give way before the power of grace, by which God had become visible in
him. God manifested himself through the virtues and miracles of the
saint. In him, therefore, one honored God, and through this veneration
one kept close to Him. At the same time one hoped to be allowed to
share in the divine favors bestowed visibly on the saint by obtaining

miracles for those who venerated the saint, for in the miracles these
favors remained operative. This was, in a nutshell, the theological
concept of sanctity, which gave a 'rational' character to canonization
and the veneration of the saints, according to the norms of a medieval
sense of reality.[1]

Historically speaking, the custom of canonization originated from
a concrete need to exercise ecclesiastical control on the desire manifested among the faithful to venerate the dead as saints, all the more
so because their mortal remains occupied an important place in this
veneration due to the miraculous power ascribed to them. Sometimes,
particularly since the seventh century, this desire led to the veneration of relics of extremely doubtful origin, and these relics had to be
given a semblance of authenticity through a Life, which was the simple
brainchild of a commercially inspired hagiographer.[2] When in the course
of the tenth century this evil had been largely overcome, and canonization, as a rule, preceded the veneration of the dead as saints, the process took place principally for pastoral reasons, in order that the
faithful, through this cult, might come closer to God and at the same
time imitate the saint's virtuous life. However, in those days, canonization acquired also a social importance of a more profane character.
The new shrine would be visited by the faithful, something which would
benefit a particular church materially as well. Moreover, canonization
often increased the social prestige of the one who had succeeded this

saint in his ecclesiastical or secular function, or of those who in
other ways considered themselves linked with him in their social status.

Thus the canonization of Edward the Confessor in 1161 was granted
by Alexander III also as a gesture towards Henry II of England, because
the latter, unlike the Emperor Frederick Barbarossa, had refused to
choose the side of the anti-pope Victor IV. The canonization of Edward
implied an increase in the prestige of the ruling princes of England,
something which the canonization of Louis IX in 1297 achieved for the
kings of France. The opposite intent was possible too: Anselm of
Canterbury's canonization in 1163 took place, among other things, because
Alexander III wishes to buttress the prestige of the then archbishop
Thomas Becket because of the conflict with King Henry II. Thus it could
occur that the petitioning or granting of a canonization was also sub-
jected to secondary norms, for example, whether or not it would be poli-
tically opportune.[3]

As we have already seen, a written _Life_ occupied an important place
in a process of canonization. It was an essential document, not only
to achieve canonization, but also to make it pastorally effective.
Naturally this mutual relation existed also between the earliest _Life_
of St. Bernard and his canonization. How important this _Life_ has been
for the promotion of his cult as a saint is evident from the multiplicity
of manuscripts in which this text was handed down.[4] It was written with
the clearly preconceived intention both to obtain his canonization, that

is, the recognition of his sanctity, and to propagate his cult from the
moment his canonization allowed. All the same, this relation is somewhat obscure, because the text of this _Life_, which was completed in
1155-1156 and received in this form the explicit approbation of the
older followers of St. Bernard, was re-written ten years later, or at
least clearly revised, while his canonization took place only on 18
January 1174.

The question that has to be answered here is the reason for this
revision of the text. Was the revision due to changes in the image of
his sanctity? The revision of the text, in fact, was followed by an
internal controversy in the Cistercian order, which in its turn resulted
in the postponement of the canonization of the first abbot of Clairvaux
to a later date. Until recently, while no relation was seen between
the _Life_ of St. Bernard and his canonization, the revision of the text
was explained by the need felt by Geoffrey of Auxerre, its author, who
was still alive, to endow the manuscript with a greater historical reliability.[5] Apart from the fact that such an explanation attributes to
Geoffrey a desire which was alien to his time, the absurdity of this
hypothesis is shown by an accurate comparison of both versions of this
Life. The image of the practice of heroic virtue by St. Bernard and the
narrative of his miracles were slightly touched up in the second version,
simply to accentuate even more strongly the special favors bestowed on
him.[6]

A better clue to the explanation of this revision is provided by
the letter which Pope Alexander III sent to the Church of France on
18 January 1174, promulgating the canonization of St. Bernard. In it
he mentions that in 1163, at the Council convened by him at Tours, a
number of important members of the Cistercian order had handed him a
request for this canonization. According to the pope, he had at the
time not been against the request, but had refused it all the same, or
at least postponed it, for a practical reason: a number of other petitions for canonization had reached him, and these he had to reject in
any case. To avoid scandal, he had also refused to deal with the petition for St. Bernard's canonization.[7]

This clarification by the pope is not plausible, if it were only
for the fact that it occurred in a letter addressed to the Church of
France, which would give it maximum publicity. Surely the scandal which
the pope had wished to avoid in 1163 would still be made in 1174. But
there is a much more likely reason why Alexander refused to deal with
the request of 1163 for St. Bernard's canonization--if one takes into
account the development of the process of canonization in the twelfth
century.

Since the end of the tenth century, it had become customary to
address petitions for canonization no longer to the local bishop, but
to the pope himself. As a result, the recognition of sanctity acquired
a greater authority, and the petitions were dealt with at councils.

86   Ideals and Reality

In the presence of the participants at the council, the <u>Life</u> of the
candidate for canonization was read aloud or translated verbally.
This was followed by a consultation and a decision. This procedure
lasted until during the pontificate of Innocent II (1130-1143). But
even at that time objections had been raised to it. It was argued
that this procedure allowed only a judgment on the edifying character
of a <u>Life</u>, while it made any research into the reliability of the narrative impossible. For the same reason Innocent is said to have refused
a previous request for the canonization of Edward the Confessor.[8] Likewise, Pope Eugene III (1145-1153) had not wanted to deal with the canonization of the Emperor Henry II during a council. He called this change
of procedure an exception, made because he wished to know more about the
candidate in question.[9] However, he did not accept for discussion any
other requests for canonization.

During the pontificate of Pope Alexander III (1159-1181) the
discussion of requests for canonization outside a council became an
unwritten rule. Its application is clear from the processes of canonization held during his pontificate. Contemporaries became aware of the
new rule simply through experience. Thus it is understandable how those
who petitioned for St. Bernard's canonization in 1163 could still cherish
the hope of obtaining it from this pope. But it becomes equally understandable why the pope, speaking of this request, did not mention the
real reason why he refused it. The withdrawal of processes of canonizatio

from the authority of the councils could provoke resistance among the

participants at these councils. All the same, it appears that those

who in 1163 requested the canonization of St. Bernard, knew why their

request was then refused. This is true, for example, of Geoffrey of

Auxerre, who, as abbot of Clairvaux, was the principal petitioner. For

it was at Clairvaux that St. Bernard lay buried, and consequently Clair-

vaux would become the center of his cult. Geoffrey had been chosen abbot

of Clairvaux in 1162, when his predecessor there, Fastred, had become

abbot of Cîteaux. The choice of Geoffrey of Auxerre was probably connect-

ed with the plans to ask for the canonization, since as a former secretary

of St. Bernard he had had an important share in the composition of the

saint's earliest _Life_. As early as 1146, he had supplied hagiographical

data to the author of the first book, William of St. Thierry. After the

death of St. Bernard, he had been involved in the choice of Arnold of

Bonneval as author of the second book, while the last three books he

wrote himself.[10]

In 1163, Geoffrey had taken part in the Council of Tours. At that

time he was probably the most important man in the order, certainly

with regard to the remembrance of St. Bernard. Shortly before the be-

ginning of this council, Fastred, abbot of Cîteaux, had died, and his

successor there, the Englishman Gilbert, had not been a monk at Clairvaux.

The real reason why the request for the canonization of St. Bernard had

not been dealt with at Tours caused Geoffrey to revise the text of this

Life.

He certainly had a right to do so, both as co-author of the Life
and as abbot of Clairvaux. The revision of the text undertaken in the
years 1163-1165 took into account the fact that, in the new petition
for canonization, the newly submitted Life would also be tested on the
credibility of the information it provided. However, since such a
narrative, dealing with the practice of virtue and with stories of
miracles, had to be to a large extent a standard text, it could no
longer contain any clues that could lead to verification. In this
way the principal motive for the revision becomes understandable. It
consisted mainly in the omission of miracle stories in which well-known
persons were mentioned as witnesses. In some cases the miracle was retained and even further elaborated, while the name of the witness disappeared, at least if at the time he were still alive. The authenticity
of the narrative was no longer allowed to be open to historical research.

This revision of the text was completed by Geoffrey in 1165. Possibly he was forced to do so, because Pope Alexander III was at that
moment demanding Geoffrey's abdication, and insisting on it, in spite
of resistance by Gilbert, the abbot of Cîteaux. At any rate, the text
did not undergo any further changes, except in three manuscripts,[11] and
when the new petition for canonization was made in 1173, this version
of the Life was submitted. So the question arises what interrelation
is there between this revision of the text, the abdication of Geoffrey

as abbot of Clairvaux and the lapse of time between this revision and
the final request for canonization. For, in spite of the fact that the
acts of the process of canonization held in 1173 clearly show the presence there of Geoffrey of Auxerre as advisor,[12] and therefore that the
Life as revised by him was submitted together with this request, this
text had been held in little esteem during the intervening years, at
least at Clairvaux. For Geoffrey's successor there, Pons of Auvergne,
commissioned Alan of Auxerre in those years to write a new Life of St.
Bernard.[13]   Alan, who had become a monk at Clairvaux in 1131, was chosen
abbot of Arrivour in 1140 and bishop of Auxerre in 1152, returned to
Clairvaux in 1167. There he worked at his task between the years 1167
and 1171. Abbot Pons, however, did not submit a request for canonization.
Probably this was not done because Alan's work did not show enough quality.
In any case, a new request was made only when Pons had become bishop of
Clermont-Ferrand in 1171, and the text as revised by Geoffrey had been
accepted once more at Clairvaux.

Thus it is clear that for a certain time the text as revised by
Geoffrey of Auxerre provoked resistance in the Cistercian order and that
this resistance led to the writing of a second Life and to the postponement of a new request for canonization. But there are no clear indications about what kind of objections were raised against the revised
text. According to Alan of Auxerre, objections had been raised against
the first Life because it did not tell the truth and because it showed

insufficient respect for ecclesiastical and secular authorities.[14]
This objection came from Geoffrey de la Roche, a cousin of St. Bernard,
who had entered Cîteaux with him in 1112 and had followed him to Clairvaux. There he had been prior until, in 1139, through the influence
of St. Bernard, he occupied the hotly disputed episcopal see of Langres.[15]

It is obvious that this Geoffrey took part in the meeting of
bishops and abbots who gathered in 1155-1156 to examine the first Life
of St. Bernard, which at that time had been completed. The result of
their verdict was that these bishops and abbots, in an introduction to
the last three books, presented themselves as the joint authors.[16]
Describing themselves in this introduction as those followers of St.
Bernard who had been very close to him, they apparently found in this
writing, to which they had added a number of passages,[17] an image of the
saint that strongly appealed to them. Because of this it is obvious
that the objections of Geoffrey de la Roche against this first Life referred to a revision of the text, which moreover he had known from first
hand since he had retired at Clairvaux in 1163. The objection of Geoffrey
de la Roche to the lack of respect for ecclesiastical and secular rulers,
could thus refer to the omission of the names of important people in the
revised text. All the same, there is also question here of a political
objection to Geoffrey of Auxerre, at least if one considers in addition
the reason given by Alexander III for wanting Geoffrey to resign.

It was said that Geoffrey of Auxerre had done great harm to Clairvaux

and with it also to the Cistercian order, because by his conduct he
had forfeited the confidence that kings and other rulers had deposited
in his predecessors.[18]   However, this argument, although it appears
purely political, also concerns the memory of St. Bernard, the predecessor par excellence, a memory which Geoffrey apparently had betrayed.
All the same, it is unlikely that the pope here refers to Geoffrey's
revision of the first _Life_.   True enough, Alexander III based his objection on complaints that had reached him from members of the Cistercian
order. With regard to the abdication of Geoffrey of Auxerre, a second
letter of the pope has survived, in which all those who complained to
Alexander about this abbot appear to be older followers of St. Bernard.[19]
Besides Alan of Auxerre and Geoffrey de la Roche, Alexander mentioned
Henry of France, brother of Louis VII and, since 1162, archbishop of
Reims, and also Cardinal Henry Moricotti.

These four persons, who in virtue of their office had probably
participated in the assembly which approved the text of the first _Life_,
appeared ten years later as decided opponents of Geoffrey of Auxerre,
speaking, moreover, in the name of many others. Their objections a-
gainst him could only indirectly have concerned his revision of the
first _Life_. Naturally they must have felt unhappy because in the new
version Geoffrey of Auxerre had replaced their introduction to the last
three books (which, however, had not been widely circulated) with a text
which made clear to the initiated that Geoffrey was their author.[20] But

the arguments of both Geoffrey de la Roche and the pope himself have
too much political content to allow the revision of the text to be the
central issue. No doubt the original text, as a remembrance of St.
Bernard, was so sacrosanct in the eyes of the older followers of the
saint that its revision must have increased their animosity against
Geoffrey of Auxerre. But their principal objection was clearly of a
political character, even if here again the memory of St. Bernard occupied a central place. In his political conduct Geoffrey of Auxerre had
in their opinion betrayed this memory, and thus inflicted serious harm
on Clairvaux. This last argument was sufficient reason for Pope Alexander
to demand Geoffrey of Auxerre's abdication, and to insist on it, in spite
of resistance by the abbot of Cîteaux.

Others who have dealt with this abdication have looked for its cause
in Geoffrey's attitude in the conflict between Thomas Becket and King
Henry II.[21] When the archbishop of Canterbury had fled from England in
the autumn of 1164, he had at first found refuge in the Cistercian monastery at Pontigny. For the English king this was reason enough to
threaten the Cistercian monasteries in his domain, which included part
of France, with reprisals. This was embarrassing for the major superiors
of the order, all the more so as it was said that the Cistercian abbots
in England had not quite agreed with Becket's attitude toward the king.
This disagreement, it was said, had been manifested in 1164 during a
meeting of English Cistercian abbots at Kirkstedt, a meeting at which

Geoffrey of Auxerre had also been present.[22] The abbot of Cîteaux

himself, represented at Kirkstedt by Geoffrey, afterward promised

Henry II that the Cistercian order would remain neutral in the conflict

between him and Becket.[23] This concession resulted, among other things,

in the punishment, by the major superiors of the order, of a monk who

had committed himself to the archbishop's cause.[24]

Alexander III, who himself strongly supported Thomas Becket's

point of view, did not agree with the order's attitude. And he consid-

ered Geoffrey of Auxerre the one mainly responsible for it. The pope

was not alone in these political objections against Geoffrey, since from

the reasons he gave in the spring of 1165 that the abbot of Clairvaux

should abdicate, it appears that these objections also existed within

the order and indeed to such an extent that they warranted his demand.

But Geoffrey's abdication did not mean the end of his influence on

Gilbert, the abbot of Cîteaux. Because the latter, after the final ses-

sion of the order's General Chapter in September 1166, went to see Becket

at Pontigny to tell him about the problems his stay there was causing for

the order. Consequently, the archbishop decided to leave Pontigny, some-

thing which both the pope, the community of Pontigny and many other Cis-

tercians regretted.[25] Also this fact was attributed, at least in the

order, to Geoffrey's influence on Gilbert. For after Geoffrey's abdica-

tion, which must have drawn a great deal of attention, he resided at

Cîteaux.

There is a curious indication that Geoffrey's attitude in the
conflict between Henry II and Thomas Becket was considered in the Cistercian order a betrayal of the memory of St. Bernard. Pons of Auvergne,
the new abbot of Clairvaux, who, as we have seen, entirely rejected the
text of the first Life, appears to have been in favor of supporting
Thomas Becket. To prove this, one cannot rely on the fact that Becket
in April 1169 was given a new opportunity, at Clairvaux, of pronouncing
an interdict against the followers of the king, because at that moment
Pons of Auvergne resided elsewhere.[26] But later, as bishop of Clermont-
Ferrand, he clearly promoted the cult of Becket, once the latter had
been canonized in 1173.[27] However, this correlation between sympathy
for Becket and rejection of the revised version of the first Life is not
yet sufficient to show that a more reserved attitude in the conflict between Becket and Henry II could be considered, in the Cistercian order,
as a betrayal of the memory of St. Bernard.

To reach that conclusion one should establish the relation between
this conflict and the one existing since 1159 between Alexander III and
the Emperor Frederick Barbarossa, because of the latter's support of
the anti-pope Victor IV. When Alexander was looking for support for
his recognition as pope, the Cistercians responded generously. Important members of the order at once committed themselves to obtain recognition for him in France and England. At the time Cistercians did not
attach too much importance to the possibly negative consequences of this

attitude for the Cistercian monasteries within the German Empire. This commitment of the order to Alexander III naturally evoked memories of St. Bernard's conduct during the papal schism of the years 1130-1138, when he had dedicated himself totally to obtaining the recognition of Innocent II by the princes of Western Europe. One could even say that the Cistercian's attitude during the schism of 1159 was determined to an important degree by Bernard's earlier attitude and by the results he had obtained. We have no concrete indications to prove this. But there is no doubt that St. Bernard's influence continued to powerfully determine the order's policy during the first years after his death.[28] Moreover, in the second book of the saint's first _Life_ ample attention had been paid to his conduct during that earlier schism. Much more indeed than the preaching of the second crusade, which had failed, this conduct could be valued as a concrete merit Bernard had gained for the Church as a whole. The positive result of his mediation in this schism must evidently have inspired the order in 1159, when it had to define its position in relation to the papal schism.

It was undoubtedly the older followers of St. Bernard among whom his influence was strongest, and who had also worked for the recognition of Alexander in 1159. To them, moreover, the conflict between Henry II and Thomas Becket appeared more than anything else an extension of this earlier conflict, the more so because Henry II, to counteract the support Becket was receiving from Alexander III, had contemplated choosing the

side of Barbarossa. Some of Henry's followers were excommunicated by
Becket because of their contacts with the emperor's party, a decision
that won the approval of Alexander III.[29] Just as a choice of Alexander III in his conflict with Barbarossa, based on a historic faithfulness to the conduct of St. Bernard, led logically to an unconditional
option in favor of Becket, so also a more reserved attitude in this
latter conflict, like the one assumed by Abbot Gilbert and by Geoffrey,
must have been obviously considered as abandonment of the position the
order had taken up in the struggle for the recognition of Alexander III.
Just as reminiscences of the earlier conduct of St. Bernard had influenced the order's determination to support Alexander, the same reminiscences continued playing their part when the order opted for Becket.
For the same reason a more moderate attitude in this conflict could be
interpreted from that point of view as a betrayal of the memory of St.
Bernard. Those who accused Geoffrey of such betrayal could, for the
same reason, also have decided to reject his revision of the first Life,
the more so because they, as early followers of the saint, considered
themselves the authors of the original version, to which they had a
strong emotional attachment.

That emotional factors played an important role in all this is
apparent also from the way the new superiors of the Cistercian order
became involved in the schism of Barbarossa. When, in 1168, Gilbert
was succeeded as abbot of Cîteaux by Alexander of Cologne, once more

a direct follower of St. Bernard, the new abbot tried to find a solution for the problems that afflicted the order as a consequence of the conflict between emperor and pope. He tried to reach a peaceful solution, which seemed possible at the death of Pascal III, the successor of the anti-pope Victor IV. Abbot Alexander offered the pope his good services and together with Pons of Auvergne he showed considerable diplomatic activity. Pons received special missions from the pope, and Rome had great expectations for his mediation efforts. However, the results he obtained were more to the benefit of the order than of the pope himself.[30] The memory of St. Bernard, which had so strongly influenced the order's option in this conflict in 1159, appeared ten years later to be no longer decisive, at least for Pons of Auvergne, however much he continued to share Becket's opinion and his aversion to the revised text of the first Life.

But his diplomatic failure, at least in as far as the curia was concerned, broke the deadlock which had been reached in the canonization of St. Bernard because of Pons' objections against Geoffrey of Auxerre. In 1171, Pons became bishop of Clermont-Ferrand. One could surmise, although without concrete indications to prove it, that this appointment was the result of Alexander's annoyance at the manner in which Pons had mediated in the conflict between pope and emperor.[31] Meanwhile, however, Geoffrey's influence in the order had started to grow again, which is evident from the role he played in the settlement of the conflict between

Becket and Henry II, whereby the archbishop had to accept Geoffrey's
point of view.[32]

Here again practical considerations of the order's own interest
had begun to predominate. Perhaps this also explains that, at Clairvaux,
Pons was succeeded by Gerard, who until then had been abbot at Fossa
Nova, and that Gerard managed to be succeeded at Fossa Nova by Geoffrey
of Auxerre.[33] From then on the resistance against the second version
of the first Life came to an end, so that this text could serve at the
request for canonization in 1173.

The series of problems that has obscured the relation between the
Life of St. Bernard and his canonization, contain another important
element. The Life described St. Bernard as a 'time-less' saint. His
earthly life played only an accidental role in it. In this respect
there was no substantial difference between the first and the second
version. However, the resistance against the second version, which led
to the postponement of the canonization, had arisen because at that moment the concrete historical memory of St. Bernard had not yet disappeared

During the first years after Bernard's death he was not yet known
exclusively as a saint. He was at least in equal measure a concrete historic person, and as such he had his followers. In that respect his
canonization in 1163 would have been premature. Time had to elapse before one would be able to venerate him as a 'time-less' saint. As long
as the revision of his Life still provoked repercussions because St.

Bernard himself still appeared as a historically known person, the time was not ripe for his canonization. Looking at it like this, one cannot really say that his canonization was postponed by the rewriting of his <u>Life</u> through the reactions it provoked. One should rather say that the canonization, as a result of these reactions, did not take place prematurely, because through them it became clear that at that moment the saint's life after death was still too much time-bound.[34]

NOTES

1. On the relationship between canonization and hagiography, see H.
   Delhaye, _Les légendes hagiographiques_, Subsidia hagiographica 18A
   (Brussels, 1905; 4th ed., 1955 [reprinted 1968]); E. Kemp, _Canoniza_
   tion and Authority in the Western Church (Oxford, London, 1948);
   R. Klauser, "Zur Entwicklung des Heiligsprechungsverfahren bis zum
   13. Jahrhundert," _Zeitschrift für Rechtsgeschichte_ LXX (1954),
   Kanonische Abteilung IX, 83-101; M. Schwarz, "Heiligsprechungen im
   12. Jahrhundert und die Beweggründe ihrer Urheber," _Archiv für Kult_
   geschichte XXXIX (1957) 43-62; B. De Gaiffier, _Etudes critiques_
   d'hagiographie et d'iconologie. Subsidia hagiographica 43 (Brussel
   1967) pp. 475-507: L'hagiographie et son publique; A. Garcia y
   Garcia, "A propos de la canonisation des saintes au XIIe siècle,"
   Revue de droit canonique XVIII (1968) 3-16.

2. Kemp, _Canonization_, pp. 27-28. J. Guiraud, "Le commerce des reliques au commencement du IXe siècle," _Melanges G. B. de Rossi_ (Paris
   Rome, 1892) pp. 73-95. H. Silvestre, "Commerce et vol de reliques
   au moyen âge," _Revue belge d'histoire et de philologie_ XXX (1952)
   721-39. On the value attributed to the relics of saints, see H.
   Fichtenau, "Zum Reliquienwesen im früheren Mittelalter," _Mitteilung_
   des Instituts für österreichische Geschichtsforschung LX (1952) 60-

3. According to M. Schwarz ("Heiligsprechungen," p. 58), there were
   other motives for requesting the canonization of St. Bernard, besid

the legitimate desire to obtain authorization to venerate him as a
saint. See A. H. Bredero, Etudes sur la Vita prima de saint Bernard
(Rome, 1960) p. 150, n. 1 (reedited in ASOC XVIII [1962] 36, n. 7).

4. Bredero, Etudes, pp. 15-24 (ASOC SVII [1961] 19-27).

5. E. Vancandard, "L'histoire de saint Bernard, critique des sources,"
Revue des questions historiques XLIII (1888) 337-89. E. Vancandard,
Vie de saint Bernard (Paris, 1895) xx-xl. R. Aigrain, L'hagiographie,
ses sources, ses méthods, sa histoire (Paris, 1953) p. 311.

6. Bredero, Etudes, pp. 138-47 (ASOC VIII, 24-33).

7. Ph. Jaffé et al., Regesta pontificum Romanorum. (Leipzig, 1885-
1888; reprinted Graz, 1956) no. 12330; PL 185:622.

8. A. H. Bredero, "The Actual Canonization of Saint Bernard," in Saint
Bernard: Studies Commemorating the Eighth Centenary of His Canonization, CS 28 (Kalamazoo, Michigan, to appear). The first request
for Edward's canonization was also refused for a political reason;
see Kemp, Canonization, pp. 76-78.

9. Regesta, no. 8882; PL 180:1118. See Kemp, Canonization, p. 79.

10. Bredero, Etudes, pp. 73-77, 111-12, 116-18 (ASOC XVII, 218-22, 256;
XVIII, 3-4).

11. MSS Dijon 659, Genoa A IV 33, Châlon-sur-Saône 6. Bredero, Etudes,
p. 56 (ASOC XVII, 58-59). Geoffrey wrote this passus about 1170;
ibid., p. 141, n. 1 (ASOC XVIII, 26, n. 7).

12. Tromund, abbot of Chiaravalle (near Milan), Letter to Gerard, abbot

of Clairvaux; PL 185:626-27. This letter was written after the
canonization had been authorized.

13. See the prologue to the Second Life by Alan, PL 185:469. Bredero,
"Actual Canonization."

14. Alan himself recognized his work as an abbreviation of an un-
finished attempt by Geoffrey de la Roche to rewrite the older version of the First Life. Alan made this attempt at the same time
that Geoffrey of Auxerre was rewriting the original text. Comparing
the work of Geoffrey de la Roche with the older version of the First
Life, Alan remarked: 'Necnon etiam, si quis diligenter advertat,
ibidem quaedam aspera inserta reperiuntur, verbi gratia contra
ecclesiasticae et saecularis potestatis authenticas sublimesque
personas.' PL 185:469.

15. G. Constable, "The Disputed Election at Langres in 1138," Traditio
XIII (1957) 119-57.

16. The text of this prologue has been preserved only in the Douai MS
372, vol. II, fol. 176. The MS originated in the scriptorium of
the abbey of Anchin (Black Monk) where it was written at the same
time that Geoffrey of Auxerre was revising the text of the First
Life. At this time there was a close relationship between the
scriptoria of the two monasteries. See Bredero, Etudes, p. 118, n. 2
(ASOC XVIII, 4, n. 5). The prologue has been edited in the MGH, SS
XXVI, 110, and by Bredero, Etudes, frontispiece and p. 40 (ASOC XVII,

17. Bredero, _Etudes_, pp. 121-22 (ASOC XVIII, 8-9).

18. Letter dated 27 March 1165 addressed to Gilbert, abbot of Cîteaux;
     Regesta no. 11169; PL 200:348: '...Non eam gratiam et reverentiam
     in oculis regum et principum prometruit, quam antecessores ejus
     promeruisse noscuntur, ipsi monasterio non modicum derogatur et
     totus ordo non minimum exinde incommodum sustinet et jacturam.'

19. Letter dated 1 April 1165 addressed to Henry, archbishop of Reims;
     Regesta no. 1171; PL 200:350. See also the letter to Henry of Pope
     Alexander, dated 25 May 1165; _Regesta_ no. 11194; PL 200:368. I have
     dealt with the problems surrounding the abdication of Geoffrey of
     Auxerre in "Thomas Becket et la canonization de saint Bernard," in
     Raymonde Foreville (ed.), _Thomas Becket: Actes du colloque international
     de Sédières, 19-24 août 1973_ (Paris, 1975) pp. 55-62. See pp. 55-56.

20. In this prologue Geoffrey calls himself: '...puer sanctitatis
     ipsius, dignationis filius, benignitatis alumnus, quem ab ejus
     uberibus post annos circiter tredecim...mors avulsit.' The _annos
     tredecim_ refer to the date of Geoffrey's conversion in 1140.

21. M. Preiss, _Die politische Tätigkeit und Stellung der Cistercienser
     im Schisma 1159-1177_. Historische Studien 248 (Berlin, 1934) pp.
     67-112. S. Lenssen, "L'abdication du bienheureux Geoffry comme
     abbé de Clairvaux," Coll. XVII (1955) 98-110.

22. Preiss, _Tätigkeit_, pp. 79 and 89. See also F. W. Powicke, _The Life
     of Aelred of Rievaulx by Walter Daniel_. (London, 1950) pp. xlix-li.

23. This concession is indirectly known from a letter of King Henry II to Abbot Gilbert; PL 190:1409; J. C. Robinson, Materials for the History of Becket. (London, 1881) V. 365. Preiss, Tätigkeit, pp. 86-87, dates this arrangement between 26 February and 27 March 1165

24. Alexander III protested this measure in a letter to the Cistercian abbots written between 1165 and 1169; Regesta no. 11435; PL 200:569

25. Vita s. Thomae, auctore Herberto de Boseham, ed. J. C. Robertson, Materials III, 398.

26. Together with Alexander, the abbot of Cîteaux, he stayed at the court of the emperor from January to the beginning of March 1169. Frederick had asked for their mediation in making a reconciliation with the pope. Immediately after this, they travelled to Rome, as is clear from a letter they wrote to William, archbishop of Sens, before leaving the German court. W. Holtzmann, "Quellen und Forschungen zur Geschichte Friedrich Barbarossa, II, Zu den Friedensverhandlungen zwischen Kaiser und Papst im Jahre 1169," Neues Archiv XLVIII (1929-1930) 400-409. The Presence of Thomas Becket at Clairvaux is mentioned in the Vita s. Thomae, auctore Willelmo filio Stephani, chap. 83 in Robertson, Materials III, 87. See also the discussions held after my paper at the Becket symposium.

27. This early veneration has been mentioned by Madame Simone Caudron in her paper at the Thomas Becket Symposium, "Les Châsses de Thomas Becket en émail de Limoges," Actes, pp. 233-41.

28. See the letter of Fastred, as third abbot of Clairvaux, to some other Cistercian abbot, chap. 2: 'Non haec vita est, quam me et te docuit pater et praedecessor noster Bernardus felicis recordatienis.' PL 182:705.

29. Regesta, no. 11275; PL 200:416 (May 1166).

30. Preiss, Tätigkeit, pp. 123-25.

31. Ibid., pp. 126-27.

32. This is evident from a letter of Thomas Becket, dated 1169, to Geoffrey of Auxerre. Robertson, Materials VII, 225-26.

33. It should be noted that the abbey of Fossanove was within the Empire, not France. Given the resistance of Henry of France, archbishop of Reims, to Geoffrey as abbot of Clairvaux, there is some reason to suppose that King Louis VII had strong feelings against Geoffrey.

34. See A. H. Bredero, "San Bernardo di Chiaravalle: Correlazione tra fenomeno cultico e storico," in Studi su S. Bernardo di Chiaravalle nell'Octavo Centenario della Canonizatione (Rome, 1975) pp. 23-48.

WILLIAM OF SAINT THIERRY'S
READING OF ABELARD'S CHRISTOLOGY

E. Rozanne Elder
Western Michigan University

'Peter Abelard is teaching novel doctrines again and writing novel-ties,' William of Saint Thierry advised Saint Bernard and the bishop of Chartres in 1138. 'Nor is it a matter of little things but of the faith of the holy Trinity, the person of the Mediator, the Holy Spirit, the grace of God, the sacrament of our common redemption.'[1] Expressing amaze-ment that the influential abbot of Clairvaux had so long kept a silence perilous in its tacit consent, William exhorted him to do battle with Abelard, and to this end he carefully counselled him in the intricacies of Abelard's errors. Of the thirteen propositions offensive to William's sense of orthodoxy--and among those nineteen delated by Bernard and con-demned at the Council of Sens--one in particular touched an area in which William had already shown himself sensitive. Item eight in the letter to Bernard accused Abelard of writing: 'That Christ, God and man, is not one of the three persons in the Trinity.'[2]

In the treatise which quickly followed the letter, William articulat-ed in minute detail his understanding of Abelard's Christology and its perversity. William was not a philosopher, certainly not of Abelard's rank, nor, I think, was he a trained theologian. A careful examination of his objections to Abelard's teaching about the person of Jesus Christ, however, reveals William as an incisive logician, a deliberative thinker and a thorough researcher of orthodox sources.

In Abelard's _Theologia_ 'scholarium,' which we know William had, the schoolman had maintained a chary attitude toward what came to be known as the communication of idioms. He objected specifically to confusing the properties of the divine Word with properties of a created being, and his students credited him with a further aversion to speaking of a part as if it were a whole. A wealth of differences separate the being of any man from that of God, they argued. 'For man is a corporeal being,' their master Abelard wrote, 'composed of members and indissoluble; but God is neither a corporeal being nor does He consist in parts so He can be dissolved. Therefore God can properly be said to be neither flesh nor man.'[3]

The consequences of this line of reasoning for Christology are obvious. William, reading the passages literally, charged Abelard with making a fundamental distinction between the Son of God and Jesus Christ, 'severing God from man,' he wrote, 'like Nestorius.'[4] In considering the persons of the Trinity, Abelard regarded Christ the eternal Son of God and Christ the man quite separately. With a flourish born of what William considered impious ignorance, Abelard had created artificial and ultimately disastrous divisions when he had maintained that: 'it must be realised that even if we concede that Christ is one of the three persons in the Trinity, we do not, however, grant that this person, which Christ is, is one of the three persons in the Trinity.'[5]

First of all it rankled William that Abelard should have considered
himself in a position generously to concede and, when it suited him, to
deny what Scripture had patently declared.[6] Irritating though he found
it, Abelard's attitude was incidental to the primary issue, his apparent
categorical separation of God from man in Christ.

In at least seeming to shatter the singleness of Christ's person,
Abelard could hardly escape the monk's ire, for William had already
stoutly defended this doctrine in his treatise On the Sacrament of the
Altar. In it he had stressed with some vigor that Christ was and forever
remained a single divine person, and that the man Jesus Christ was the
same person and so was one with God.[7] And he had specified Christ as
the naturae utriusque res, the reality to which human and divine natures
were united.[8] Until he took issue with Abelard, William had seldom concerned himself with the explication of doctrine, yet on this one point
at least he had already taken a strong and unequivocal position--which
indicates that he had given careful thought to the question. His rebuttal
of Abelard's teaching seems likely, therefore, to have resulted not from
a quick and pious impulse, but from a long-considered and strongly-held
conviction.

By 'this person which Christ is,' Abelard--as William read him--meant
a man, a corporeal and dissoluble being assumed by the second divine person in the Incarnation. God, incorporeal and indissoluble, could not

properly be said to be man. To admit the Incarnate Christ into the Godhead seemed to Abelard tantamount to saying that God had, at a point in
time, been added to. In Abelard's declared opinion, it would be 'to
confess a new or novel God.'[9] William assessed this opinion as destruct-
ive of the singleness of Christ's person. He appears to have thought
that the schoolman viewed the Incarnation either as a jumbled mixture or
as a cooperation of separate persons, the eternal person of the Son and
the human person whom He assumed. Against the notion of compositeness,
William time and again quoted an Augustinian maxim that the Word endured
immutably in His own nature, in which nothing composite with which He
might subsist should be suspected.[10] Division of Christ's person and commixture of his human and divine substances William found as abhorrent as
he declared Christian tradition did.[11] Christ's humanity, like that of
all human persons, had been created by God and was consequently a creature-
his authority for this was Gregory the Great.[12] The eternal, uncreated
Word had assumed a creature but, William read Abelard to say, a creature
cannot be part of his Creator. The man Christ cannot be part of the uncreated God who created him. If not part of God, this human creature
which Christ assumed could not be a person of the Trinity. This logical
sequence led William to conclude that Abelard had posited an eternal uncreated person, the Word, and a human person, Christ, united with each
other yet forever distinct.

If Abelard insisted that the man Jesus Christ, united with the Son
of God, could not be one of the persons of the Trinity, while at the same
time he maintained that Christ the Son was God from eternity, then, William calculated with exasperation, he substituted by his argument a quaternity for the Trinity. Turning Abelard's own arguments and phraseology a-
gainst him, William reasoned:

> If in the Trinity, which God is, there are three
> persons (which he himself does not contradict),
> and if Christ, God and man, is one person (which
> again he does not contradict), and if he neverthe-
> less in no way concedes this person to be one of
> the three persons in the Trinity, then, we have
> now a new God from him, that is, a fourth person
> in the Trinity with God.[13]

To eradicate the notion of quaternity, William appealed to his favorite authority, Saint Augustine, who had stated without equivocation
that the assumption of manhood by the second person of the Trinity had
in no way increased the number of persons within that Trinity.[14] Because
Christ was eternally God the Son and remained God the Son even when man
in time, William believed (and thought all Christians should believe)
that God, the Son of God, was born, suffered and died. Yet his divine
nature did not merge with his human. The natures remained distinct;
the person was single. 'I say,' William advised his readers:

> let us and let every tongue confess Him, confess
> that He is in the glory of God the Father, that
> He is [there] for no other reason than because
> He is one of the three persons within the majesty

> of the Highest Trinity but in this manner that
> He is Himself also the Son of God, that is,
> conjoined or rather united to the Son of God
> in unity of person, just as we also believe
> that God the Son of God was born in time and
> suffered by reason of that very same unity of
> person, without any calumnies about new novelties
> in God.[15]

To counter Abelard's objection further, William underscored the distinction between the human and divine natures of the single person Christ.
God, he pointed out, is omniscient. God alone knows the day of judgement. God the Son, equally God, knows the day of judgement. When the
Son of God became man, he remained God, and because of his divine nature
he continued, as man, to know the day of judgement. This knowledge he
did not possess by reason of his human, finite nature; but, because His
divine nature was united perfectly to His human, he knew it in His humanity as well as in His divinity.[16] So also in His humanity but not by
reason of His humanity, He remains one of the three persons of the Trinity.
Eternally God, He remained God when He took on manhood. He assumed a
man and became thereby truly man, a creature, but He remained God, and
the man He assumed became the Son of God He eternally is--one person.
Just as Christ knew in His humanity what by His human nature He could
not know, William argued,

> so likewise we say that Christ, the son of man,
> in that human nature but not by reason of it,
> is one of the three persons in the Trinity
> according to that union which it has with God;

> because just as God incarnate became the son of
> man on account of the man assumed, so too the
> man assumed was made the son of God because of
> the God assuming him.[17]

To reinforce his case still further William called up a passage he ascribed to Pope Saint Leo concerning the mutability of the Incarnate Word.
The passage read: 'The Word of God did not change into flesh or the
flesh into the Word, but each remains in each and Christ remains one in
both, neither divided by diversity nor confused by commixture.'[18] The
text stipulated, and William concurred, that although Christ had been
begotten in one way (<u>aliter</u>) by His Father and in another by His mother,
he was not one person (<u>alter</u>) from His Father and another by His mother.[19]
Christ, God and man, remained inalterably one, single person.[20] William
could not insist too strenuously on that unity of person. As Son of God
Christ remained, as God is, immutable, 'but in the Word alone. And the
son of God was buried,' William echoes here a formulary of his earlier
eucharistic treatise, 'but in the flesh alone.'[21]

Because Abelard had granted that within the Trinity there are three
persons of one substance and, furthermore, that one of these persons, the
Son, became man while yet remaining God in what Leo had called the 'enduring
unity of person,'[22] William concluded that the schoolman had overstepped his
evidence and illogically contradicted it. 'As God the Father and God the Son
are one substance in the Trinity but not one person,' William made comparison
'so in the form of the Mediator, God and man are of one person but not

of one substance.'23 Consequently, he contended against Peter Abelard,
'this person Christ, who is God and man, is, according as He is God,'
one of the three persons of the Trinity.24

By stating that the person Christ, 'according as He is God' is one
of the persons of the Trinity, William tended slightly towards agreement
with his adversary. Anticipating Abelard's probable protestation that
this had been almost his own original point, William leapt to the heart
of the matter to head off this objection:

> He [Abelard] will say: therefore He is not [one
> of the three persons in the Trinity] according
> as He is man. Certainly, but the man is also
> there because of the inseparable unity by which
> He is one person with God.25

Mindful of Abelard's scruples against introducing by this assertion a
creature into the Godhead, William insisted that the identification of
'this person which Christ is' as a person of the Trinity did not consti-
tute the entry of a new person into that Trinity. The man Jesus had
never existed as a person before He became united with the person of the
Son of God. He began to be and to be God simultaneously.26 Abelard's
distinction between the third person in the Trinity and 'this person'
had therefore no meaning by William's interpretation. The 'persons'
are a single person. Since the man Jesus did not exist until completely
and utterly one with God the Son, to 'allow' the incarnate Christ into
the Triune Godhead is not to introduce a new person or to make up a new

or novel God. The very idea horrified William.

> God forbid that by this argument we should assert
> something new in God when, as Pope Leo and
> Augustine agreed, we say that this man was pre-
> destined from all eternity to be God incarnate
> and glorified to this status in God's good time,
> and that He began to be and to be God simultan-
> eously because He was only one God.[27]

This is the reason, William argued, that Christ's human mother is
correctly called the mother of God. The Son whom she bore was not conceived as a man who thereafter became God as well as man. At the instant
of His conception He was man, fashioned out of her (ex ea), and God insofar
as He began to be God-man from her (de ea).[28]   As God, Jesus Christ could
say 'I and the Father are one'; as man He confessed, 'The Father is
greater than I.'[29] He who said both was one person, eternally, indivisibl
immutably, whom 'we call God the Son of God,' William wrote, 'in that He
is one substance with the Father and the Holy Spirit, whom we call man the
Son of man in that He is one person with God the Son of God.'[30] Christ
is--in the words of Augustine--a single person 'so unchangeable from each
nature that the designation of each demands the other.'[31]

William's adamant defense of the unity of Christ's person and his
consequent placement in the Trinity of 'this person which Christ is'
convinced Saint Bernard, who latched on to the Nestorian tag[32] without
apparently appreciating the full thrust of William's objection. The
Council of Sens in its turn duly condemned Abelard for teaching 'that

neither God and man nor this person which Christ is, is one of the three
persons in the Trinity.'[33]

For all his success, William had not finished with the matter. He
undertook to refute Abelard's errors more thoroughly in his *Aenigma fidei*,
written not long after the condemnation at Sens and the most meticulously
theological book William ever composed. In it he riveted his attention
on the God revealed more than, as was his wont, on the man seeking God.
In the *Aenigma*, for the first and only time, William maintained that the
Son had remained wholly God while becoming wholly man, that part of Him
had not become man while another part remained God.[34] He can only have
bothered with this uncommon distinction because of his recent concern
over Abelard's teaching. Amid the gossip circulating about the schoolman was a rumor, preserved by Gerhoch of Reichersberg, that Abelard had
taught that Christ was *deus ex parte et homo ex parte*.[35] Abelard's actual
statement, contained not in the *Theologia 'scholarium'* available to William
but in the *Theologia christiana*, read *ex divinitate et humanitate una est
compacta persona et pro parte Deus pro parte homo*.[36] That William felt
called upon for the first time in his life specifically to deny the 'part-
ness' of Christ may indicate his awareness of vague charges if not knowledge of Abelard's *Theology*. It may also indicate that, having sent off
the *Disputation* to Bernard, William inquired further into Abelard's theories

In the _Aenigma_, as in the _Disputation_, William began to teach that Christ's divine nature had not been changed in the Incarnation. The concept _natura_ _non_ _mutata_ antedates William by centuries and the places in which he could have found it are manifold. Against Abelard, he had quoted St Leo.[37] Augustine had used it. So, too, according to the _Epitome_ of Abelard's student, had Ambrose.[38] During the twelfth centur it had been incorporated into the works of Anselm of Canterbury, Willia of Champeaux and Abelard.[39] Because William first used the phrase in the _Disputation_ against Abelard, in whose works it occurs, his awarenes or perhaps re-awareness, may have resulted from his reading of Abelard' detested _Theologia_. He may have borrowed from Abelard in order to refu Abelard.

At one point in the _Aenigma_, William stressed the unity of Christ' person to the point of overcorrecting Abelard's supposed slight. Zealo to safeguard this inseparable unity and so Christ's place in the Trinit William stated without preface or apology that divinity had suffered in the flesh. He added immediately that divinity did not, however, 'co-su with the flesh because in His own nature, divinity remained forever im- passible.'[40] In protecting the unity of person which he was convinced Abelard had threatened, William momentarily allowed his rhetoric to ove whelm his usual caution. By saying 'divinity' suffered rather than 'Go suffered, as he did a moment later,[41] William himself overran the limi of orthodox expression, transgressing a cardinal rule of the communication of idioms. His statement is as extreme in its way as Abelard's was in the other. William's motive in this momentary lapse seems clear. By the hyperbole of his assertion, he hoped to counter once and for all Abelard's 'severing [of] God from man, like Nestorius.'

NOTES

1. Ep 326 (inter Bernardi); PL 182:531B (order reversed): 'Nec de minimis
    agitur, sed de fide sanctae Trinitatis, de persona Mediatoris, de
    Spiritu sancto, de gratia Dei, de sacramento communis redemptionis.
    Petrus enim Abadlardus iterum nova docet, nova scribit....'

2. Ep 326, 3; PL 182:532B: '8. Quod Christus Deus et homo non est tertia
    persona in Trinitate.'

3. Theologia 'scholarium' III; PL 178:1197B: 'Homo quippe res corporea
    est, et membris composita ac dissolubilis. Deus vero nec corpora res
    est, nec in partibus constat ut dissolvi potest. Deus igitur nec
    caro, nec homo proprie dicendus est.' See Epitome 24; PL 178:
    1733D: 'Impropria igitur sunt, ut pars pro toto accipitur. Saepe nam-
    que contingit, totum pro parte partemque pro toto accepi, ut anima,
    cum pars sit hominis, pro homine ponitur....Eodem modo cum dicimus:
    Deus est homo, pro parte verum est et est sensus: Deus est uniens sibi
    hominem.'

4. Adv Abl VIII; PL 180:276D: '[Iterum dicit de persona Mediatoris,] Deum
    ab homine secernens, sicut Nestorius....'

5. Adv Abl VIII; PL 180:276D-77A: '"Sciendum," ait, "est quod licet con-
    cedamus quod Christus tertia sit persona in Trinitate, non tamen con-
    cedimus quod haec persona, quae Christus est, sit tertia persona in
    Trinitate."' See Epitome XXIV; PL 178:1732B.

6. Adv Abl VIII; PL 178:277A: '"Hoc," inquit, "concedimus, illud non
    concedimus," tamquam de Christo, sive in Christo nil sit, vel esse pos

nisi quod ille concesserit.'

7. Sacr altar I; PL 180:348B.

8. Sacr Altar I; PL 180:346B: '[Christus] qui ex unitis naturis in
    idipsum naturae utriusque res est, neutro carens, in utroque Deus
    et homo Christus....'

9. Theologia 'scholarium' III; PL 178:1107B: 'Homo, quippe res corporea
    est, et membris composita ac dissolubilis. Deus vero nec corporea
    res est, nec partibus constat ut dissolvi possit. Deus igitur nec
    caro nec homo esse proprie dicendus est....Absit autem ut aliquam
    rem Deum esse ponamus, quae non semper extiterit, aut non semper Deus
    fuerit. Hoc quippe est Deum novum vel recentem confiteri....' (The
    phrase 'Deum novum vel recentem comes from Psalm 80:10 and Deut. 32:17.)

10. Adv Abl VIII; PL 178:278C, 279C, 280B. Augustine, Epistola 169, ii,
    7; PL 33:745: '...Permanente tamen Verbo in sua natura incommutabiliter,
    in qua nihil compositi cum quo subsistat ulla phantasia humani animi
    suspicandum est.'

11. Adv Abl VIII; PL 178:278C: 'Ubi sicut audire refugit fides Christiana
    in Christo Deo et homine personae divisionem, sic etiam abhorret divinae
    substantiae cum humana substantia confusionem, sive commistionem.'

12. Adv Abl VIII; PL 178:277D, quoting Gregory the Great, Epistola 39; PL 77:
    1097C: '"...Ex humanitatis natura non habuit [scientiam diei judicii]
    ex qua cum angelis creatura fuit."'

13. Adv Abl VIII; PL 178:277C: 'Ad quod dicimus, quoniam si in Trinitate, quae Deus est, tres sunt personae quod ipse non contradicit, et Christus Deus et homo una est persona, quod etiam ipsum non contradicit; quam tamen tertiam in Trinitate esse personam nullatenus concedit; jam utique recentem ab eo Deum habemus, quartam scilicet in Deo cum Trinitate personam....'

14. Adv Abl VIII; PL 178:277D: 'Sed sicut dicit beatus Augustinus ad Evodium, "assumpto homine nequaquam personarum numerus auctus est sed eadem Trinitas mansit."' Augustine, Epistola 169; PL 33:745.

15. Adv Abl VIII; PL 178:278A: 'Ipsum, inquam, et nos, et omnis lingua confitetur quia est in gloria Dei Patris: quod non est aliud, quam quia est tertia persona in majestate summae Trinitatis, sed secundum hoc quod et ipse est Dei Filius, hoc est in unitate personae conjunctus vel potius unitus Filio Dei, sicut et Deum Dei Filium natum temporaliter credimus, et passum, secundum eamdem personae unitatem, absque omni calumnia recentis in Deo novitatis.'

16. Adv Abl VIII; PL 178:277BC: 'Incarnatus enim Unigenitus Dei, factusque pro nobis homo perfectus, in natura quidem divinitatis novit diem et horam judicii, sed tamen hunc non ex natura humanitatis novit. Quod ergo in ipsa humanitate novit, non ex ipsa novit, quia Deus homo factus diem et horam judicii non nisi per divinitatis suae potentiam novit.'

17. Adv Abl VIII; PL 178:277C: 'Unde et nos similiter dicimus, Christum

Filium hominis in ipsa natura humanitatis suae, sed non ex ipsa, secundum eam quam cum Deo habet unionem, tertiam esse in Trinitate
personam, quia sicut incarnatus Deus factus est filius hominis propter hominem assumptum, sic assumptus homo factus est Filius Dei propter assumentem Deum.'

18. Adv Abl VIII; PL 178:278D: 'Item Leo papa de Christo:..."Nec tamen
Verbum in carnem, sive caro in Verbum mutata est; sed utrumque manet
in utroque, et unus in utroque Christus, nec diversitate divisus, nec
diversitate divisus, nec commistione confusus."'   This passage, no
longer considered a genuine part of Leo's Tome, occurs there in a published edition of 1700 (Sancti Leonis magni papae magni opera omnia,
II, Appendicula sermonum [Lyon, 1700] p. 193.

19. Adv Abl VIII; PL 178:278D: '"Nec alter est ex Patre alter est
ex matre; licet aliter sit ex Patre, aliter ex matre."'

20. Adv Abl VIII; PL 178:277D: 'Et Christus Deus et homo una est persona.'

21. Adv Abl VIII; PL 178:278C: 'Unde idem Filius Dei incommutabilis est,
atque coaeternus Patri; sed in Verbo solo. Et sepultus est Filius Dei,
sed in carne sola.' See Sacr altar·I; 348B.

22. Adv Abl VIII; PL 178:279A: '"...manente unitate personae...."'

23. Adv Abl VIII; PL 178:270A: 'Sicut enim in Trinitate Deus Pater et Deus
Filius unius substantiae, sed non unius personae, sic in forma Mediatoris Deus et homo sunt unius personae, sed non unius substantiae.'

24. Adv Abl VIII; PL 178:279B: 'Nos vero dicimus, secundum praemissas
    sententias Patrum, quia Christus Deus et homo haec persona, secundum
    quod Deus est, tertia est in Trinitate persona.'

25. Adv Abl VIII; PL 178:279B: 'Dicet: Ergo, non secundum quod homo est.
    Utique, sed est ibi etiam homo, propter inseparabilem unitatem, qua
    una est persona cum Deo.'

26. Adv Abl VIII; PL 178:279BC: 'Sed permanente divinitate Filii Dei in
    sua natura, sicut dicit B. Augustinus, incommutabiliter, sine omni
    composito humani phantasmatis, cum quo subsistat, mirabili et incompara-
    bili susceptione in unitatem personae homo ei est appositus, sive aptat-
    non prius creatus et postmodum assumptus, sed simul in ipsa assumptione
    creatus. Et sicut dictum est, simul coepit esse, et Deus esse, sed
    gratia, non natura, nomine vel persona, non essentiali substantia.'

27. Adv Abl VIII; PL 178:279B: 'Absit autem ut per hoc recens aliquid
    asseramus in Deo, cum, sicut Leo papa sentit, et Augustinus consentit,
    hominem ab aeterno ad hoc praedestinatum, et in tempore beneplaciti Dei
    in hoc glorificatum, simul dicimus coepisse esse, et Deum esse, cum non
    sit nisi unus Deus.'

28. Adv Abl VIII; PL 178:280AB: 'Propter haec omnia dicimus Mariam theoto-
    con, hoc est matrem Dei, Christum genuisse Deum et hominem unam per-
    sonam; hominem, in quantum ex ea esse coepit; Deum in quantum de ea
    Deus et homo esse coepit.'

29. Adv Abl VIII; PL 178:280A, citing John 14:28 and 10:30. See Augustine, <u>Contra Sermonem Arianorum</u> 8; PL 42:689.

30. Adv Abl VIII; PL 178:280B: '[Fatemur] Deum Filium Dei, in quantum una ipse substantia cum Patre et Spiritu sancto est; hominem filium hominis, in quantum ipse cum Deo Dei Filio una persona est....'

31. Adv Abl VIII; PL 178:279C, quoting Augustine, <u>Contra sermonem Arianorum</u> 8; PL 42:688: '"...ex natura utraque constantem, ut quaelibet earum vocabulum etiam suum impertiat alteri...."''

32. Bernard, Epp 192, 330, 331; PL 182:358D-59A; 535B-36A; 536C-37B. '...Cum Nestorio Christum dividens hominem assumptum a consortio Trinitatis excludit' (Epp 330 and 331).

33. Mansi, <u>Sacrorum Conciliorum nova et amplissima collectio</u>....(Florence, 1767; reprinted Graz, 1961) 21, 568: 'Quod nec Deus et Homo neque haec persona quae Christus est, sit tertia persona in Trinitate.'

34. Aenig 96, ed. M.-M. Davy, <u>Deux</u> <u>traités</u> <u>sur</u> <u>la</u> <u>foi</u>: <u>Le</u> <u>miroir</u> <u>de</u> <u>la</u> <u>foi</u>;' l'enigma <u>de</u> <u>la</u> <u>foi</u>. Bibliothèque des textes philosophiques (Paris, 1959) p. 174; PL 180:438D: 'Neque enim pars ejus remansit in Patre et pars ejus venit in Virginem, cum totus in Patre remaneret quod erat, et totus fieret in Virgine quod non erat. Sic ergo verus Deus ac summus totum hominem in se accepit.'

35. Gerhoch of Reichersberg, <u>Epistola</u> 21; PL 193:576D: 'Iterum alia vice, cum essem Romae, [et] quidem Lateranensis canonicus nomine Adam noviter

de scolis magistri Petri Abaelardi egressus, conabatur astruere Christum

ex parte Deum, et ex parte hominem esse....'

36. Theologia christiana IV, 44; PL 178:1274B.

37. Adv Abl VIII; PL 178:278D. See Sacr altar I; pl 178:346A; Aenig 92,

Davy, p. 170 (PL 180:437A); and 94, Davy, p. 172 (PL 178:437D)--taken

from Augustine, De trinitate XV, 11, 20; OL 42:1072.

38. Epitome 24; PL 178:1733B.

39. Anselm, Cur Deus Homo 7, ed. F. S. Schmitt, II, p. 101; William of

Champeaux, Sentences, ed. O. Lottin, Psychologie et morale aux XIIIe

et XIIIe siècles. (Louvain, Gembloux, 1959) V, 262, p. 213; Abelard,

Theologia 'scholarium' III; PL 178:1106 and 1108.

40. Aenig 94; Davy, pp. 172-174; PL 180:438B: 'Passa enim est divinitas

cuncta que carnis erant in carne; quia passibilem carnem cum humanis

affectibus Deus suscepit; non tamen compassa est cum carne, quia

impassibilis semper in sua natura divinitas permansit.' See ibid.

96; Davy, p. 174; PL 180:439A.

41. Aenig 96; Davy, p. 174; PL 180:439A: 'Ideo enim in carne Deus passus

est; quia passibilem carnem accepit. Ideo autem carni compassus non

est....'

HUMILITY AND THE SACRAMENTS OF FAITH

IN WILLIAM OF SAINT THIERRY'S SPECULUM FIDEI

Chrysogonus Waddell, OCSO
Abbey of Gethsemani

Like his great and good friend Bernard of Clairvaux, William of Saint-
Thierry was endowed with a prodigious ability to assimilate and to make his
own ideas and expressions borrowed from many different sources. Indeed, a
certain amount of William's literary out-put consists of little more than
patristic and biblical excerpts strung together so as to form some kind of
a coherent whole. The De sacramento altaris, for instance, ends with a
florilegium of such texts used by William to undergird his own preceding
treatise.[1] So also, two of his commentaries on the Song of Songs, consisting respectively of texts by Ambrose[2] and Gregory the Great,[3] contributed massively to his later and highly original Expositio altera super Cantic
Canticorum;[4] and in his prologue to his Expositio in Epistolam ad Romanos,[5]
William describes his role as author-compiler in terms of a bird with
borrowed plumage: if the original owners of the feathers were to demand
back their plumage, William would be one bare little bird without a feather
of his own.[6]

But even when William is less explicit as regards his sources, the
knowledgeable reader is aware that whole paragraphs are sometimes cribbed
straight from Augustine, or that William must have written this or that
folio with his copy of Gregory of Nyssa open before him on his work-desk;[7]
and Etienne Gilson claims that, to the really perceptive ear, there are

echoes of Pseudo-Denis to be found even in William's literary style.[8]
At times, one even has the impression that William of Saint-Thierry is
imitating William of Saint-Thierry.

But no matter how derivative William might be by reason of his sources,
what he does with this material is often astonishingly original.
Cassian once wrote that the monk should so interiorize the texts of the
psalms, that when he prays them, they become, as it were, his own new
creations. This is what William often did with his biblical and patristic
sources.

The purpose of this paper is to draw attention to one or two such
pages in William's Speculum fidei,[9] written probably between 1140 and
1143, in the immediate aftermath of William's polemic against Master Peter
Abelard, Prince of Dialecticians.[10]

This treatise represents a systematic attempt to deal with some of
the problems touching on the genesis, development and structure of the
act of faith. These were, for William and his co-evals, no merely speculative problems. The quality of their faith determined the quality of
their whole life in Christ, and there were monks in William's monastic
milieu whose faith seemed to rest on flimsy foundations indeed. It was
symptomatic of William's pastoral realism that he broke off his lofty
considerations on the Song of Songs in order to address himself first to
the refutation of Peter Abelard, and then, in a more positive way, to a

systematic treatment of matters touching on the act of faith.

Not unexpectedly, the role of reason in the genesis and evolution
of the act of faith looms large on William's horizon, and, for the first
half of the treatise, so often as William touches on the relationship
between reason and faith, he writes almost exactly what the reader of
Anselm, or of Peter Lombard, or of Thomas Aquinas, would expect him to
write. Faith requires the submission of reason to divine authority;
faith is based, not on the immediate evidence of the revealed truth, but
on God's authority; faith is not acquired by logic and dialectics; humility and absolute submission of reason to authority are essential condi-
tions for the subsequent understanding of what one believes.[11] Indeed,
so insistent is William on the problems posed by reason, that the reader,
though he recognizes the orthodoxy of each of William's statements, begins
to wonder whether, deep down, this champion of faith can envisage reason
other than as a most unfortunate obstacle to a really serious spiritual
life. William almost seems to look on reason in much the same way Teresa
of Avila, centuries later, looked on the imagination in certain kinds of
prayer: the mad woman of the house.

Strange to say, it is later on in the Speculum, in sections dealing
with new subject-matter, that William's insight into the relationship between faith and reason finds a particularly rich and original expression.
Midway through the treatise, he suddenly interrupts his penetrating discuss-

ion about the man whose whole being strains to attain to an intellectual understandng of the faith he professes. Without warning, he moves from the level of reason to another level:

> Fear not, servant of God; let your feet not stumble,
> nor your footsteps slip. Men without faith ask for
> signs, and men of hesitant faith seek for wisdom.
> As for you, embrace Christ crucified....If you heed
> the flesh with its senses, [he] will appear foolish
> and weak, but if, with the Apostle Paul, you have
> the mind of Christ, you will understand that the
> Word of God is sovereign Wisdom....[12]

And, with the help of Pauline texts on the wisdom of God seen as foolishness by men (1 Cor 1:23-24), William goes on to show that 'the foolishness of God's Wisdom is the flesh of the incarnate Word,' and that fleshly-minded men can find healing only in the flesh of the Word made flesh (which William equates with the foolishness of the preaching of the gospel and with the simplicity of faith).[13]

> Become foolish, then, in order to become wise; and the
> economy of the Mystery [of Christ] hidden from before all
> ages in God the Creator, will become clear to you. Become
> weak with the weakness of God, and you shall learn what
> is the immeasurable greatness of his power in us who
> believe according to the working of his great might.[14]

The import of what William is saying becomes all the more astonishing when we situate ourselves in the intellectual climate of the early twelfth century. Western European man was at last beginning to exploit his intellectual resources in a way undreamed of before the rediscovery of Aristotle and the revival of dialectical discourse. A new universe was waiting to be explored, and there were many understandably eager to exploit to the full the resources offered by dialectics and the new learning. The frontiers of the then known world of ideas were waiting to be crossed, and the experience must have been as heady as it was for Columbus sailing across an uncharted ocean to discover a New World, or for the astronauts landing on the moon.

But here is William telling us to forget all that, and to embrace Christ crucified. Is he being reactionary? anti-intellectual? Not in the least. Because, for William, as for the Cistercians in general, there was nothing static in the experience of the monk who resolutely entered into the poverty of the 'sacraments of faith'--and by 'sacraments,' William usually (but not consistently) means sacraments in the early patristic sense, that is to say, those sacred realities which express and give access to yet deeper, more divine realities: the Sacred Humanity of the incarnate Word, the Scriptures, the Church and the whole system of sacrament-signs (baptism, Eucharist, etc.).[15]

It is true that we have been created for eternity, and that our spirit, which is capax Dei, has by its very nature a certain affinity with the divine, eternal realities.[16] It is also true that, by reason alone, we can attain to a true, even lofty knowledge about God: we can know that He exists, and we can know something about His providence and his attributes.[17] But a knowledge of God such as this is not what the monk is after. Rather than

preoccupy ourselves with this type of rational, discursive knowledge abou
God, we have to enter with courage and conviction into a quite different

universe. It is not an inaccessible God outside space and time, but the

incarnate Word of God who is the proper object of our faith. And when

William speaks of the Incarnation, he includes all that goes with it--the

earthiness and materiality of birth, suffering, death on a cross; a sacra

mental system in which spiritual realities become accessible only through

material substances as humble as water, bread, wine and oil; sacred books

written in an often uncouth indiom and teeming with events and sayings

offensive to right reason. All this is somewhat scandalous when we consi

the spiritual nature of man, created in the image and likeness of God.[18]

But once we have entered into all the lowliness of this humble econo

of salvation, things begin to happen. Because, the life of faith, rooted

as it is in the scandal of the Incarnation, has its own in-built dynamism

William distinguishes three degrees of knowledge in this growth in faith.

The first degree he describes in terms of somewhat grudging 'hospi-

tality'"

> 'He who believes will be saved...,' says the Lord.
> So the first degree consists of not refusing the
> grace of hospitality to those things which came to
> us from outside ourselves...[that is to say, the
> whole economy of salvation as described by the
> gospels, in contrast to the truths we can deduce
> about God by reflecting on our own spiritual
> nature]; one simply obeys the Lord, and gives
> one's simple assent.[19]

This rather strained 'hospitality' leads, however, to a more intimate type of relationship--one of 'friendship.'

> The second degree consists of a familiar friend-
> ship based on good will: like a friendship between
> men who commune and share in the same bread and in
> the same chalice.[20]

But this deeper, more intimate perception of the divine realities

grows into an even richer experience, much more intimate:

> The final degree is a sort of marriage in the
> depths of the soul--a marriage between the
> truths [of faith] which have been received
> from outside oneself, and the immanent truths
> [that is, those accessible to man by means of
> his faculty of reason].[21]

In other words, all the 'philosophical' truths we can know thanks to

reason--truths such as God's existence, His providence, His attributes--

are now known in a manner radically different from the way these truths

are known by the dialectician. This is now no merely speculative, abstract

knowledge, but a 'taste-and see' experience of the living God, and experi-

ence which admits of an ever growing perfectibility.

This presentation of faith in terms of a dynamic growth in which the

subject is transformed in proportion as the realities of faith are pro-

gressively interiorized, is perfectly in line with the type of experience

described in the very heart of the Rule of Saint Benedict, in Chapter VII

'On the Degrees of Humility.' In 1959, Placide Deseille, OCSO, published

an important article[22] in which he analyzed with finesse the doctrine

contained in this chapter, and showed that this teaching, mediated to

Benedict by a line running from the <u>Rule of the Master</u> back to Cassian,
back to Evagrius and finally back to the common <u>doctrina</u> of the desert
fathers, had the same inbuilt dynamism. In the first degree of humility,
the monk is possesed by an almost animal fear of an angry God. Depress-
ing as this starting-point might sound, it is, after all, only a starting point. And the monk who manages to ascend all twelve degrees of
humility attains at last to a perfection of love and interior freedom
in which all that had been done, in times past, with constraint from
without, is now done spontaneously, by second nature, as it were, out of
love for Christ and for the sheer joy of virtue. William, it would seem,
has treated the evolution of the act of faith in terms of the same dynami

From the twelfth century until the time of the Council of Trent,
theologians in general agreed that one of the reasons for the institution
of the sacraments was our need to be exercized in the virtue of humility.
A line of development can be traced from Hugh of Saint-Victor,[23] to Peter
Lombard,[24] to Thomas Aquinas,[25] and to Bonaventure.[26] The variations
are many, but the main theme rings clear. By his sin of disobedience,
Adam turned from God, the uncreated substantial Good, to a material,
created good inferior to man's spiritual nature. Consequently, God, in
his justice, has willed that we regain our lost likeness to God by means
of an economy of salvation essentially bound up with material realities.
Since man remains spiritual by nature, this dependence on material reali
ties as vehicles of grace involves a real humiliation.[27]

All this sounds vaguely similar to William's insistence on the humble, lowly nature of the 'sacraments of faith.' But nowhere in Hugh of Saint Victor or in the later theologians do we find, in this sacramental context, anything resembling William's teaching about the radical dynamism of that faith which, adhering to Christ crucified, expands in a love and knowledge of the deepest sort possible.

One final note. William was not the only Cistercian who had a predilection for what was poorest and most humble as a means of entering more perfectly into the deep things of God. Saint Bernard's devotion to the Sacred Humanity of Christ was an expression of the same basic approach. Perhaps the 'mystique' of poverty characteristic of the earliest Cistercians, but soon lost, was the fruit of the same type of experience; and much the same could be said for the ideas expressed by the White Monks in the areas of art, architecture, liturgy, music. In their own way, they too were interested in passing beyond the frontiers of the then known world of ideas, and, in their own way, perhaps they succeeded.

NOTES

1. PL 180:341-66.

2. PL 15:1947-2060.

3. PL 180:441-74.

4. PL 180:473-546.

5. PL 180:547-694.

6. PL 180:547. The figure of the bird is borrowed from Horace.

7. William's sources have been studied by Dom Déchanet, Aux sources de
   la spiritualité de Guillaume de Saint-Thierry (Bruges, 1940).

8. The Mystical Theology of Saint Bernard (London, New York, 1940) p. 219
   n. 22.

9. The best edition is the one by J. M. Déchanet, OSB, Guillaume de Saint
   Thierry: Le miroir de la foi. (Bruges, 1946). Also excellent is the
   edition by M.-M. Davy, Deux traités sur la foi. (Paris, 1959). The
   text is also in PL 180:365-98.

10. In the Déchanet edition, pp. 11-17 and 36-40.

11. In the Déchanet edition, Chapitre III, pp. 74-93 (PL 180:372-76), pass

12. Déchanet, pp. 112-13; PL 180:381b.

13. Ibid.

14. Ibid.; biblical references from Eph 3:9 and 1:19.

15. Excellent note on William's concept of sacramentum in Déchanet, p. 25
    with valuable remarks about William's witness to an aspect of twelfth
    century sacramental theology which deserves closer study.

16. Déchanet, pp. 134-35; PL 180:386bc.

17. Déchanet, pp. 144-45; PL 180:389d.

18. In the Déchanet edition, Chapitre VI, pp. 116-29 (PL 180:382-85),
     passim.

19. Déchanet, pp. 138-39; PL 180:387b.

20. Ibid.

21. Ibid.

22. "A propos de l'épilogue du chapitre VII de la Règle," Coll. 21 (1959)
     289-301.

23. Summa sententiarum, Tract. IV, Cap. I; PL 176:117-18 (Hugh's author-
     ship of this treatise is disputed); and De sacramentis legis naturalis
     et scriptae; PL 176:34.

24. Petri Lombardi Libri IV sententiarum, Lib. IV, Cap. 5, ed. Quarrachi
     (Florence, 1916) II, 747.

25. Summa theologiae III, q. 61, a. 2.; In IV sententiae, dist. 1, q. 1,
     a. 2, 1 ad 2um.

26. In IV sententiae, Dist. I, Pars I, q. 1, ed. Quarrachi (Florence,
     1949) editio minor, IV, 5-6.

27. See Innocenzo Colosio, O. P., "La prassi sacramentale come esercizio
     di umilità," Rivista di Ascetica e Mistica 9 (1964) 101-116.

WILLIAM OF SAINT THIERRY'S EXPOSITION

ON THE EPISTLE TO THE ROMANS

John D. Anderson
Johnson O'Connor Research Foundation

Christ's summation of the Law in terms of love of God and love of neighbor guided the inquiry of the early Cistercians as they sought for an authentic monasticism. The monk before God and the monk before his fellow-monk were themes which gave direction to the literary endeavors of the twelfth-century Cistercians. This was a century that produced literally dozens of commentaries on that classic love song of Christ and the soul, the Canticle of Canticles.[1] This was a century that saw the composition of that masterpiece on Christian friendship, Ailred of Rievaulx' De amicitia spiritali.[2] And these were but manifestations of a growing re-emphasis on the theme of self-knowledge which was so vital for the life of the soul. Ambrose in his Exposition on Psalm 118 had said nosce teipsum,[3] and William of Saint Thierry, feeling the immediacy of this admonition, made it part of his collected passages from Ambrose which might help him comment on the intimate relationship between Christ and the individual monk.[4]

Among the early Cistercian writings William's Exposition on Romans is something of an anomaly, for it departs from the object of most Cistercian exegesis, the Canticle of Canticles.[5] It perhaps reflects something of William's experience at the school of Reims before he became a monk,[6]

in that the Epistle to the Romans was one of the most popular books for
commentary in the schools. In any event, there is only one other twelfth-
century commentary of Romans by a Cistercian to which I have been able
to find reference, the commentary attributed to Guerric of Igny by Charles
DeVisch in his seventeenth-century catalog of Cistercian writers.[7] But
this work is not extant and is of very doubtful attribution. In fact,
later editors of Guerric do not even mention it.[8]

Behind William stands a long tradition of commentary on Paul's Epistle
to the Romans. There are commentaries on this Epistle by several early
writers in the West.[9] Likewise, there is Origen's Commentary of Romans
which Rufinus rendered into Latin in the early fifth century and whose
use became commonplace in Western exegsis of Romans.[10] For example, the
Origen-Rufinus Commentary was used in the commentaries on Romans written
by Rhabanus Maurus and Sedulius Scotus in the ninth century, and by Anselm
of Laon in the Glossa ordinaria in the early twelfth century, and in the
middle of that century by Peter Abelard, William of Saint Thierry and
Peter Lombard in their commentaries on the Pauline epistle.

The Exposition on Romans by William was written at Signy as were
William's other works which rely on Latin translations of Greek sources.[11]
Printed in Migne's Patrologia Latina, itself a reprint of Tissier's edition
from the seventeenth century, the Exposition is found in a single twelfth-
century manuscript from the library of Signy and now in the municipal

library of Charleville: MS 49. The manuscript contains two parts: the
first is an eleventh-century collection of Paul's _Epistles_ with marginal
and interlinear glosses from Augustine, Gregory, Leo, Basil and Origen,
with one attributed in the manuscript to Plato, but which is actually
Augustine. These are in at least three hands, one of which may be that
of William himself. The second part of the manuscript is William's _Expo-
sition_ on _Romans_.

It is William's use of the Origen-Rufinus _Commentary on Romans_ on
which I wish to focus in the next few pages. But it may be easier to
understand this use of Origen after some preliminary observations. The
earliest extant source for the Matins readings used by the early Cistercians is the _Breviary_ of Stephan Harding, a document from about 1130.
Included among the lections read at Matins are works which were attribute
to John Chrysostom and to Origen. Here, indeed, there seems to be evider
of an early Cistercian propensity for Greek writers. However, when compared with the ninth-century _Homiliary_ of Paul the Deacon which provided
the core of the readings used in the Cluniac usage of Molesme from which
the Cistercians received their _Homiliary_, it can be seen that all of the
Greek readings used by the Cistercians were taken from the traditional
Cluniac homiliary. Thus, in the lections, the Cistercians read passages
from Greek authors, but passages sanctioned by a monastic tradition of
almost 300 years. This is typical of the way the Cistercians chose their

sources.

Two further observations: one concerns the presence of Origen in the West; the other, the nature of Rufinus' translation of Origen's _Commentary_. In the Middle Ages, from the ninth to the twelfth century, Origen was ubiquitous, especially in the monasteries. It is true that he was used with caution.[12] Nevertheless, he was looked upon in the Carolingian monastic revival as a spiritual mentor, a guide and an inspiration. Benedict of Aniane, the great monastic legislator and reformer of the Carolingian age, praised Origen as a model for monks.[13] The _Homiliary_ of Paul the Deacon, commissioned by Charlemagne, contains six readings attributed to Origen (all are apocryphal). These readings formed part of the Matins lections in the West from the ninth century until the reform of Pius V in the sixteenth century. As already mentioned, the earliest known Cistercian lectionary contained some of these same Origen readings.[14] In addition, Origen was read by Cassiodorus, Gregory the Great, Alcuin, Sedulius Scotus, Rhabanus Maurus, Amalarius of Metz, John Scotus Erigena, Notker Balbulus, Peter Lombard, Bernard of Clairvaux, William of Saint Thierry, Peter Abelard and Hugh, Andrew and Richard of Saint Victor.[15] Origen is represented in most of the libraries whose twelfth-century collections can be reassembled.[16] In short, Origen was part of the tradition of spirituality in the West, especially the tradition of monastic spirituality.

The second point is the peculiar nature of Rufinus' technique of
translation. Perhaps a better word would be transmutation. Rufinus
brought the riches of the East to the West, but in the process he unabash-
edly altered what he read, to conform to his own Western point of view.[17]
In this, Rufinus was far from unique: Jerome and Hilary of Poitiers,
among others, both modified Eastern texts for Western ears.[18] There is
no question here of the accuracy of Rufinus' renderings of the Greek text.
He was not, strictly speaking, translating. He was providing Latin versions of Greek writings for the spiritual instruction and edification of
his contemporaries.[19] Therefore, when William of Saint Thierry said that
he used Origen in his Exposition on Romans, this admission must be understood with significant qualifications. William was using Origen, bowd-
lerized, as it were, for a Western audience. Furthermore, William also
adapted the text of the Origen-Rufinus commentary for his purposes.

The text of Origen's Commentary on Romans which William used at Signy
is extant today in the municipal library of Charleville in MS 207, six
folio volumes of Origen's works. These volumes are in Latin like all the
works in the Signy library which are by Greek authors.[20] In addition to
this we have in Charleville-Signy MS 49 a Latin text of Paul's Epistle to
the Romans with glosses, eleven of which I have found in William's Exposition. Thus, we have the version of Paul's Epistle with which William
worked; we have William's own admission that he was using Origen in his

<u>Exposition</u> <u>on</u> <u>Romans</u>, and we have the copy of the Origen-Rufinus <u>Commen-</u>
<u>tary</u> which he used.

Now, the question remains: how did William utilize Origen in his
exegisis? What use did he make of the commentary of Origen? Bouyer says
that in his <u>Exposition</u> <u>on</u> <u>Romans</u> William

> exerted himself to bring about a synthesis between
> the two great systems of thought which the problem
> [of grace and freewill] had called forth in early
> Christianity: those of Augustine and Origen. The
> masterly way in which he combined the basic princi-
> ples of the two thinkers...and made them supplement
> each other is the measure of his stature as a theo-
> logian.[21]

This is, indeed, lofty praise, but remember, this is the same Bouyer who
sees in William's <u>Enigma fidei</u>, 'the direct influence of Origen...given
precision and balance by St. Athanasius and the Cappadocians.'[22] And
this, Bouyer says about a work for which not a single Eastern source has
been found.[23] On the contrary, in the <u>Enigma fidei</u> William's discussion
of the problem of man's vision of God is based on his reading of Augustine's lengthy <u>Epistle 147</u>, which provided William with an approach to
the problem as well as its solution. William's understanding of the identit
of the Holy Spirit with all that is common to both Father and Son is
throughly Augustinian, and absolutely not Eastern.[24] This, by the way, is
an understanding reiterated by William in his <u>Exposition</u> <u>on</u> <u>Romans</u>.[25]
William's entire treatment of the Divine Names utilized Augustinian categories and progresses along Western lines, with no hint of dependence on

Dionysius the Areopagite. The definition of persona which William accepted, cujus pro sui forma certa sit agnitio, was taken from Boethius.[26]
In short, the Enigma fidei is a Western theological statement.

William's use of Origen in his Exposition on Romans does not justify the description by Bouyer. For the most part, William borrowed spiritual vignettes and passages which gave added dimension to the statements
of Paul. In this, William was doing essentially no more than had been
done by Rhabanus Maurus and by Peter Lombard in their commentaries on
Romans. In fact, in many instances the same sections of Origen-Rufinus
were used by William and one or the other of these commentators. For
example, William and Rhabanus both borrowed the Origen-Rufinus section on
Rom. 1:4 Qui praedestinatus est Filius Dei in virtute. William said:

> Now, according to the Greek translation, he is
> not predestined, but destined, who was always
> God, and he came in power, that is, in that
> which he was. For Christ is the power of God
> and the wisdom of God.[27]

Immediately before this in William's Exposition is a quotation from Augustine which also occurs in Lombard's Commentary.[28]

William's commentary has many sections of direct address. Throughout his Exposition William broke off from his narrative and addressed God
in prayer. In this way William's text differs from those of Rhabanus and
Lombard. Rhabanus was a compilator; he was passing on the fragmented
comments of the Fathers in the manner of a catena. He dutifully cited
his authors and even instructed the reader to mention these authors so

his hearers will know whose opinion was being read to them.[29] Lombard,
on the other hand, wrote as a <u>scholasticus</u>. His text is for students.
It is analytical and pedantic. It gets involved in controversial topics
such as the Christological debate of the <u>assumptus homo</u>, which involves
the personality of Christ.[30] Lombard gave the Hebrew, Greek and Latin
form for Paul's name. William, on the other hand, was concerned more
with the meaning of the name: it signifies a man who is humble and tran-
quil and on whom the Holy Spirit rests.[31] In some respects this difference is a matter of emphasis. William's tone and purpose were irenic.
He did not intend to write a treatise dealing with questions of heresy
or controversy. He wrote to preach God's glory, and he wrote compelled
by the joy of the contemplation of God's grace. Paul had written against
the Jews, the Fathers had commented on the <u>Epistle</u> to defend the faith
against heretics, but William wrote to foster humility and true devotion.
This was the intention of a monk admonishing his brothers to respond in
the leisure of the cloister to a God whose love endures forever.

This was William's purpose as stated in the Preface to his <u>Exposition</u>.
He wrote as a monk for other monks. Passages which had little application
for his monastic purposes were passed over quickly. For example, on
<u>Romans</u> 1:26ff., with the statements on homosexuality, William simply said
that the passage is somewhat offensive, <u>kakemphaton</u>, using a grammatical
term drawn ultimately from Quintillian.[32] William's overview of the
<u>Epistle</u> is essentially Augustinian. From Augustine's comments on <u>Romans</u>

he saw four states or levels in men's development: _ante_ _legem_, _sub_ _lege_,

sub _gratia_ and _in_ _pace_.[33] This Augustinian scheme is basic to an under-

standing of the entire _Epistle_ as William pointed out in his _Exposition_:

> These four distinctions are operative throughout
> the body of this Epistle, at one time concerning
> the man of God as an individual; at another, the
> people of God as a community.[34]

Our author's understanding of original sin and _Romans_ 5:12 is thorough

ly Augustinian down to the damnation of unbaptized children.[35] Here in

the discussion of Adam's sin the reader gets the clearest view of the

kind of use William made of Origen. Rufinus' rendering of the Greek makes

the statement:

> All men who are born, and have been born, in this
> world were in Adam's loins when he was still in
> paradise, and all men were expelled from paradise
> with him and in him when he was driven out.[36]

William used this text with a most telling alteration. He said:

> All men were in Adam's loins when he sinned and
> in him they sinned and with him they were expelled
> from paradise.[37]

Insistence on inherited guilt characterizes William's interpretation of

Romans 5:12, and it was repeated time and again throughout William's com-

mentary.[38] This position separates William's reading of _Romans_ from any-

thing that can be called Eastern or Greek. William's stance was diametri-

cally opposed to that of the East wherein man suffers a weakening and in-

herits an inclination toward sin, but has no share in Adam's guilt. Con-

sequently it is simply not true to suggest that in William we can hope to find a blend of Augustinian theology and eastern Orthodox theology.

This article has been an attempt to define the context of William's <u>Exposition</u> <u>on</u> <u>Romans</u>. Much remains to be done on the <u>Exposition</u> itself. This paper is merely an introduction. Here I am primarily concerned with an approach to William's <u>Exposition</u>, and in fact to all that William wrote.

To sum up, William was a man in touch with his tradition, not a man reaching outside that tradition. Whatever William's use of Greek works, he remained within the Western tradition in his theology. His worth as a monastic writer must be assessed accordingly. His is the contribution of a monk nurtured by Western monasticism. His quest was for the traditional sources of monastic life in the West. William was most profoundly influenced by Augustine, and to a lesser extent by Ambrose, Gregory, Leo, Hilary etc. His view of original sin, his theology of grace, his understanding of the Trinity, his treatment of the Divine Names, his solution to the problem of faith and reason, his definition of <u>persona</u>, were all Western and in the Latin tradition of the West. The last word on William will not be said until an investigation is made of his dependence on Augustine, Gregory, Ambrose and the other giants of Western theological thought.

William's significance, therefore, is not in a general use of the writings of the Greeks, or in a profound grasp of Eastern theology, as some have suggested. The exciting thing about William of St. Thierry is

his mature awareness that renewal involves a return, that is, a return
to the sources to achieve the enlightenment upon which all renewal must
be predicated. He had a thirst for an authentic monasticism. And who
was his guide? It was Benedict.[39] Benedict had said: read Basil,
and the monks of the West read Basil. He had recommended Cassian,[40]
and they read Cassian. But why Origen? Because the tradition of Western
monasticism said: read Origen. Origen was, in spirit, if not in fact,
the monk par excellence for the West. It was he who spoke most eloquent-
ly to the monk of that heightened sense of awareness of human helpless-
ness and divine compassion which can be nurtured, perhaps best in the
monastic life.

William did not seek to change the Western monastic tradition; he
sought to renew contact with that tradition; He did not judge his past,
much less did he turn his back on it and look to the East for something
better. Orientale lumen is not the battle cry of a new monastic Hellen-
ism. This term expressed a sentiment which was in fact, traditional,
with all that this word conveys that is positive, constructive and creati
As Rozanne Elder has pointed out, the sentiment is at least as old as
Cassian in the West.[41] Orientale lumen speaks of every monk's longing fo
a long-passed Golden Age. But William was no nostalgic dreamer. True,
monasticism first appeared in the East, but that same monasticism in all
of its vitality and spiritual dynamism was no more distant than Benedict'
Rule. In William's eyes Benedict's monasticism was not a watered-down

version, a second best, an imitation. It was that same life of the Desert. And it was re-contact with this life-force, Benedict's monasticism,
which William strove to achieve. This, I believe, is the key to William's
Exposition on Romans and to all that he did and wrote.

NOTES

1. J. Leclercq, The Love of Learning and the Desire for God (New York, 1961) pp. 90-91.

2. Peter of Blois rearranged Ailred's treatise and presented it as his own later in the twelfth century. During the next two centuries several compendia or summaries of the treatise by Ailred were written. These are published by A. Hoste in CC, continuatio medievalis, I.

3. PL 15:1402D.

4. Ex scriptis Ambrosii; PL 15:1951D.

5. Joachim of Flora, while not representative of Cistercian exegetes, has extant works on the Apocalypse. The Commentary on Ruth ascribed to Isaac of Stella is of very doubtful authenticity.

6. It seems necessary to say Reims rather than Laôn since the only manuscript evidence, the Vita antiqua, names Reims as William's place of study. While there are those who suggest Laôn, no real evidence has been produced to back this claim.

7. Bibliotheca scriptorum sacri ordinis Cisterciensis (Cologne, 1655) p. 131.

8. CF 8, pp. xviii-xix. Also, the Commentary on Romans attributed to Gilbert of Hoyland by DeVisch, Bibliotheca, p. 126, is spurious; see Friedrich Stegmüller, Repertorium biblicum medii aevi (Madrid, 1950) no. 2497.

9. Augustine, CSEL 84; Pelagius, PLS 1:1112-81; Ambrosiaster, CSEL 81, pars I.

10. Adolf Harnack, <u>Die Überlieferung und der Bestand der altchristlichen Litteratur</u> (Leipzig, 1893) pp. 400-401, lists sixteen manuscripts of Origen's <u>Commentary on Romans</u> in Western <u>scriptoria</u> before the thirteenth century.

11. J. Déchanet, <u>Aux sources de la spiritualité de Guillaume de Saint-Thierry</u> (Bruges, 1940) p. 57, n. 1.

12. Rhabanus Maurus, <u>Praefatio altera</u> to his <u>Ennarationes in epistolas beati Pauli</u>; PL 111:1276A. Also, Leclercq, <u>Love of Learning</u>, pp. 101-102.

13. J. Leclercq, "Les <u>Munimenta fidei</u> de S. Benoit d'Aniane," <u>Analecta Monastica</u> I (1948) p. 74.

14. Bruno Griesser, "Das Lektionen- und Perikopensystem in Stephans-Brevier," C Ch 71 (1964) and 73-92 for the listing of the patristic readings for Matins.

15. M. L. W. Laistner, <u>Thought and Letters in Western Europe, A.D. 500-900</u>, (Ithaca, 1931) adds Julian of Toledo (p. 169) and Radbertus (p. 304). For the fullest treatment of Origen's influence in the West see Henri DeLubac, <u>Exégèse Médiévale</u> (Paris, 1959) I, 221ff.

16. Leclercq, <u>Love of Learning</u>, p. 100.

17. J. E. L. Oulton, "Rufinus's Translation of the <u>Church History</u> of

Eusebius," <u>The Journal of Theological Studies</u> 30 (1929) 150-74. See
pp. 153-56 especially. For useful bibliography on Rufinus' translations see Francis X. Murphy, <u>Rufinus of Aquileia, His Life and Works</u>
(Washington, D. C., 1945) 192-94.

18. M. Monica Wagner, <u>Rufinus the Translator</u> (Washington, D.C., 1945)
     pp. 12-13, 21.

19. Wagner, <u>Rufinus the Translator</u>, p. 97.

20. This fact has been verified by an examination of the MSS from Signy
     by Madame Hubert Collin, the wife of the Charleville archivist. The
     results of this examination have been conveyed to me by letter.

21. Louis Bouyer, <u>The Cistercian Heritage</u> (Westminster, 1958) pp. 84-85.

22. Bouyer, <u>The Cistercian Heritage</u>, p. 116.

23. See CF 9, Introduction and Notes; also my paper "The Use of Greek
     Sources by William of St. Thierry Especially in the <u>Enigma fidei</u>,"
     in M. Basil Pennington (ed.), <u>One Yet Two: Monastic Tradition East
     and West</u>, CS 29 (Kalamazoo, Michigan, 1976) pp. 242-53.

24. Vladimir Lossky, <u>The Mystical Theology of the Eastern Church</u> (Cambri
     1968) pp. 81, 213.

25. PL 180:561C and 591D.

26. PL 64:1343D-44A.

27. William's text is PL 180:550C. See Origen-Rufinus, PG 14:849B, and
     Rhabanus Maurus, PL 111:1285B.

28. See PL 191:1314A where Lombard names Augustine as his source.

29. PL 111:1276A.

30. PL 191:1312.

31. PL 180:549B.

32. Quintillian, Institutiones 8. 3. 44.

33. PL 180:570; from Augustine, PL 35:2065ff.

34. PL 180:571A.

35. PL 180:599.

36. PG 14:1009D-1010A.

37. PL 180:596C

38. PL 180:594, 595, 599.

39. Before he became a Cistercian William spent approximately twenty years
     as a Black monk at Saint Nicaise in Reims and at Saint Thierry right
     outside of Reims.

40. Benedict, Regula, Chapter 73.

41. Michael Petschenig, Ioannis Cassiani Conlationes XXIIII, CSEL 13
     (Vienna, 1886) p. 311, especially lines 10-14. This is in the
     Preface to Part Two of the Collations.

CHIMAERA OF THE NORTH:

THE ACTIVE LIFE OF AELRED OF RIEVAULX

Douglass Roby
Brooklyn College of the City University of New York

The subject of this paper, Aelred of Rievaulx, is often referred
to as the Bernard of the North.[1] Like Bernard he was both the perfect
type of the Cistercian abbot, devoted to his community and to monastic
otium, and also a great public figure, obliged by his position and tal-
ents to mix frequently in public affairs. It is one of the tragedies
of the Reformation in England that the collection of over three hundred
of his letters, known to have existed as late as the sixteenth century,
has not survived.[2] It would have enabled us to be a great deal more
specific about the ways in which Aelred found it possible to reconcile
the public and private sides of his abbatial responsibilities.

Nevertheless, the loss of Aelred's letters has not left us entirely ignorant of his public life. The Life of Aelred,[3] written by his
infirmarian, Master Walter Daniel, is primarily concerned with demonstrating Aelred's sainthood, but gives an occasional glimpse of Aelred's
vast public undertakings; Aelred's sermons[4] have survived only in fragmentary collections (not all of them adequately edited to this day), but
they also prove that he preached at synods and other gatherings of non-
monastic clergy. Aelred's expository works also contain occasional
allusions to his activities outside the monastery, though these must be
treated with some reserve: it is not self-evident that since Aelred describes the Battle of the Standard[5] with some vividness he was necessari-

ly present at Northallerton. Finally, the examination of charters and

arbitration settlements is occasionally rewarding: Dom Alberic Stac-

poole has discovered a few occasions not previously noticed where Aelred

acted as witness or assesor in ecclesiastical cases, generally in the

north of England.[6]

An examination of this evidence for Aelred's activity outside of

Rievaulx is interesting not only for the better picture it gives of

Aelred's personality and sense of values, but also for the light it can

shed on the workings of the Cistercian constitution in its formative

days. Since modern research has shown that the _Carta caritatis_ and the

first _Instituta_ of the General Chapter did not spring full grown from

the head of Stephen Harding but evolved under the pressure of circumstan-

ces,[7] it is more important than ever to examine closely exactly what the

circumstances were which occupied and occasionally pre-occupied a busy

Cistercian abbot. In cases like this, the life of Saint Bernard may be

rather misleading: as a figure of European reputation, called on to

intervene in every dispute from a disputed election to a suffragan bish-

opric to the preaching of the Crusade, Bernard is hardly typical of the

Cistercian abbot. Aelred, however, as abbot of a prosperous if somewhat

out of the way community, respected in his neighborhood but hardly an

international figure, may provide a far more convenient yardstick for

measuring the activities of the hundreds of abbots who met at Cîteaux

for the General Chapter.

Once having become a monk at Rievaulx in 1134, Aelred's public life can be divided into two categories. By far the larger number of his travels and public appearances must have been on the business of his order: the rounds of visitation to the five daughter houses which Rievaulx founded in his lifetime, and the visits to Cîteaux required by the Carta caritatis.[8] Unfortunately, these activities have left very little trace in surviving records, and it is by no means easy to know how regular Aelred was in the performance of these duties. (Nor is it possible to postulate that since Aelred was an excellent medieval abbot that he saw his duty of visitation in terms of the absolute obligation imposed on a modern abbot.) On the other hand, Aelred's much more sporadic activities as a peacemaker and ecclesiastical judge have left marks scattered through the records of medieval England, marks which allow us to trace a minimum profile of his activities, even if, as is likely, many of the records are defective.

Looking first at Aelred's activities outside the sphere of his responsibility to the Carta caritatis, it comes as no surprise that Aelred took a considerable part in the ecclesiastical affairs of the North. Born into a family of hereditary priests while such a situation was still entirely reputable,[9] and fostered in the court of the king of Scots,[10] Aelred was accustomed from his earliest youth to both the ecclesiastical and the diplomatic manners. It was only natural that this talented young man from a prominent clerical family (we can perhaps think of the clerical dynasties of the eighteenth-century Church of England) should have been in line for episcopal preferment in Scotland,[11] and should have been sent on a dip-

lomatic mission of unknown character to the archbishop of York in 1134.[12]

(It should be remembered that the independence of the Scottish Church

was not recognized until 1192, and that York was attempting to make its

claims to metropolitan authority over the Scottish sees a reality, in

part to compensate for the losses it had suffered to the see of Canter-

bury since the Conquest.)[13]

It is somewhat ironic that Aelred's first known activity outside of

Rievaulx after his conversion should have been a visit in 1138 to Hexham

to witness the final surrender of his father's hereditary rights to the

recently founded (1113) Austin canons of Hexham.[14] (It is possible that

in the same year Aelred was present at the Battle of the Standard, fought

at Northellerton between invading Scots under Aelred's foster brother

David I, king of Scots, and English forces under Rievaulx' founder, Walter

Espec.[15] There is, however, no solid evidence for his presence: Aelred's

vivid discriptions of the last minute quarrels in the Scottish army were

probably common knowledge, derived from disgruntled captives after the

battle, and the speeches of the protagonists are clearly in the ancient

historical tradition of speeches which ought to have been made, not direct

reportage. As a simple monk, recently professed, it seems less than like-

ly that Aelred would have been allowed so far from his monastery without

urgent need.)

Nevertheless, Aelred's childhood friendship with King David I, and

his more than passing acquaintance with Walter Espec soon proved useful:
we have evidence that Aelred accompanied his abbot to Walter's castle of
Wark on Tweed, in the debated lands of the Anglo-Scottish border, when
the homage of that important fortification was conceded to David as
part of the peace settlement following the Scottish defeat at Northallerton.[16]

The last public activity of which we have any information before
Aelred's election to the abbacy of Revesby was in some ways the most influential for his later career: in 1142 Aelred accompanied his abbot on
the long journey to Rome, to plead the Cistercian case in the disputed
election at York, following the death of Archbishop Thurstan.[17] Aelred
has left us no account of his visit, and Master Walter only records that
Aelred pleaded his brief with skill. From the letter of introduction to
the Speculum caritatis, however, we know that Aelred had come to the attention of Saint Bernard himself, and a stop at Clairvaux en route to Rome is
a logical deduction.[18] The impetus which Bernard's authority gave to
Aelred's literary career, although not strictly part of his public life,
must have been crucial to his general development, overcoming his reluctance
to publish the notes which he seems to have been working on even before
his appointment as novice-master.

In 1143 Aelred was appointed abbot of Revesby, a daughter of Rievaulx,
in the process of foundation, and for the next five years his labors as
abbot of a struggling new community seem to have fully occupied his time.

In 1147 however, Abbot Maurice of Rievaulx, finding the cares of administration too onerous, resigned his office, and the election was given
to Aelred, whose success at Revesby was thus ratified. Almost immediately Aelred found himself called away from his new responsibilities to act
as judge in an involved case of ecclesiastical protocol: Aelred joined
the bishop of Durham in settling a dispute between the monastic chapter
of Durham and its prior over precedence in the choir.[19] (Since Aelred
was only installed at the end of November, it is possible that it was
his personality and family connection, rather than simply his position
as an impartial mediator, which was decisive in the invitation.)

Over the next few years, and with increasing frequency until hinder-
ed by physical incapacity, Aelred found himself in demand as judge, mediator and witness for charters of exceptional importance. In 1154 Aelred
was called to Furness in Lancaster to judge a dispute between Savigny
(mother house of a congregation which entered the Cistercian fold en bloc
in 1147) and her daughter house of Furness, which had been Cistercianized
by a mission from Rievaulx in 1148, over the control of Byland.[20] In
this case Aelred's interest was compound: not only had Rievaulx eased
Furness' entry into the customs of Cîteaux, but Byland was Rievaulx'
nearest neighbor—so near in fact that the ringing of its bells had confused the monks of Rievaulx and caused Byland to move to a new site in
1148 out of ear-shot of its neighbors.[21] In 1159, on his way
back to Rievaulx from a visitation of his scottish daughters, Aelred stopped

in Durham and witnessed two charters concerning the relations between
Durham and York.[22] In the same year, and perhaps on the same expe-
dition, Aelred found time to visit and be edified by Goderic of Finchale,
as attested by the biography of that interesting pirate turned hermit.[23]

Probably in the next year, Aelred was at the Gilbertine house of
Watton, not far east of York, where a scandal had arisen through the se-
duction of one of the nuns by a canon of the house. Aelred, in his own
account of the case,[24] records that he was invited to be judge by Gilbert
of Sempringham himself. We do not know if this was Gilbert's first contact with Aelred, other than by reputation--they could have met at the
General Chapter in 1147 when Gilbert pleaded unsuccessfully for the incorporation of his order into Cîteaux[25]--but once again the impression
he made was obviously favorable: in 1164 Aelred was at Kirkstead in
Lincolnshire to witness an agreement between the Cistercians and Gilber-
tines over such practical matters as the prevention of rivalry between
the granges of the two orders.[26]

By 1164 Aelred's life was drawing to a close, and the account of
his faithful infirmarian, Master Walter, vividly describing the arthri-
tic agonies which the climate of the north--and perhaps Aelred's fondness
for that ultimate weapon of English asceticism, the cold bath--was terribly vivid. "His body, looking by the fire like a leaf of parchment, was
so bent that his head seemed altogether lost between his knees."[27] Indeed
Aelred's illnesses were a long standing problem; Walter indicates that

as early as 1157, the year in which the abbots of Scottish houses were

excused from attendance at the General Chapter except once in four years,

Aelred had received a broad dispensation from choir and other regular

obligations on account of his bad health.[28] (No trace of this dispensa-

tion is to be found in the records of the Chapter, but if it were not

entirely warranted it would surely have been attacked as other portions

of the Life were, and defended by Walter in his reply to Abbot Maurice.)[29]

This evidence of serious illness, especially in Aelred's last four

years, makes it very difficult to judge the reliability of the evidence

for his presence at Westminster on the occasion (1163) of the translation

of the relics of Saint Edward the Confessor, the newly canonized patron

of the House of Plantagenet. Aelred certainly wrote both a lesson for

the feast, and a revised version of Osbert of Saint Clair's Life for his

kinsman Lawrence, abbot of Westminster.[30] We know that Aelred was as

far south as Westminster in March of that year; we have a copy of a con-

cord between the bishop of Lincoln and the abbot of Saint Albans to which

he was a witness.[31] In general, however, the most recent opinions seem

to doubt his actual presence at the celebration: in spite of the asser-

tions of several later chronicles, if he had been well enough to travel,

he would probably have gone to the General Chapter instead. (That Aelred

was not adverse to attending such events in principle can be surmised

from his presence in 1155 at the translation of the relics in Hexham.

There he not only wrote a short work on the saints of Hexham, but also preached in the familiar precincts of his ancestors' church.)[32]

Having surveyed very briefly the scope of Aelred's activities outside the monastic world, we can now turn to the murkier question of his
activity outside Rievaulx, but within the Cistercian Order. This is a
subject, unfortunately, on which we have only the barest scraps of information, and it is axiomatic that the weakest of arguments is the argument from silence. The abbot of Rievaulx is not mentioned in the surviving records of the General Chapter; there are no visitation records
of any English or Scottish monasteries until hundreds of years after
his death.

What we can say with assurance is this: at least from the time of
the revision of the Carta caritatis in 1152 it was a serious and formal
obligation of every Cistercian abbot to attend the General Chapter at
Cîteaux each year, unless excused--as the Scottish abbots were in 1157.[33]
We do have records of Cistercian abbots not long after Aelred's time
being severely censured for non-attendance, and it is reasonable to suppose that Aelred, of all people, was not conspicuously flouting this rule
When looked at in the concrete, however, the situation becomes more diffi
cult. The distance from Rievaulx to Cîteaux was over 1000 km, a distance
which would have involved at least two months travel for the round trip,
even when autumn storms did not interrupt or delay the Channel crossing.
For a man in delicate health, as Aelred obviously was for at least his
last ten years, such a journey must have been an ordeal, and we can at

least suspect that the dispensation from choir obligations mentioned by
Master Walter, even if it did not specifically include the obligation
of the General Chapter, must have been considered as *prima facie* evidence of sufficient ill health to dispense Aelred from regular attendance.

The only positive evidence that Aelred did make the journey on at
least some occasions, aside from a late reference by Reginald of Durham
to a lost work of verse, composed while enroute to Cîteaux,[34] is the sermon recently discovered by Aelred Squire, which was preached at Troyes.[35]
The bishop of Troyes from 1145 till 1169 was Henry of Carinthia, a Cistercian of Morimond and friend of Saint Bernard; to stop en route to
Cîteaux at Troyes was almost as inevitable as the stop at Clairvaux,
Rievaulx' own motherhouse--although we have no positive evidence that
Aelred actually used this highly probable route. (Thus we can speculate
on meetings between Bernard and Aelred on which Aelred's lost correspondence might shed light, but Master Walter does not mention any contacts,
and we have no proof of a meeting after 1142 when Aelred was not yet novice-
master.)

The other great obligation of visitation for a Cistercian abbot,
imposed in the earliest versions of the Carta caritatis, is that of an
annual tour of inspection of daughter houses. On this point there is
no room for equivocation: "The abbot of a mother house shall visit annu-
ally all the filiations of his own monastery. And if he should visit
the bretheren more frequently than this, let it be to them a subject of

joy."[36] The phenominal expansion of the order, and especially of the
four eldest daughters of Cîteaux, soon made this simple provision a
physical impossiblity--Saint Bernard would have been hard pressed to
visit all the forty-nine daughters of Clairvaux in a year had he had
nothing else to occupy his time--and the rider was attached in later revisions of the Carta: "either in person, or by one of his co-abbots."[37]

The difficulties of Rievaulx in Aelred's time were not so serious;
Rievaulx had only five daughters: Melrose and Dundrennan in Scotland,
and Rufford, Revesby and Warden in England. These houses were also geo-
graphically arranged as to make it possible to include them on circuits.
One long swing to the north and west would take Aelred to Melrose in the
borders and then south and west again to Dundrennan in the wild Celtic
wilderness of Galloway. That Aelred did make this journey we have some
evidence; Master Walter recounts a strange story (which Powicke notes
as having analogs in Irish mythology) of the cure of a man who swallow-
ed a frog, as well as the settlement of disputes between warring tribal
chieftans.[38] Nevertheless, Master Walter's accounts leave more questions
unanswered than answered. Powicke has also pointed out that the chronolog
of Walter's account is confused, and the simplest explanation seems to
be that he confused three rather widely spaced visits to Scotland, in
1159 (perhaps the same trip on which he met Saint Godric of Finchale),
1165 (when Aelred is recorded as having been in Kircudbrightshire on
Saint Cutherbert's Day, 20 March) and as late as 1166 (when there is evi-

dence from a chronicle that he visited Melrose).[39] This confusion, of
course, does not prove that Aelred was in Scotland only on those dates,
but it does at least encourage speculation that his visitations were not
strictly annual affairs. Melrose, on the other hand, being closer to Rievaulx, having Aelred's old foster brother Waldef as its abbot, and being
a convenient stopping place for a visit to the ambulatory court of the
king of Scots, was probably visited frequently; Dundrennan in the damp
wilds of Galloway must have been much less inviting. (The nearest abbey
whose abbot could have been deputed to visit Dundrennan was Holmcultram,
founded from Melrose itself about 1152; one can easily imagine Waldef
making a visitation journey to both abbeys and then reporting his findings
to Aelred when he made his canonical visit to Melrose's own mother house.)

For Rievaulx' English daughters we have no information at all. Since
all three could have been visited with only minor digression while on the
way to the General Chapter, we can assume that they were visited at least
as often as Aelred went to Cîteaux; greater precision than that seems impossible.

Having come to the end of our information about Aelred's activities,
inadequate though it is, we can venture some general conclusions about
Aelred and perhaps Cistercian abbots in general.

In the first place, Aelred, like so many great Cistercians of the
first generations, came from that social class which George Orwell characterized as lower-upper-middle. As such he was both well educated and very

well connected: his fosterage at the court of Scotland especially

brought him into contact with most of the ruling class of North Britain.

It is in this light that the pattern of most of the activities outside

Rievaulx other than visitations is clearest. Aelred continued to visit

the court of Scotland, continued his relation with Waldef of Melrose and

above all continued his connections with the churches of Hexham and Dur-

ham in which his family had been powers for generations. Even in his

trips to the south, we find that Aelred appeared at Westminster, where

his kinsman Lawrence was abbot. In this sense, Aelred was still very

much the member of a special class of feudal socity; in spite of the

conscious rejection by the Cistercians of so many ties to the feudal

world, Aelred's life was a round of visits to his relatives and peers.

This aspect of the Cistercian life, recently developed by R. W. Southern

in his Western Society and the Church in the Middle Ages,[40] has been

the object of some criticism. Perhaps further investigation of the world

in which Cistercians actually moved would help to clarify the ambivalent

relationship to feudalism which characterized the first generations of

Cîteaux.

Secondly, when we look at the very scanty and inadequate data about

Aelred's visitations and attendance at the General Chapter, another shad-

owy pattern may emerge. Although a long way from Cîteaux, Rievaulx was

not burdened with a great number of daughters, nor were a great number

of separate journeys necessary to visit them all. Nevertheless it is

difficult to imagine that Aelred was able to satisfy the letter of the
law as far as his visitations were concerned, especially after 1157
when his health became a serious problem. (Nor can failing health have
been uncommon among Cistercian abbots, elected for life and frequently
indulging in youthful excesses of asceticism.) It seems only fair to
assume that the elaborate system of annual visitations, legislated in
the Carta caritatis and the Instituta of the General Chapter, was less
a matter of invariable practice than an ideal.

Since the time of the Council of Trent the attitude of the Roman
Catholic Church toward the observance of the law has been one of almost
Prussian severity. It is therefore very difficult for us, accustomed to
the hard, clear lines of the Codex juris canonici to appreciate what must
have been the attitude toward law before the appearance of Gratians'
contribution to the Corpus. A paper which I gave at this Conference
last year commented on the free and easy attitude toward the law of transitus ad aliam religionem displayed by many twelfth-century authorities;
on at least one occasion Saint Bernard himself frankly violated a solemn
agreement on transitus which he had sealed only a few years before. This
is not to say that Aelred, Bernard, or any other twelfth-century churchman
despised the law; on the contrary, they were representative of a very
legally minded age. But it does suggest that the letter of the law was far
less important than the spirit. Just as we have come to realize that the
purpose of the Cistercian reform was to return to the purity of the Rule,

even though the rejection of oblates and the inclusion of the lay brothers were not in the _letter_, so we may be able to see an attitude toward the _Carta caritatis_ which did not make a fetish of its intentions.

1. David Knowles, The Monastic Order in England, 2nd ed. (Cambridge, 1963) p. 240.

2. Walter Daniel's Life of Ailred, ed. and trans. F. M. Powicke, Nelson's Medieval Texts (London, Edinburgh, 1950) p. c.

3. Ibid.

4. PL 195, and C. H. Talbot, Sermones inediti b. Aelredi Abbatis, Series Scriptorum S. Ordinis Cisterciensis (Rome, 1952).

5. PL 195:701-712.

6. A. Stacpoole, "The Public Face of Aelred," Downside Review 85 (1967) 183-99, 318-25.

7. For a bibliography to 1956, see D. Knowles, "The Primitive Documents of the Cistercian Order," in Great Historical Enterprises (London, Edinburgh, 1963) pp. 198-222. There is a new edition, Les plus anciens texts de Citeaux by J. de la Croix Bouton and J. B. Van Damme, Cîteaux Commentarii Cistercienses, Stuida et Documenta II (Achel, 1974).

8. Chapter 1-4.

9. C. Brooke, "Gregorian Reform in Action," in Medieval Church and Society (New York, 1972) pp. 69-79.

10. Powicke, Life, pp. 2-13. See A. Squire, Aelred of Rievaulx (London, 1969) pp. 4-15.

11. Powicke, Life, p. 3: 'Whence the King loved him exceedingly and every day was more and more considering how to advance him, so much so, indeed, that if he had not unexpectedly entered the Cistercian Order he would have honoured him with the first bishopric of the land.'

12. Ibid., p. 10.

13. Fliche and Martin, Histoire de l'Eglise 9b, 262-63. R. W. Southern, St Anselm and his Biographer (Cambridge, 1963) pp. 135-42.

14. Squire, Aelred, pp. 8-11.

15. PL 195:701-712. See W. L. Warren, Henry II (Berkeley, 1973) pp. 180-81.

16. Stacpoole, "Public Face," p. 193.

17. Powicke, Life, p. 23. See D. Knowles, "The Case of Saint William of York," in The Historian and Character (Cambridge, 1963) pp. 76-97.

18. Aelredi Rievallensis opera omnia, edd. A. Hoste and C. H. Talbot, CC continuatio medievalis (Turnhout, 1971) pp. 3-6. See A. Wilmart,

19. "L'instigateur du Speculum caritatis," RAM 14 (1933)

19. Stacpool, "Public Face," p. 193.

20. Knowles, Monastic Order, pp. 249-51.

21. D. Knowles and R. N. Hadock, Medieval Religious Houses: England and Wales (London, 1971) pp. 116-17.

22. Powicke, Life, p. lxiii.

23. Knowles, Monastic Order, p. 263.

24. De sanctimoniali de Watton, PL 195:789-96.

25. Knowles, Monastic Order, pp. 206-207.

26. Stacpoole, "Public Face," p. 194.

27. Powicke, Life, p. 79.

28. Ibid., p. 39.

29. Ibid., pp. 66-81.

30. Ibid., pp. 41-42. See p. xlviii.

31. Stacpoole, "Public Face," p. 194.

32. Squire, Aelred, pp. 112-15.

33. Powicke, Life, p. 39n.

34. Squire, Aelred, p. 64.

35. A. Squire, "Two unpublished Sermons of Aelred of Rievaulx," Citeaux 11
     (1960) 110-16.

36. Trans. from L. Lekai, The White Monks (Okauchee, 1953) p. 269.

37. J. Turk, Cistercii statuta antiquissima (Rome, 1949) p. 130.

38. Powicke, Life, p. 48n.

39. Ibid., p. xciv.

40. R. W. Southern, Western Society and the Church in the Middle Ages
     (Harmondsworth, 1970) esp. pp. 250-72.

NEGATION AND APOCALYPSE:

STYLE AND VISION IN AELRED OF RIEVAULX

Mary Harris Veeder
Indiana University Northwest

In offering a literary analysis of Aelred's De institutione inclusarum, I realize that my approach will seem narrower than those which many other commentators have taken.[1] Certainly Aelred's literary artistry is only one aspect of what makes him so monumental a figure. I hope, however, that a close examination of aspects of the plan and style of his work will add to our sense of how humane and masterful a director of souls and institutions Aelred of Rievaulx was.

I should define immediately the first term I use in my title--negation. I mean negation in two senses. In order to direct us toward spiritual excellence, Aelred uses exempla which present graphically our fallible natures, our negative qualities; he also uses negative syntactic constructions to reinforce our sense of these negative qualities. I focus on negation because of its centrality to the eremitic life. The flight to the desert--whether in early Egypt or twelfth-century England--is in itself an act of rejection, a negation of the world. Although this act of negation served the positive purpose of spiritual elevation, negation itself was fraught with danger. The recluse might feel so proud, so superior to his fellow humans, that there would never be any movement beyond the initial gesture of rejection to the positive pursuit of God's love. The structure of the De institutione parallels

the ideal of progress from negative to positive spirituality. Aelred
moves us from a discussion of outer man to a knowledge of inner man,
from the negative traits which we should reject to the goals which we
should seek, from the world of time to the timeless world of the heavenly Jerusalem. Then, since we have not yet in our lives reached the
moment of actual Apocalypse, Aelred ends his work by returning to himself as the combination of negative rejection and positive action. My
paper will be organized around the movement of Aelred's work, examining
the stages of the journey from negation of the world to positive union
with Christ.

Let us look first, then, at the beginning of the De institutione,
and study the examples of negative strategy and negative syntax which
we find there. Although many other spiritual advisors certainly use
negative examples to warn their listeners away from deleterious courses
of action, what makes Aelred's work especially effective is the combination of negative examples with many negative syntactic constructions.
Let us consider the strategy of those negative examples first. Aelred
must convince us of how wicked we could become if his instructions were
not followed. Thus, in the section regarding the outer man, we find not
a mere listing of prohibitions, but vivid portraits of anchoresses untrue
to their calling and all too true to the negative possibilities of human
nature.

Vix aliquam inclusarum huius temporis solam inuenies,

ante cuius fenestram non anus garrula uel rumigerula
mulier sedeat, quae eam fabulis occupet, rumoribus
ac detractionibus pascat, illius uel illius monachi,
uel clerici, uel alterius cuiuslibet ordinis uiri
formam, uultum moresque describat, illecebrosa
quaeque interserat, et puellarum lasciuiam, uiduarum
quibus licet quidquid libet libertatem, coniugum in
uiris fallendis explendisque uoluptatibus astutiam,
depingat. Os interea in risus cachinnosque dis-
soluitur, et uenenum cum suauitate bibitum, per
uiscera membraque diffunditur.

How seldom nowadays will you find a recluse alone.
At her window will be seated some garrulous old
gossip pouring idle tales into her ears, feeding
her with scandal and gossip; describing in detail
the face, appearance and mannerisms of now this
priest, now that monk or clerk; describing too
the frivolous behavior of a young girl; the free
and easy ways of a widow who thinks what she
likes is right; the cunning ways of a wife who
cuckolds her husband while she gratifies her
passions. The recluse all the while is dissolved
in laughter, loud peals of laughter, and the
poison she drinks with such delight spreads
throughout her body.[2]

By giving us this portrait of negative traits, Aelred is able to empha-

size the dangers that must be overcome before spiritual excellence can

be obtained. To see the virtues which Aelred is implicitly advocating

here, we must pass, as readers, through the negative details; what we

must do as Christians to imitate the virtues is, analogously, to put

our negative potentiality behind us. Further, we see what happens if

such a course of action is now followed. The aliquam inclusarum of

the first line is seen by the end as only os and uenenum. We see the

disintegration of the anchoress happening literally before our eyes.

The portrait of the anchorite schoolmistress provides another negative example.

> Sunt quaedam inclusae quae docendis puellis oc-
> cupantur, et cellam suam uertunt in scholam.
> Illa sedet ad fenestram, istae in porticu resident.
> Illa intuetur singulas, et inter puellares motus,
> nunc irascitur, nunc ridet, nunc minatur, nunc
> blanditur, nunc percutit, nunc osculatur, nunc
> flentem pro uerbere uocat propius, palpat faciem,
> stringit collum, et in amplexum ruens, nunc filiam
> uocat, nunc amicam.

> It is not unknown for a recluse to take up teaching
> and turn her cell into a school. She sits at her
> window, the girls settle themselves in the porch;
> and so she keeps them all under observation.
> Swayed by their childish dispositions, she is
> angry one minute and smiling the next, now threat-
> ening, now flattering, kissing one child and
> smacking another. When she sees one of them
> crying after being smacked she calls her close,
> strokes her cheek, puts her·arms round her neck
> and holds her tight, calling her: 'My own baby
> girl, my own pet.'[3]

As Aelred in the previous example showed the disintegration of aliquam

into os and uenenum, so here he shows us that memoria dei, so valuable

for the anchorite, can disappear in the distractions of the daily routine

of teaching children. The repeated nunc shows us a soul locked into

particular temporal moments, each moment succeeded only by another

equally limited one. The quick stop and start motion of each clause

emphasizes the futility of such a life for the anchorite: it goes

nowhere.

At the end of this section, Aelred offers Saint Agnes and a monk

who fears for his chastity as exemplars. They do not at first glance

seem to be negative examples, because they are both spiritually successful; in each case, however, the lesson they finally teach is a negative
one. For example, when telling of the angel protecting Agnes in the
brothel, Aelred says to the recluse: ...non certe angelus tuo casto
ceerit cubiculo, qui prostibulo non deerit ("...you may be sure that
the angel who was present in the brothel will not be absent from your
chaste cell").[4] Non...deerit: to not be absent means, of course, to
be present. Why then does Aelred not say that the angel will be present.
Aelred's choice of double negation emphasizes how instable a foundation
there is for any spiritual pride or sense of final achievement. The
protection of the angel is not denied, but assurance is given cautiously
indeed. Finally, of course, Aelred wishes the exemplum to offer en-
couragement. Yet even the final comment to the recluse, on God's help,
is negatively phrased: ubi multa carnis afflictio, aut nulla aut parua
potest esse delectatio ("for when the flesh is sorely afflicted there
can be little or no pleasure").[5] Aut nulla, aut parua: the rigid aut
framework makes us realize, even as we come to nulla, that it will be
balanced with another possibility which turns out to be parva. Thus
Aelred refuses to offer ascetic practices as guarantors of perfection.
Even if you fast, he will not guarantee the total absence of delectatio.
He ends with parua, not with nulla, because complete triumph can never
be assured in the temporal world.

The same insistence on the lack of positive certainty and on the

certainty of negative possibilities is found at the conclusion of the
monk's prayer to Christ. When fasting and freezing immersions fail to
bring his flesh totally under control, the monk prays directly to
Christ. His motion is worthy enough but he does so only to make an
improper request: orat, plorat, suspirat, rogat, adiurat, obtestatur,
ut aut occidat, aut sanet ("he prayed, wept, sighed, implored, be-
sought, insisted that he either kill him or heal him").[6] The monk is
demanding certainty. Aelred's comment in reply is all the more stark
after the flourish of the question: Praestatur ad horam refrigerium,
sed negatur securitas ("He was granted some temporary relief but refused lasting tranquillity").[7] Negatur securitas: securitas is denied
because, to a Christian in pursuit of perfection on earth, securitas
is standing still, a deadly lack of motion toward perfection.

All these early examples of negative behavior or negative possibilities in man teach the same lesson: the battle for sanctity lasts
as long as life, hence there is always the possibility of failure.
There is no positive assurance of salvation.

Aelred's emphasis on man's fallible, negative qualities is, as
we have seen, made more effective because it is emphasized by and reflected in his stylistic use of negative syntax. Let us concentrate
briefly upon his style now, particularly his repetitions of non and nulla.

> Non circa cellulam eius pauperes clament, non
> orphani plorent, non uidua lamentetur.

> Her cell is not to be besieged by beggars, nor
> by orphans and widows crying for alms.[8]

In this example, Aelred is discussing the effects of true poverty on
the recluse's daily life. True poverty will mean the absence of clamor
at her door. The negative presentation does not, however, serve only
the purpose of showing her that she gains an absence of noise. That
advantage could have been stated positively: "Let there be quiet and
peace and solitude around your dwelling." Aelred's negative statement
allows him to introduce what could happen into the very sentence that
promises it will not. The danger appears especially strong because it
is made present, in the sentence: circam cellulam ejus pauperes cla-
ment...orphani plorent...uidua lamentetur. Only the one negative word
in each case, non, separates the anchorite from the cacophony that de-
stroys memoria Dei.

> Itaque claustralibus nulla debet esse pro pauperi-
> bus sollicitudo, nulla pro hospitibus suscipiendis
> distentio, quippe quibus nulla debet esse de crastino
> cura, nulla cibi potusue prouidentia. Nutriantur
> potius in croceis, spiritualibus pascantur deliciis.
>
> So monks of the cloister should not be troubled
> with any concern for the poor or distracted by
> the reception of guests; indeed they should not
> even have any care for the morrow, no anxiety
> over food and drink. Let them rather feed on
> saffron and take their pleasure in the things
> of the spirit.[9]

Severing themselves from the essence of Christianity, its charity, is
what hermits' severest critics accuse them of. Here, in exploring the

analogy of Martha and Mary, Aelred would appear to encourage such
criticism. Aelred's point, however, is that these negations are not
nihilistic. And the pattern of their presentations emphasizes the
positive quality of these negations which bring the soul salvation
through the eremitic life. Nulla...sollicitudo, nulla...distentio...
nulla...cura, nulla...prouidentia: these negations are the way to
the goal. But they must be seen in living it. Aelred carefully sur-
rounds the nulla clauses with qualifying context: it is specifically
among the claustrales that such negations are positive. More importantly, the nulla pattern leads us, literally and stylistically, to the
state where spiritualibus pascantur--so obviously the green pastures of
the Good Shepherd. Negation has thus brought the recluse where all
Christians find the ultimate positive goal.[10]

As he did with the material from Agnes' life and from the life of
Christ, Aelred uses the details of his own life as a model of the way
in which a vision of man's negative qualities can be the beginning of
a positive motion toward God. For his Christian family and survival
through the physical perils of childhood, Aelred thanks God and then
proceeds to lament his own youthful rejection of God. Following this
comes the more general meditation found in the Migne text.

Walter Daniel's Life of Aelred indicates no such actual period
in Aelred's life. In fact Daniel makes a point of asserting Aelred's
purity in those years.

> For he practised from his boyhood spareness of
> living. In his dress he eschewed all superfluity,
> vainglory and wantonness, turning his vesture into
> a symbol and forecast of the admirable poverty of
> his later life. He avoided elaborate confections,
> as the wear of the proud and effeminate....His
> graciousness and good will were so great that in-
> jury did not stir him up to anger, nor slander
> provoke him to vengeance....[11]

Walter's intent was hagiographical, of course. Either Walter's sta-

ture as an intimate biographer or a similar hagiographical impulse

seems to have caused early editors to omit the sections detailing

Aelred's youthful follies from their texts. That Aelred's admissions

of early transgressions are, however, not so opposed to the aims of

hagiography as those early editors judged, such critics as M. Courcelle

and Father Dumont have made clear. The _pattern_ of Aelred's life, not

the early events themselves, is saintly, for this pattern is that of

Augustine's life: led astray in his youth, he is redeemed by the

prayers of a faithful woman--in this case his sister--who is obviously

analogous, in her faithfulness, to Monica. The point is thus not whether

the events actually did happen, but that Aelred has presented them as

fitting into a pattern traditional in hagiographical works. Thus Aelred

offers his life as another example of the negative becoming positive

model. If we see Augustine here, we can then see how positive the model

is, for the subject of our attention is not Aelred's defection but God's

mercy and benevolent care.

Ultimately a Christian's life, under God's merciful direction, progresses toward the Last Judgment and the new order that Apocalypse

brings. The structure of Aelred's De institutione likewise moves

toward the importance of the apocalyptic events, the end of negation

and, for the blessed, the beginning of union with God.

> Hanc cuius natura non horret, cuius non expauescit
> affectus? Nam bestiae fuga, latibulis, et aliis
> mille modis mortem cauent, uitam tuentur.
>
> Is there anyone who has not a natural repulsion
> for death, who does not feel a dread of it?
> Wild beasts guard themselves from death, pre-
> serve life by flight, hiding-places and a thou-
> sand other devices.[12]

This hardly seems the picture of beginnings. What prevents Aelred's

judgment from being a solely dark vision, however, is his insistence

on looking beyond death to Judgment and beyond Judgment itself, to

the visio pacis, the heavenly Jerusalem. Definition by negation has,

of course, long been a Christian tradition in defining God and heaven.

Revelations 21:4, for example, is preceeded by the descriptions of the

plagues. Such other authors as John of Fécamp and Alcher of Clairvaux

also followed this pattern.[13] The tradition of combining Last Judgment

terror with a vision of heaven's peace is, however, certainly well suit-

ed to Aelred's task as he saw it.

> Nullus igitur ibi luctus, fletus nullus, non dolor,
> non timor, non tristitia, non discordia, non inuidia,
> non tribulatio, non tentatio, non aeris mutatio uel
> corruptio, non suspicio, non ambitio, non adulatio,
> non detractio, non aegritudo, non senectus, non
> mors, non paupertas, neque tenebrae, non edendi,
> non bibendi uel dormiendi ulla necessitas, fatigatio

nulla, nulla defectio.

Quid ergo boni ibi est? Vbi neque luctus
neque fletus, neque dolor est neque tristitia,
quid potest esse nisi perfecta laetitia? Vbi
nulla tribulatio uel tentatio, nulla temporum
mutatio uel aeris corruptio, nec aestus uehementior
nec hiems asperior, quid potest esse nisi summa
quaedam rerum temperies et mentis et carnis uera
ac summa tranquillitas? Vbi nihil est quod timeas,
quid potest esse nisi summa securitas? Vbi nulla
discordia, nulla inuidia, nulla suspicio nec ulla
ambitio, nulla adulatio, nec ulla detractio, quid
potest esse nisi summa et uera dilectio? Vbi
nulla paupertas nec ulla cupiditas, quid potest
esse nisi bonorum omnium plenitudo? Vbi nulla
deformitas, quid potest esse nisi uera pulchritu-
do? Vbi nullus labor uel defectio, quid erit nisi
summa requies et fortitudo? Vbi nihil est quod
grauet uel oneret, quid est nisi summa facilitas?
Vbi nec senectus expectatur, nec morbus timetur,
quid potest esse nisi uera sanitas? Vbi neque
nox neque tenebrae, quid erit nisi lux perfecta?
Vbi mors et mortalitas omnis absorpta est, quid
erit nisi uita aeterna?

So there will be no mourning, no weeping or pain,
no fear, no sadness, no discord, no envy, no
tribulation, no temptation, no variable weather,
no overcast skies, no suspicion, no ambition, no
adulation, no detraction, no sickness, no old age,
no death, no poverty, no darkness, no need to eat,
drink or sleep, no tiredness, no weakness.

What good then will be lacking? Where there
is no mourning or weeping or pain or sadness, what
can there be but perfect joy? Where there is no
tribulation or temptation, no variable weather or
overcast skies, no excessive heat or harsh winter,
what can there be but perfect balance in all things
and complete tranquillity of mind and body? Where
there is nothing to fear, what can there be but
total security? Where there is no discord, no
envy, no suspicion or ambition, no adulation or
detraction, what can there be but supreme and true
love? Where there is no poverty and no covetousness,
what can there be but abundance of all good things?

> Where there is no deformity, what can there be
> but true beauty? Where there is no toil or weakness,
> what will there be but utter rest and strength?
> Where there is nothing heavy or burdensome, what
> is there but the greatest ease? Where there is no
> prospect of old age, no fear of disease, what can
> there be but true health? Where there is neither
> night nor darkness, what will there be but perfect
> light? Where all death and mortality have been
> swallowed up, what will there be but eternal life?[14]

Non, nec, nihil and nulla deny to a heavenly world qualities of whose

existence Aelred himself has made us so aware through the negative

strategy of his work: dolor, tentatio, temporum mutatio, mors et

mortalitatis. In the process of making heaven attractive by showing

it the reverse of earthly vexations, Aelred emphasizes also that those

vexations can only be escaped in heaven, that they can never be escaped

on this earth. The most basic structuring device of this passage, the

division into vbi and quid potest esse nisi mirrors the oppositions

found in our response. Aelred makes us desire heaven so much because

he has made us so acutely aware that we do not have it. The pattern of

contrasts in the passage polarizes the two sides of our response, yet

still yokes them into the harmony of syntax, which reflects the harmoni-

ous ordering of all things finally by God.

Yet syntax is not enough. Because there is more to heaven than

the mere absence of earthly pain, and because the recluse and reader

may not be able to bear many more negatives without being overwhelmed

by this world, Aelred then switches his tense to that of prophetic certainty. <u>Videbitur</u> occurs six times in rapid succession. There the

Creator and courts of angels are seen directly, positively, <u>non</u> <u>per</u>

<u>speculum</u> <u>in</u> <u>enigmate</u>, and not with the stylistic equivalents of

<u>specula</u>--negative images.

> Videbitur in se, uidebitur in omnibus creaturis
> suis, regens omnia sine sollicitudine, sustinens
> omnia sine labore, impertiens se et quodammodo
> dispertiens singulis pro sua capacitate, sine
> sui diminutione uel diuisione. Videbitur ille
> uultus amabilis et desiderabilis, in quem desi-
> derant angeli prospicere. De cuius pulchritudine,
> de cuius lumine, de cuius suauitate, quis dicet?
> Videbitur Pater in Filio, Filius in Patre, Spiritus
> sanctus in utroque. Videbitur <u>non</u> <u>per</u> <u>speculum</u> <u>in</u>
> <u>aenigmate</u>, <u>sed</u> <u>facie</u> <u>ad</u> <u>faciem</u>. Videbitur enim
> sicuti est, impleta illa promissione qua dicit:
> <u>Qui</u> <u>diligit</u> <u>me</u>, <u>diligetur</u> <u>a</u> <u>Patre</u> <u>meo</u>, <u>et</u> <u>ego</u>
> <u>diligam</u> <u>eum</u>, <u>et</u> <u>manifestabo</u> <u>ei</u> <u>meipsum</u>.
>
> He will be seen in himself, he will be seen in
> all his creatures, ruling everything without
> anxiety, upholding everything without toil,
> giving himself and, so to speak, distributing
> himself to one and all according to their capa-
> city without any lessening or division of himself.
> That lovable face, so longed for, upon which the
> angels yearn to gaze, will be seen. Who can say
> anything of its beauty, of its light, of its
> sweetness? The Father will be seen in the Son,
> the Son in the Father, the Holy Spirit in both.
> He will be seen not as a confused reflection
> in a mirror, but face to face. For he will be
> seen as he is, fulfilling that promise which
> tells us: 'He who loves me will be loved by my
> Father, and I will love him and show myself to
> him.'[15]

Ultimately, however, we are recalled to the limitations of our humanity

and we return to the use of negation. After a brief moment when we do not see _per speculum_, the section ends

> Quid est hoc? Certe quod oculus non uidit, nec
> auris audiuit, nec in cor hominis ascendit, quae
> praeparauit Deus diligentibus se.

> What is this? To be sure, what eye has not seen
> nor ear heard, nor heart conceived, what God has
> prepared for those who love him.[16]

Aelred's work is not yet completed. In the epilogue he returns to

the personal tone with which he began. He speaks directly to his sister,

summarizing the sections of the work, showing that the interior and ex-

terior rules she sought are provided. His last words, then, are of him-

self.

> Si qua igitur in huius libelli lectione profecerit,
> hanc labori meo uel studio uicem impendat, ut apud
> Saluatorem meum quem expecto, apud Iudicem meum quem
> timeo, pro peccatis meis intercedat.

> If anyone makes any progress as a result of reading
> this little book, let her make me this return for
> my toil and my care, to intercede for my sins with
> my Savior whom I await, with my Judge whom I fear.[17]

Such an ending is conventional, of course. Its use of negative realities

to generate positive spiritual impetus makes it, however, especially ap-

propriate for Aelred's use here. The particular elements in Aelred's

conclusion reveal it to be not an ending but a beginning. For the

recluse, so long and so dangerously removed from the Christian community,

it is especially true that salvation is to be gained only on a personal

level, only by applying the literary lessons to one's own life. No man

was ever saved by syntax alone. Aelred offers himself as the final

exemplum, the bridge between the literary vision and the act of life.
In what he says of himself in the conclusion we see the qualities
which his work has shown us are essential to the Christian life:
joyful expectation (_saluatorem_ _meum_ _quem_ _expecto_) balanced with a
sense of Judgment's negative potential (_Iudicem_ _meum_ _quem_ _timeo_) and
a final awareness of fallibility (_peccatis_ _meis_). The portrait shows
both positive and negative aspects, what is gained, what failings remain. Thus he confesses himself one of us, on the way to salvation,
to the positive through the negative. The task is now the reader's,
to follow Aelred in living as we have while reading.

NOTES

1. Aelred of Rievaulx, De institutione inclusarum, ed. C. H. Talbot, in Opera Omnia I, edd. A. Hoste and C. H. Talbot (Turnholt, 1971) pp. 635-82. The English translation used is by Mary Paul Macpherson, OSCO, in The Works of Aelred of Rievaulx, I, Treatises, The Pastoral Prayer. CF 2 (Spencer, Massachusetts, 1971) pp. 41-102.

2. Inst incl p. 638; Macpherson, p. 46.

3. Inst incl pp. 640-41; Macpherson, p. 49.

4. Inst incl p. 652; Macpherson, p. 65.

5. Inst incl p. 652; Macpherson, p. 66.

6. Inst incl p. 653; Macpherson, p. 67.

7. Inst incl p. 653; Macpherson, p. 67.

8. Inst incl p. 639; Macpherson, p. 48.

9. Inst incl p. 661; Macpherson, p. 76.

10. The meditations on Christ's life--while they do make us aware of the negative, that not all men received Him into their hearts --also emphasize positive movement. Aelred's main effort with the reader here is to induce--by the use of present tenses and dramatic participation--a closeness to Christ, a closeness that will make rejection of the world and awareness of human falli-bility significant.

11. Walter Daniel, The Life of Ailred of Rievaulx, trans. and ed.

F. M. Powicke (London, 1950) pp. 4-5.

12. Inst incl p. 677; Macpherson, p. 97.

13. As cited by Sister M. P. Macpherson, see John of Fécamp, Liber
     meditationum, c. 21 (PL 40:917); Soliloquum animae ad Deum, c. 35
     (PL 40:895); Alcher of Clairvaux, De diligendo Deo, c. 18 (PL 40:
     862f).

14. Inst incl p. 680; Macpherson, pp. 100-101.

15. Inst incl p. 681; Macpherson, p. 101.

16. Inst incl p. 681; Macpherson, p. 102.

17. Inst incl p. 682; Macpherson, p. 102.

Charles Dumont OCSO
Abbaye de Scourmont

There is perhaps no work which bears better witness to the humanism of the twelfth-century Cistercians than the Treatise on Spiritual
Friendship of Aelred of Rievaulx. When we speak about humanism during
the twelfth century, however, we must be clear about what we mean, for
humanism is a very general, and even ambiguous, term which signifies
something different in almost every century. We must remember also
that in more recent times a rationalistic type of humanism has broken
the harmony of the Christian synthesis of man achieved during the renaissance of the twelfth century. It would be erroneous, and indeed a
great mistake, to think of Aelred as clandestinely smuggling profance
literature, the De amicitia of Cicero, into the cloister under the cloak
of piety. Such a compromising attitude would be completely contrary to
the Cistercians' spirit of authenticity and loyalty. There is no reason
to doubt Aelred's sincerity when he writes:

> Cicero's book on friendship, I remembered, had
> at one time given me great pleasure; but now,
> on reading it again, I was astonished to find
> how little it touches me....Thinking this over
> from time to time, I began to wonder whether
> Cicero's ideals could find support in Scripture,
> and I read and reread what the Fathers had to
> say about friendship in their works.[1]

In doing this, Aelred was actually doing exactly what the Fathers themselves had done, and he knew this very well. He points out this characteristic of the Fathers' works: "They were as skilled in divine things

as they were perspicacious in the wisdom of the world, and they were
able to transpose and elevate everything good they had found in profane learning so that it might serve for the strengthening and benefit
of the Church...."[2]

In the Mirror of Charity he quotes the most eloquent of the phil-
osophers, Cicero, with reference to his excellent doctrine on temper-
ance and sobriety. But to these two virtues, sobrietas et justitia,
the Apostle added a third one, pietas,--sobrie, juste et pie vivamus
in hoc saeculo--so that no philosopher might boast of having reached
the fullness of truth. This pietas, most surely, is purity of intention;
it is love, the only way.[3] Having quoted Terence's witty satire of a
"yes man" and explained it in a traditional way, Aelred adds, "It may
be that Terence borrowed these ideas from our treasury of Scriptures
and clothed the words of the prophets with his own," and he continues
by quoting Isaiah 30:10 and Jeremiah 5:31.[4] Everything coming from
pagan or profane literature had to be rendered relevant and assimilated.
This transposition constituted the excellence of the method of the Fathers which Aelred wanted to follow. For this very reason he condemns
those who "looking with scorn upon the whole line of the Fathers because
of their rustic simplicity, run instead after I do not know what sort of
silly new fancies of the scholastics." Aelred made this sarcastic remark
about the people who were seeking arguments which would permit them to
introduce into our churches the horrible and noisy new instrument of

music which is called the "organ"![5]

Aelred applied to Cicero's De amicitia the same method which he admired in the Fathers. What was lacking in Cicero was the scientia salu-
taris: the science of salvation, that is, of charity. Now charity is
the fullness and perfection of the affectus of love, and the whole of
Cistercian spirituality was deeply rooted in this basic natural virtue
of Love. Each time that Aelred makes a synthesis of the spiritual itin-
erary, he begins by recalling the universal order existing in the cosmos,
as it was described by the Stoics: love holding everything together and
maintaining harmony in the universe. The Cistercians had been familiar
with this teaching of Cicero and Seneca, and it exercised a great influence on their philosophy, especially on their ethical doctrine of moder-
ation and a balanced life. This stoic influence has not been emphasized or studied enough, but it is perhaps one which is as important as Neo-
platonism. Love is the principle of order in the universe. Love, any
kind of love, has a dynamic power, but it must be put to use according
to the laws of nature and reoriented, brought back to its source from
which it may then flow forth in all its purity.

If one wishes friendship, as a value, to stand on its own feet, as
some modern theologians of human values do, one would do well to read
the treatise of Cicero. With its noble Roman sobriety, it still has
great charm for a modern reader, and we could say that if Aelred was no
longer attracted by Cicero's book because he could not find the name of

Jesus there, many modern readers may not feel attracted to Aelred's b
book because this name may seem to them to appear too often! If, however, one desires a doctrinal work on Christian friendship, a theology
of this very human reality, there is no other treatise or piece of writing in the whole history of Christian spirituality better than this work
of Aelred.

Jean Leclercq has pointed out that Saint Bernard's ascetical and
mystical teaching must be understood as being primarily intended for
monks. It is very important that we keep this in mind, because when
we read the works of Saint Bernard or Saint Aelred we will never, or
very seldom, be reminded of this fact. The reason for this is simply
that, for them, everyone was supposed to be a monk, and lay people were
somehow likened to the monks by their generosity in almsgiving, or by
imitation of their life. It was difficult for them to imagine that one
could be saved in the world, just as sometimes today, unfortunately,
some monks consider the opposite to be true! The Cistercian Fathers,
then, did not very often stress the value of the elements of monastic
discipline, but it is equally important for scholars who want to understand the founders of Cîteaux, as for Cistercian monks of today, to have
a clear idea of the pattern of Cistercian life, and especially of the
relationship between theory and practice in the ancient sense of the
words: theoria and practiké, that is, the coherence and unity existing
between the active and contemplative elements of monastic discipline.

This subject, as Professor McGinn recently pointed out, has need of extensive study.

There is what might be called a "basic course" in the <u>schola caritatis</u>, this school where one learns how to love. Saint Bernard develops this in his three steps of humility and truth, and Saint Aelred in the <u>Mirror of Charity</u>, with the three Sabbaths. According to Aelred, in the <u>schola caritatis</u> the monk learns, through the experience of conversion, to love himself, and learns to love others by widening and opening his heart in the practice of brotherly love in community, so that he may acquire a greater capacity for loving, and make himself capable of love of God.

The second step is the most important insofar as the formation or reformation of a man is concerned. If Aelred's ascetical doctrine of love uses the language and psychology of courtly love, a discovery of the twelfth century, theologically speaking it is based on the patristic doctrine of man created in the image of God. An image is in conformity with its model, with its exemplary cause, to the degree that it adheres to it. It is a dynamic relationship. The man who cleaved to God is made one spirit with Him. This cleaving <u>is</u> charity. The monastic community, therefore, is to be seen as the milieu, at once necessary and efficacious, for this restoration of the likeness of God which has been lost by the sin of selfishness, egoism, <u>propria voluntas</u>, and singularity. This truth was so important for the Cistercians that if we make abstraction of it, their spirituality becomes totally incoherent and incomprehensible.

Just as they found in the doctrine of the Stoics the balance coming
from the golden mean and alternance, which permitted them to face the
problems of human life: person and society, solitude and communication,
work and leisure, so in Cicero they found the principle of following
nature as a guide: sequi naturam. Now when Aelred read natura in Cicero
he understood this "nature" as being applied to man as he was created by
God in the garden of Eden. Natura still had its etymological meaning of
nascor, that is, what man was born for, what he was made for. And what
he was made for was to love, to love God. The image of God in man was
damaged, but not completely destroyed or ruined. Memoria Dei could be
understood as being the divine archetype in the depths of the soul, rediscovered with the help of Revelation. This is the source of the confidence which the Cistercians had in human nature, and especially in its
principal affectus: love.

Quite by chance, a few days ago I was looking through a classic of
sociology, one of the first works of Max Weber, and came upon this remark
which I think is very much to the point, and may be quoted here because
it shows, negatively, how trust in man is based on traces of the divine
left in his nature:

> The Calvinist doctrine of the utterly corrupted
> nature of man and its consequent doctrine of
> predestination in its extreme inhumanity pro-
> duced a feeling of unprecedented inner loneliness
> of the single individual....The effect of this
> most extreme form of exclusive trust in God [is

> evident in the strikingly frequent repetition,
> especially in English Puritan literature, of
> warnings against any trust in the aid of friend-
> ship of men. One had to distrust even one's closest
> closest friend. Humanity in relation to one's
> neighbor has, so to speak, died out.[6]

Since the soul has affinity with the Word, and since like attracts

like, love is a thrust (élan) of the soul which only needs to be straight-

ened out to take its right orientation once again toward God and the

sharers of its own nature: all men. For Aelred the three loves (of self,

of others and of God) are inseparable and interacting. This is a very

interesting doctrine, and an original one. One cannot love oneself with-

out loving God; one cannot love others if one does not love oneself, etc.

And the process is not a kind of one-way traffic. One does not practice

brotherly love in order to reach the love of God, and once arrived there,

kick away the ladder. Aelred says specifically that we learn

from the love of God how to love our brothers, and we can descend the

steps and repose pleasantly in the love of our fellowmen.

Now we come to the doctrine of friendship, which is a more particular

and authentic kind of charity. You know his theory, somewhat naive but very

significant, of the distinction between charity and friendship. Adam and Eve

were friends. By the fall, they lost this easy type of charity. Charity be-

came difficult. It is necessary to love one's enemies, to love everyone.

Still, friendship remains possible with a few persons, and ultimately

will be possible with all, when God will be all in all.

The experience of friendship is a means of perfection, indeed only

a degree short of perfection. From being a friend of a man, one becomes
a friend of God, for it is basically the same experience of conformity
of wills. Perfect union of two wills: this definition given by Cicero
and Sallust is brought up when these two classical authors are discussed
in the first dialogue. Love of God is essentially the union of a human
will with the will of God. In the charm of friendship there is an experience of this. It is a step. It is not yet perfect. The next step,
e vicino, is friendship with Christ Himself. Aelred repeats this doctrine
five times in his treatise. Once again, this is not to be seen as one-
way traffic. Aelred will explain the disinterestedness of human friendship by even going so far as to compare it with the experience of union
with God in love. Usus eius fructus eius, as Saint Bernard says, speaking of love. The reward of friendship is friendship itself. It is a
reward which will reach its fullness only when the friends will be totally
absorbed, together, in the contemplation of God.[7]

Mutual understanding makes of a friend the voice of authentic conscience, of one's true self. He wants his friend, as indeed God wants
him, to become what he is, to become a friend of Christ. If
we connect the Greek principle of "the like seeks the like" with the doctrine of the likeness of God in man, we can understand what Aelred means
when he says, "From friendship with man one may eventually pass over into
friendship with God, because of the likeness which exists between the two.

In contrast with passing feelings, our love of God must be judged by the way in which our will is firmly joined to God's will. When the soul

is thus united to God, the Spirit of God may transform its whole will,

completely, into His own kind and quality, so that adhering to it in an

indissoluble bond of unity, the Spirit is made one with the will of man.

You know the naive illustration of a kiss as being the meeting of two

spirits. The kiss of the Spirit is an experience of union of two spirits.

Talis conformitas maritat animam verbo. Complexus plane, idem velle et

nolle idem unum facit spiritum de duobus.[9]

We may say that in all human experience there lies ambiguity. Per-

haps it is because of this danger of ambiguity that in recent times the

monastic tradition of friendship has been lost to a large extent. Ambigu-

ity, however, is unavoidable when human existence is the source of ex-

perience, but is not to be considered as being something which will be

misleading. "All spiritual teaching is based on ambiguity. The passage

to another order is not paralogism, because the life of God is not a su-

perior life, vaguely analogous to the one from which we started, but with

no real kinship with it. It is the fullness of life, in which all life

is eminently contained. Between the realities indicated by the term of

'life' it establishes a symbolical relationship, in the original and rad-

ical sense of the word...."[10] What Henri de Lubac says here of life can

be said of love or friendship. This can be found in Cistercian spiritual-

ity. Aelred expressed it in the Mirror of Charity, written when he was

still a young monk. Having probably met with criticism, he answered:

"If you want to criticize this doctrine of mine, remember that Christ had a friend, Saint John." He thus shows that Christ sacramentalized friendship, for every word or gesture performed by Christ has been sacramentalized, and friendship is included among these. It was transformed when Christ showed his friendship for man during his human life In suae dilectionis transformans...caritatis sacratissimum genus amici

Let me conclude this paper by widening the horizon, and intimating that Aelred's doctrine is one that is very up-to-date. In closing, I would like to quote a reflection of an American phenomenologist, an existentialist, who writes:

> ...If theologians cannot speak perceptively about
> the mystery of human love, how can they hope to
> communicate the meaning of divine love as an
> existential power...?[12]

NOTES

1. Spir amic, Prologue; CC, Continuatio medievalis, [CCM,I] (Turnhout, 1971) p. 288.

2. 'Tanto in divinis fuisse prudentiores quanto in sapientia illa mundiali fuerant perspicaciores....Talis fuit beatissimus martyr Cyprianus, talis Ambrosius, talis Augustinus, atque Hieronymus, qui totum, quod de scientia hauserant saeculari, ad firmamentum profectumque Ecclesiae transtulerunt.' Oner 28; PL 195:479C. Compare In festo s. Benedicti, sermo 3; PL 195:248A: 'In regula eius refulget aurum beatissimi Augustini, argentum Hieronymi, bis tinctus coccus Gregorii, sed et sententiae sanctorum Patrum, quasi lapides pretiosi.' In Assumptione, sermo 25; PL 195:360B: 'Certe animo cupida salutis, studiosa perfectionis, vitam, mores, doctrinamque sanctorum circuit Patrum.' Spec car II, 24: 'Inde etiam in claustris monachorum grues et lepores, damulae et cervi, picae et corvi: non quidam Antoniana et Machariana instrumenta, sed muliebria oblectamenta.' Oner 11; PL 195:403C: 'Considerent quos scientiae radios, quae virtutum lumina, quae caritatis scintillas, quae spiritualium correptionum fulgura suis emittebant temporibus, Gregorius, Augustinus, Ambrosius, Hilarius. Et ut ad viciniora veniamus, recogitent nostri, quomodo suis eluxerint temporibus, [Martinus,] Cuthbertus, Dunstanus [Wilfridus].' Oner 11, PL 195:404B: 'Ubi sumus, numquid in coelo, numquid ibi, ubi quondam Antonius, Marcarius, Hilarion?' Spec car

III, 34: 'Caeterum qui vitiorum impugnationem atque remedia ple-
nius nosse desiderat, legat librum Joannis Cassiani, quem de insti-
tuendis abrenuntiatibus intitulavit.'

3. Spec car III, 75; CCM, I, 141. The reference to the De rege Rejotar
   of Cicero should have been indicated in this new edition.

4. Spir amic III, 111; CCM, I, 343.

5. Spec car II, 69; CCM, I, 99: 'Totam Patrum serietatem quasi rustici-
   tatem contemnat ac iudicet, modo cantandi, quem Spiritus sanctus pe:
   sanctissimos Patres quasi per organa sua, Augustinum videlicet, Am-
   brosium, maximeque Gregorium, instituit: hiberas, ut dicitur, nae-
   nias, vel nescio quorum scholasticorum nugas vanissimas anteponens.

6. Max Weber, The Protestant Ethic and the Spirit of Capitalism (New
   York, 1958) pp. 104 and 106.

7. Spir amic II, 61; CCM, I, 313.

8. Spir amic III, 87; CCM, I, 336: '...Ab hominis ad Dei amicitiam,
   ob quamdam similitudinem diximus facilius transeundum.' See Spir
   amic III, 127; CCM, I, 347. Spir amic III, 134; CCM, I, 349. Spi:
   amic II, 14; CCM, I, 305.

9. Bernard of Clairvaux, SC 83, 3.

10. Henri de Lubac, Further Paradoxes (London, 1958) pp. 93-94.

11. Spec car III, 110; CCM,I, 159.

12. William A. Sadler, Jr. Existence and Love, a New Approach in Exist
    tial Phenomenology (New York, 1969). The quotation is from Chapte
    VIII, "Love and the Ultimate Meaning of Existence," p. 356.

FOR THE SANCTITY OF BERNARD OF CLAIRVAUX

Hugh McCaffery, OSCO
Mount Melleray Abbey

Saint Bernard's first work, On the Degrees of Humility and Pride,
had gone forth, copy had bred copy and circulated it still farther,
when it was brought to Bernard's notice that he had added to a quotation from Mark 13:32; 'nor the Son' had, conveniently for the author's
argument, become, 'nor the Son of Man.' Was this, one wonders, a case
of Bernard's remembering his Eriugena--that Irishman again--too well?[1]
Whatever the excuse, it was only fitting that, having given some penetrating doctrine on humility, he should provide a practical demonstration in a brief Retractatio.

It could be too much to claim that Clairvaux's wide-awake abbot
never again added a word to a Scripture text,[2] but it is no exaggeration
to suggest that subsequently--indeed, very shortly after The Degrees,
he made a mistake; the mistake great writers often make of casting
pearls before posterity, of expecting posterity to be less cleverly
impatient and stupidly slow than, in fact, it turns out to be. He
did so when he wrote a masterpiece, 'In Praise of the Virgin Mother.'
It was not, as were his other writings, provoked by obligation or
occasion, but was quite simply something his devotion drove him to
when he found the opportunity;[3] the heart has reasons, and all that.

However he did it so well that, had he never written anything else on
Mary, he had let himself in for the sometimes dubious distinction of
being dubbed a mariologist. Such a calamity would have been much less
had zeal unmatched by knowledge not tended to claim for him, if not
the post of Mariologist-in-Chief, a position of Chiefly and Exclusively
Mariologist.[4]

Posterity, no doubt, has the right to discover what an author's
contemporaries did not see in his life and works, but it has no right
to distort what, in fact, is there.[5] The evidence of Bernard's writings
proves how correctly two intimate witnesses of his ways and writings
place the emphasis of his teaching. William of Saint Thierry makes,
as was to be expected, Bernard's dream-vision of Christ's birth the
root-cause of 'In Praise of the Virgin Mother.' It is only after stating that the child Bernard's far from childish affections were drawn to
the new-born Child that William, with characteristic accuracy, mentions
Bernard's devotion to Mother and Child.[6] Geoffrey of Auxerre echoes
this when he holds that 'In Praise of the Virgin Mother' and 'On how
God should be loved' exemplify Bernard's religious devotion.[7]

Yet what could well take the cake as dismissal of excessive mario-
logical claims for Clairvaux's, in every sense, proto-abbot is a sermon
of Isaac, abbot (1147-1167) of Stella. This sermon is Isaac's second
sermon for Mary's Assumption and contains express reference to Saint

Bernard's sanctity and to his sermons on the <u>Song of Songs</u> and not a word about his devotion to Mary! This is very interesting and revealing, but what is somewhat amazing, if you know anything at all about Abbot Isaac of Stella, is his high esteem for Bernard's holiness.

While some years younger than Bernard,[8] Isaac was very much a contemporary of the latter, and a fellow Cistercian abbot. He was, however, no sat-at-the-feet sort of disciple like Guerric; nor was he an imitator and commentator-developer like Aelred. He was not a <u>Song of Songs</u> sermons continuator as were Gilbert of Swineshead and John of Ford, nor was he a convert from Abelard's 'academy' in the way of Geoffrey of Auxerre. True, he did not manage to avoid all contact with Clairvaux, Alcher of that abbey was the recipient of Isaac's <u>On the Soul</u>; still, the monastery of Stella was a daughter-house, adopted not born, of Pontigny, and Isaac moved very decidedly in a different theological orbit.

Some description has been left us of what Bernard looked like in both youth and age; there is no clue as to Isaac's appearance.[9] Given that both had a sense of humor,[10] the Laurel and Hardy scene William of Saint Thierry provides when depicting shy and haggard Bernard and his sleek and handsome Cistercian companion going to William of Champeaux's headquarters for Bernard's priestly ordination[11] offers, perhaps, some idea of the contrast in physique between the delicate and emaciated abbot of Clairvaux and the doughty, energetic abbot of

Stella. At very least it is a comfort to know that one Cistercian--

does William's *monacho quodam Cisterciensi* mean "a monk of the abbey

of Cîteaux"?--though on in years, was a credit to the diet.

No doubt, Bernard and Isaac in the days of their pilgrimage

agreed on many points; with their differing temperaments, however,

the best they could often do was to agree to differ. Take, for in-

stance, the attitude an abbot should adopt towards his monks. Ber-

nard urged superiors to be like considerate mothers[12]--quite Galatians

4, incidentally--and some of his letters and sermons are, some will

complain, painfully maternal.[13] Looking at the question, and from

the angle of the monks, Isaac encourages his brothers to welcome a

strict abbot, that, like Christ, their outer selves should be cruci-

fied. With typical independence he adds that if their abbot is not

severe with them, then it is up to them to be severe with themselves.[14]

This preference for martinets and not infrequent use of Rule of

Saint Benedict language never led Isaac to much employment or enjoymen

of military terminology in his writings of whatever kind. Bernard not

only used warfare imagery and gladly provided a 'spiritual directory'

for the Templars, he expertly provoked renegade Robert with both

motherly and soldierly language.[15] The lion and the lamb shared the

peace and fire in his heart.

Isaac's disapproval of the soldier-monks of Calatrava was, it seems, not just pastoral or statesmanlike prudence, but far deeper and more personal.[16] Sturdy and intense, he may well have dreaded forestalling the prowess of the cleric mentioned by Joinville in his Histoire of Saint Louis. This courageous churchman killed, in no halfhearted manner, three "sergents" who had sent him home in his shirt; a state of high dudgeon did not leave much room for the Sermon on the Mount.

Choleric to whatever degree, Isaac may have been a cleric before becoming a monk. Comparing his words on confession with those of Bernard on the same subject[17] is not a little like perceiving the different emphasis of a parish priest and of a father of monks coming through. Bernard is anxious about the interior dispositions of the penitent; the obligation of confession to a priest is Isaac's point. Isaac, moreover, wrote a short treatise on the Mass,[18] recalling, to even the last and least cistercianologist, the still more extensive one written by Baldwin of Ford,[19] who had joined the Order from what is so ambiguously called the secular clergy.

Whatever Isaac's status, clerical or not, before his monastic initiation, there is a Melchisedech aspect to him; indeed, three aspects: the dates of his birth and of his death are unknown and he has a special devotion to the sheer greatness of God.[20] That we know he

was an Englishman comes as near undiluted chance as makes no difference.[21]
The mystery of him, the 'oddity' that strikes the uninitiate, he would
consider, without a doubt, as a very great compliment indeed, as no
small tribute to the thoroughness that he brought to his monastic living.

Thanks to William of Saint Thierry and other Bernard evangelists
we have some notions about Bernard's schooling and its severity.[22] What
Isaac studied and where must be chemically extracted from his writings,
in the light of what was fermenting in the first half of the twelfth
century in the Europe then emerging. With inexactitude to infuriate
an ecumenical council of experts, it may be stated that, whereas Bernard
became a monk after high school, Isaac joined Stella monastery after
university, quite possibly after being a master in the schools.[23] Abbot
Isaac knows what is good for his monastic audience,[24] writes to Bishop
John of Poitiers[25] and to Alcher of Clairvaux[26] as an authority, no mere
scribe.

Bernard was forever apologizing, even if it was not exactly in
the manner of his Apologia. He stressed his 'rusticity' not only to
Haimeric, Cardinal Chancellor--he gave him a poke in the ribs, as
well--but to one of those shirkers our zealous abbot of Clairvaux kept
encountering once in a while, young uncle-fixated Fulk.[27] And even
when he prescinded from his being a monk and not a student (scholasti-

cus), he betrayed his temperament and his training, plus his lack of a
certain kind of it, by much use of two very similar and restraining
texts: "Search too high, and brightness shall dazzle thee" and "Seek
not what is far above thee; search not beyond thy range."[28] Isaac
never used either text; he bulldozed his way forward, in all piety,[29]
went on surefooted and steadily, like a tireless ox, with his investi-
gatio.[30] His thinking was of the School of Chartres type.[31] Bernard
was for vestigatio;[32] his reverence in the face of mystery, his hovering
like an eagle over the depths,[33] all go to show his sympathy with the
School of Laon;[34] not to mention his debt to William of Saint Thierry
who, some think, was of that allegiance.[35] Bernard resembled the law-
abiding creditor willing to wait until things are brought out to him.[36]
Isaac was like the 'bold' young man of the Song of Songs, looking in
through each window in turn, peering through the lattices.[37]

It would be no easy task to discover which of these two Bible-
full abbots was the more biblical. Bernard was, perhaps, the more play-
ful.[38] Isaac knew the Bible backwards: if account is taken of his
liking for using texts in reverse word-order.[39] What is most noticeable, though, is how careful (?) he was to differ from Bernard, be it
a case of a Bible personage or incident or of a more or less basic
text--basic, that is, to the theology of either preacher.

With a sort of smirk, Isaac referred more than once to his Old

Testament namesake, taking "Isaac" to mean "Laughter" and all manner

of joyousness,[40] and insisted on seeing him, so correctly, as a figure

of Christ[41] and as on the up and up, as growing ever wealthier.[42]

Bernard, on the other hand, saw Isaac, Holy Isaac of Old Dispensation,

as old and blind, as trusting his hands more than his ears, putting

feeling above faith, and being fooled thereby.[43]

Ever a careful man, Bernard was quite sure that the water poured

into the water-jars at Cana represents a good, healthy, reverential,

Holy Rule. Chapter Seven fear of God--Jansenists and Jansenists of

Jansenists cannot grasp such fear as this; neither can such imagine

that confidence can be taught--that when it has filled the earthen

vessel it is changed into the wine of love.[44] Isaac was willing to

admit this interpretation, but he did not insist on it; the water

could stand for the need to make oneself a fool for Christ or for pre-

Christian exegesis.[45]

Divergences such as these are far less important, if important is

the word, than the fact that each had a different favorite among the

non-Pauline Letters: Isaac preferred James, Bernard opted for John. If

it is a question of the First Letter of John, each had a particular

basic text: Bernard was keen on "God is love;"[46] as becomes a James

fan, Isaac would have chosen "God is light."[47] He never used the "God is

love" text. Love he preferred to regard as the way to light, which,

admittedly, is quite Bernard, the Bernard of The Degrees of Humility
time. Far from having any objection to the "God is light" text,
Bernard used it, just as Isaac did, in the form "God is all light,"
although in a different kind of context.[48]

Preference for James means, among other things, that Isaac had
some acquaintance with Pseudo-Denis, and, in particular, with his
Celestial Hierarchy. Bernard, for his part, and thanks to Saint
Gregory the Great,[49] was rather impressed by the Nine Choirs[50] idea.
Though he got good value out of the "being, power, operation" triad
that lies behind the Threefold Three Hierarchies,[51] Isaac had, prac-
tically, no use for the Nine Choirs of Denis' Heaven.[52] The techni-
cality of The Divine Names and, still more, the divine "darkness" of
Letter to Caius and The Mystical Theology appealed to him instead.[53]
It is almost a joke that just when our two abbots agreed to accept Denis'
"pantheism" they not only differed, but Bernard showed himself more textual-
ly dionysian, using esse omnium of God, while Isaac has omnium essentia.[54]

Any expectation that our two Cistercian senators viewed monastic life
in the same way is, as by this time you could suspect, doomed to disappointment. Bernard, though much too clearsighted and experienced to
indulge in any kind of complacency where monks were concerned, tended
to regard Cistercian living, at least at Clairvaux, as something achieved,
a high plateau stretching out into the foreseeable future,[55] false bre-

thren--a particularly sore point with the holy abbot[56]--to the contrary

notwithstanding. The spaceship Clairvaux, it would seem, only needed

maintenance; mid-course correctional burns were unthinkable.

Isaac, at best, managed to survive shipwreck and crawl ashore at

a tiny Malta called Ré.[57] The abbey of Stella had, quite likely, never

been able fully to adapt to Cistercian usages. The reasons for Isaac's

settling at Ré are far from clear, but there can be no doubt that, if

hard work and genuine solitude were essential to his plans, he certain-

ly achieved them.[58] With so grim a background and even without it,[59]

it was to be expected he would have regarded monastic living as serious and

virile.[60] Bernard would have agreed, emphatically,[61] and would have hastened

add that monastic observance is a game,[62] a playing the fool,[63] a volun-

tary imprisonment,[64] staying at home knitting instead of going to the

wars of the 'active' ministry.[65] While both writers would have conceded that

a genuine monk shares in the crucifixion-resurrection continuum, Ber-

nard was more achievement-conscious.[66] And, as Isaac would have stressed with

all his characreristic vigor, Bernard had the God-given right to be so.

Disagree with Bernard he would, but he would admire him all the

more and with complete sincerity. Aristotle, to judge by some accounts,

did not much like to look up to Plato, but then, he was no saint; the

heavenly drew him not at all. Not so God's saints: an Ignatius of

Loyola, a John Bosco could and did look up to men among their companions

who differed from them in every possible way. It is no small sign of
Isaac's holiness that he valued that of Bernard so highly. And so to
Isaac's Second Sermon for the Assumption.

This sermon is based on three texts from the Song of Songs: 'Who
is this that makes her way up the desert road, erect as a column of
smoke?' 'Who is this whose coming shews like the dawn of day? No moon
so fair, no sun so majestic, no embattled array so awes men's hearts.'
'Who is this, that overflowing with delight, makes her way up from the
desert, leaning upon the arm of her beloved?'[67]

As might be expected, these three texts were taken as sign-posts
to the usual three stages/ages of spiritual progress. Isaac could have
found them so utilized in Bernard's ninety-first De diversis. And,
sure enough, they agreed pretty much in their application for first two
texts. Mention of 'moon...sun' and 'embattled array' gave Isaac a
reason or, at least, an excuse for making the ascent to God a five-
step affair, his favorite stairway to the Happy Ending that is the end
of ends.[68] Yet to Mary he would apply the last and highest of the three
texts only. Bernard, in his Second Sermon for the Assumption, thought
the second text was suitable, in part, to Mary; in his Sermon for our
Lady's Birthday he used the whole of it of her. Where his divergence
from Isaac comes out still more pointedly is that when he applied third
Song of Songs text to Mary, in his Fourth Sermon for the Assumption and

in his sermon for her Birthday, he carefully left out "leaning upon

her beloved." Whether he, in fact, held for the Sponsa Christi idea

of Mary or not[69]--Isaac certainly did[70]--he, as was his way,[71] left

it an open question.

Where, however, Bernard would be anything but open to theological

or any other reasoning would surely have been to Isaac's express men-

tion of Bernard and, of all things his sanctity, in a sermon on the

Assumption! And, yet, not only was there sound theology in such com-

parison, Bernard accepted the principle involved.[72] As Isaac put it

in a classic text, 'What is said [in Holy Scripture] of the Church,

as a whole, is said of Mary, in a special way, and of the individual

believer as such.'[73]

The last quarter or so of Isaac's second sermon for the Assumption

of the Blessed Virgin goes something like this:

> The first degree of holiness...is to have light
> in oneself[74] through innocence that comes of
> justification.[75] The second, is to give light
> to others by good deeds, that they may go in
> the same direction.[76] The third is to so burn
> with holy zeal that the light of the just may
> grow still brighter.[77] The fourth degree is
> holiness so great, a certain presence so com-
> pelling as to seem awesome.[78]
>
> Sinlessness, however, so complete, so thorough
> as to never fail oneself nor another is scarce-
> ly possible in this life.[79] Good deeds must,
> usually, be showy if they are to shine; good
> zeal is hardly possible without some impatience;
> a well-ordered, quietly controlled gathering

is not likely to prove awesome. Hence the reason
for that third appearance of one overflowing with
delight; no sun here to scorch in the day-time,
no moon to affect in the night; in other words,
no offence given by deed or denunciation, but,
rather, such gentleness and charm as calms and
pleases, of the kind described in the words:
'He won the approval of all mankind,'[80] 'The
Lord gave him renown by striking terror into
his enemies and, at his word, abated prodigies.'[81]

And yet we had sight[82] of a man who was in some
way more than a man.[83] Some people were offend-
ed by his reforming efforts and his rebukes and
complained about him--in his absence, that is.
His presence brought such delight and devotion,
his countenance was so terribly lovable and
lovingly terrible, his lips overflowed with
such gracious utterance,[84] that there and then
they were pacified and, blaming themselves for
blaming him, they could only love, praise and
spread the good news of all that he did.[85]
Yes, this holy man did overflow with delight,
as may without any doubt be discovered in his
writings, and most of all in his Sermons on
the Song of Songs. We are speaking, of course,
of Saint Bernard, abbot of Clairvaux.[86] To
the absent he was something to dread: sun and
moon and an army in battle-array. Those in
his presence he filled to the full with the
delight with which he himself continually overflowed. His love made him awesome to all; the
awe he inspired made him lovable; half-hearted-
ness, impatience, envy, none such found a foot-
hold in either his words or his warnings. This
and no other, dearest friends, is the highest
degree of holiness attainable in this life.

The first degree, then, is the innocence that
harms no one.[87] The second is the generosity
that does good as far as it is able and desires
to do it to all without exception: benevolent
without and beneficent within limits. The
third degree is the zeal that, inspiring the

friend of the Bridegroom for love of the Bridegroom, does not allow the Bride's love to cool
in the slightest. The fourth is the authority
that wins universal respect, though it be power-
less save for the charm of virtue and renown for
sanctity. The fifth degree is the love that all
find so tremendously and alluringly attractive;
high holiness makes it so beautiful, delight in
virtue so lovable.[88] Such was God's holy Mother
during her mortal life, and still more so was
she in the death we celebrate today, in her
going up today to her Son, to whom may she deign
pray for us, to him, who with the Father and the
Holy Spirit, lives and rules, God for ever and
ever. Amen.[89]

Isaac did not consider Bernard a mariologist because, it seems,

he rated him far higher.

NOTES

1. Eriugena, De divisione naturae, II, 28; V, 38 (PL 122:595, 1017).

2. Bernard adds "exceedingly" (nimis) to Song of Songs 1:2 in SC 19,
    1 and SC 20, 9.

3. As the prefatio to this work shows.

4. Roschini has entitled a book on Bernard's teaching on Mary: Il
    dottore Mariano. In the preface to the Spanish Mariological
    Society's Estudios Marianos (1954), Bernard is "el Doctor Máximo"
    of Mariology.

5. A masterly misrepresentation of Bernard's doctrine on Mary's
    meditation is found in Yves Congar's Christ, Our Lady, and the
    Church (London, 1957) pp. 71-76. Leaving aside the questionable
    method and its pitiful result, to take Bernard as a typical pur-
    veyor of Mary-talk is merely a display of ignorance.

6. Vita Bern, I, 2, 4.

7. Vita Bern, III, 8, 29.

8. Bernard was born in 1090; Isaac seems to have come into the world
    in 1100 or so.

9. For Bernard's appearance, see Geoffry of Auxerre, Vita Bern, III,
    1, 1.

10. For example, Bernard, Hum 40, 42; Apo 20; and Isaac, Sermo 38
    and Sermo 48 (PL 194:1819AB, 1854B).

11. Vita Bern, I, 7, 31.

12. SC 23, 2.

13. For instances: Epp 143 and 144; SC 10, 1; Sept 1, 2.

14. Sermo 15 and Sermo 27; PL 194:1739A and 1780CD.

15. Ep 1, 10 and 13.

16. Sermo 48; PL 194:1854B.

17. Isaac, Sermo 11 (PL 194:1728-29); Bernard, SC 16, 9ff.

18. Ep off mis; PL 194:1889Bff.

19. Tractatus de sacramento altaris, SC 93 and 94.

20. For this devotion, see Sermo 19; PL 194:1755ff.

21. Ep off mis; PL 194:1896AB.

22. See William of St Thierry, Vita Bern, I, 1, 3, for a remark by
    Bernard on the severity of his teachers. See also Jean Leclercq,
    Saint Bernard mystique (Bruges, 1948) pp. 18-19.

23. Isaac is styled Isaac magister in three manuscripts of his Ep off
    mis according to Gaston Salet in his "Introduction" to the SC
    edition (130) of Isaac's sermons. At the very least, magister
    supports his having received a good literary and theological for-
    mation and points to his renown. See Gaetano Raciti, "Isaac de
    l'Etoile et son siècle," Cîteaux 13 (1962) 18-34, 133-45, 205-216.

24. See, for example, Sermo 18; PL 194:1750A.

25. Ep off mis; PL 194:1890C.

26. Ep an; PL 194:1875B.

27. Ep 2, 1.

28. Proverbs 25:27--met with in SC 26, 2; see also SC 3, 2; 31, 3;
    38, 5; 62, 4-5; Nat 1, 2; I Nov 5, 12; etc.

29. Isaac refers to Proverbs 25:27 in his Ep an; PL 194:1875C. His
    hinting at both Proverbs 25:27 and Ecclesiasticus 3:22, in Sermo
    22 (PL 194:1761B) shows how differently--from Bernard--he regarded
    them. Isaac's insistence on seeking or inquiring "piously" (pie),
    while stemming from St Augustine (for example, Confessions V, 3,
    5, or De quantitate animae XIV, 24), could have come, more immedi-
    ately, from Eriugena (for instance, De divisione naturae I, 67; II,
    24; V, 30; PL 122:511, 579, 940).

30. For example, Sermo 8 and Sermo 16; PL 194:1717B, 1744A.

31. For Isaac as a "Chartres school" man, see Bernard McGinn, The
    Golden Chain: A Study in the Theological Anthropology of Isaac
    of Stella, CS 15 (Washington, D.C., 1972) pp. 8-10.

32. Bernard's vestigatio--he uses, in fact, various forms of the verb
    vestigare--is to be seen, for example, in Adv 2, 5; QH 13, 6; Ann
    1, 5; I Nov 5, 8 and 9 and 12; Csi V, 2, 4. Yet he does 'lapse'
    into investigare in SC 1, 5 and SC 38, 5.

33. Ann 2, 1.

34. The 'School of Laon' approach is described in C. H. Talbot's

'Intellectual Background,' pp. 13-14 of his edition of Aelred's
De anima (London, 1952).

35. On William of St Thierry and the School of Laon, see McGinn,
The Golden Chain, p. 236.

36. Deuteronomy 24:10.

37. Song of Songs 2:9. See Isaac, Sermo 20; PL 194:1756C.

38. For example, the quarrel among the virtues in Ann 1, 9-11.

39. Instances of such reversing seem particularly frequent in Sermo 17;
PL 194:1748AC, 1749AB.

40. Sermo 7 and Sermo 27; PL 194:1715D, 1780A.

41. Ibid. Matthew 3, 17, has undoubted links with Genesis 22, 2.

42. See indications in note 40.

43. SC 28, 7-8; Tpl VII, 13; yet see SC 71, 4, with express quotation of
Genesis 27, 9.

44. P Epi 1, 4-5; 2, 8-9; SC 54, 11-12.

45. Sermo 10; PL 194:1726A.

46. SC 83, 4; Dil XII, 35; Sept 2, 3.

47. Sermo 16 and Sermo 22; PL 194:1742D, 1761D.

48. Bernard, Csi V, 4, 10; Isaac, Sermo 17 (PL 194:1746A).

49. Gregory the Great, Moralia in Job XXXII, 23, 48; XL Homiliarum in
Evangelia, Liber II, Homilia XXXIV, 7 (PL 76:665, 1249).

50. SC 19, 2-6; Csi V, 7-11.

51. He merely refers to them as a convenient 'nine' in his Ep an;

PL 194:1880B.

52. Eriugena, with much good sense, suggests that the "being and power and operation" found in Denis' Celestial Hierarchy, chap. 11, is the basis for the three hierarchies; Expositiones super hierarchiam coelestiam, 11 (PL 122:230AB). It seems likely that this 'being and power and operation' triad is fundamental to Isaac's Sermones 19-24; PL 194:1752C-72A.

53. The first sentence of Epistola...Gaio monacho (PL 122:1177A) is used twice by Isaac: Sermo 4 and Sermo 22; (PL 194:1701D, 1761D).

54. Bernard, SC 4, 4; Csi V, 13; Isaac, Sermo 22 (PL 194:1764D). Denis' most 'pantheistic' statement, God as esse omnium ('the very being of every being') is found in his Celestial Hierarchy, chap. 4; PL 122:1046BC. Omnium esse--the equivalent of esse omnium--found in Eriugena, De divisione naturae, I, 3 and 12 (PL 122:443B, 454A), can be said to be Denis, De divinis nominibus, I (PL 122:1114C): 'omnium est causa, et principium, et essentia.'

55. Ded 3, 3.

56. Sept 1, 5; SC 24, 2.

57. For a dramatic description of his situation, see Sermo 18; PL 194: 1749D-50A.

58. Sermo 14 and Sermo 15; PL 194:1737AC, 1740AB.

59. The sermon mentioned in the following note may belong to Isaac's

days at Stella.

60. Sermo 2; PL 194:1696B.

61. For example, Ded 3, 3; QH, prefatio.

62. Ep 87, 12; see Div 41, 6.

63. Ibid.

64. QH 9, 1; Ded 1, 2.

65. SC 12, 9.

66. Ded 1, 5.

67. Song of Songs 3:6, 6:9, 8:5.

68. Sermo 4 (PL 194:170D-702A); EP an (PL 194:1880AB).

69. For Mary as sponsa Christi, see, for example, Miss 2, 2; SC 45, 2; O Asspt, 15. In this last reference the Assumpta is 'leaning on her beloved'!

70. Sermo 52; PL 194:1867C.

71. Jean Leclercq provides a good sample of Bernard's non-polemical spirit in his "Le mystère de l'Ascension dans les sermons de S. Bernard," Coll. XV (1953) 81ff.

72. For example, SC 12, 11; 68, 7; 69, 1.

73. Sermo 51; PL 194:1863B.

74. See John 8:12.

75. Literally, 'of justice'; Romans 3:25-26.

76. Literally, 'may follow him'; see John 8:12.

77. See Proverbs 4:18; John 15, 2.

78. See Esther 15:9; this very chapter of Esther is mentioned early
    on this same Sermo 52 (PL 194:1867B).

79. Because of the consequences of Original Guilt; see Isaac, Sermo
    7 (PL 194:1713CD).

80. Ecclesiasticus 44:27; in the Clementine Vulgate this text seems
    to refer to the Old Testament Isaac.

81. Ecclesiasticus 45:3.

82. See John 1:14. This assertion is usually taken to mean Isaac
    had really met Bernard; see McGinn, The Golden Chain, p. 3.

83. Used in Denis, Epistola 4 (PL 122:1178A) of Christ.

84. This echoes Psalm 44 (45):3. Geoffrey of Auxerre (Vita Bern III,
    3, 7) applies this same Psalm verse to Bernard.

85. Literally, 'praised and preached' (laudarent, praedicarent);
    compare the Preface for Masses of Our Lady.

86. Is 'saint' from Isaac himself?

87. See II Corinthians 6:3.

88. Words from the Song of Songs 6:3, found in the Office of the
    Blessed Virgin and in that of Virgins.

89. Sermo 52; PL 194:1869-70.

THE CHRISTOLOGY OF JOHN OF FORD

Edmund Mikkers, OCSO
Sint Benedictusabdij, Achel, Belgium

John of Ford, a Cistercian author who lived about 1200, was hardly known some years ago. The publication of his great Commentary on the Canticles proved him to be one of the most important authors of the Cistercian order.[1] In the exegesis of the Canticles, he can be placed in the same tradition with St Bernard and his patristic predecessors, Origin, Gregory of Nyssa, St Ambrose, Gregory the Great and John's twelfth-century predecessors.[2]

For John the Canticle is above all a sacred chant, an allegory on the most intimate relations between God and the soul. The names he uses, chant of love, spiritual chant, the sweet chant of the holy epithalamy, indicate an allegoric exegesis, a spiritual and ascetical-mystical one, an explanation that only could be inspired "by the spirit of love, by the spirit who is love."[3]

John of Ford knows how to use the images and symbols of the Canticles to express and to deepen the most fundamental doctrines of the faith and at the same time to explain the divine abundance of gifts toward men and the whole creation, as well as the spiritual experiences of one living united with God. The basic elements of his doctrine, theological as well as spiritual (if we could make a distinction), are a firmly structured christology and an ecclesiology. On these basic elements he builds a very deep spiritual doctrine with all its particu-

larities. The difficulty, perhaps, is that he does not expound his
teaching in a systematic way. But we hardly can expect that from a
monastic author who is a witness of the monastic-patristic tradition
and who has no connection at all with the scholastic movement of his
time.[4]

The christology of John of Ford has two aspects, dogmatic and
spiritual, because his spiritual doctrine is nothing but a concrete
application of the reality of incarnation and redemption in each
human life and especially in the monastic life. The reason for this
position is quite clear. In the whole Christian and patristic tradition the bridegroom in the allegorical explanation of the Canticles
is Christ, by his divinity and by his spirit living in the church and
living in each member of the church. John of Ford expresses that idea
in a very concrete way: 'Christ is the Beloved of the Father, Christ
is the Beloved of the church, Christ is the Beloved of a single soul.'[5]

John insists on a profound connection and unity between the different aspects of the mystery of incarnation, the human life of Christ,
the mystery of redemption by the death and resurrection of the Lord.
In this he is a typical representative of 'monastic theology,' in which
reading and meditation on the scriptures, theological reflexion, prayer
and admiring contemplation are joined together in a single text or
sermon. In his works, one can find hardly any trace of the dialectical
method or a logical succession of ideas.

In this paper I shall try to put together some main lines of the christology of John of Ford, an outline that will help to understand this author. The principal headings of this analysis are: (1) the names of Christ; (2) the doctrine of **incarnation**, the holiness of Christ, the Hypostatic Union, the soul of Christ, the human infirmity of Christ, the <u>necessitates</u> <u>Christi</u>; (3) the doctrine of **redemption** (the acceptance of the redemption by the Son of God, how redemption takes shape in us); and (4) prayers to Christ.

THE NAMES OF CHRIST.

Perhaps no other Cistercian author, not even St Bernard, uses more names of Christ than did John of Ford. This must be ascribed to familiarity with the scripture--witness the easy use he makes of it-- and, perhaps, to literary inspiration. But John's very use of those names shows his approach to the mystery of the Incarnation as re- vealed in the text of the Canticles and other biblical sources. The words should be taken in their whole allegorical and symbolic meaning, which they already received in the patristic tradition. Many of the images taken from the Old Testament have their fulfillment in the person of Christ.

In the New Testament texts themselves, there are many names of Christ used in a symbolic sense. John uses these, for example: new Adam,[6] second Adam,[7] true lamb or paschal lamb,[8] angel of the great counsel,[9] tree of life,[10] true David,[11] true Solomon,[12] our Zorobabel (as an image of the role of Christ after the redemption accomplished by his death and resurrection),[13] the true light,[14] lord of the whole creation,[15] image of divine majesty, form and image of the father,[16] bread of life, he who comes from heaven,[17] priest and king,[18] source of light, source of justice and holiness,[19] etc.

John uses many other names, yet more allegorical, taken from the text of the Canticles or from other sources, and sometimes these are quite unusual. Sometimes too it is rather difficult to translate them or to grasp immediately their meaning in the context. Some examples: generous eagle,[20] the arbor sinapis,[21] the most select grape;[22] also some words of the Canticles: goat, lavacrum, the wood and the lily, a sweet smelling cedar,[23] a fishhook to catch the faithful,[24] the source of living waters,[25] shepherd and meadow,[26] etc.

Another not less important series of names describes the role of Christ in the church, the various functions of Christ in the community of the faithful. Most of these names are clear enough: he who is zealous for human salvation (aemulator salutis humanae),[27] the admirable workman,[28] the head of the church, the head of the martyrs,[29] he who fulfills the will of God,[30] the crown of those who fight for him,[31] the principle of our restoration,[32] the sacrament of our salvation,[33] the sign and the image of God, restoring in us the original image of God.[34] To this category belong the other names; Christ is called the goal, the object of our praise, he to whom all our praise is directed.[35]

The intimate relation between Christ and the single soul is indicated in the words of the Canticles: the spouse, bridegroom, the
beloved, the most beloved, the most beautiful, but also in many other
names: the master,[36] the friend or the greatest friend of all friends,[37]
the sum of all our desires,[38] the sole patience of those who suffer,[39]
the most beautiful solitude,[40] etc.

Generally speaking, in the context of John's sermons these names
receive a much larger and broader signification and meaning than they
have alone, because the author supposes during his whole explanation
the presence of such an image. A more complete list of all the names
of Christ may be found in the Indices to the critical edition.[41]

THE DOCTRINE OF INCARNATION.

In nearly all his sermons John of Ford speaks in some way about
Christ, and therefore too about the mysteries of Christ ('The Jesus
is truly the matter, the goal, the end of this whole song'[42]), but, in
sermons seven to ten, John gives a more or less complete theological
explanation of the mystery of Christ, and these sermons may be considered as a kind of summary of his christology.

In the beginning of sermon seven, John says that he will not teach
anything other than what is taught by the church.[43] This statement
is important in relationship to the theological opinions he quotes
further on. He is afraid of any kind of speculation because he believes that love is the better way to understand and to know Christ

than intellectual reasoning. Christ should be known by the way of
our _affectus_. The Son himself is the most beloved of the Father,
source therefore of all love, united with the father in unity of
nature (<u>unitas naturae</u>) by a singular cohesion and oneness.[44] He
also is the Wisdom, the Truth, the Holiness and the Kindness of the
Father, and his human life is only the exterior revelation or manifestation of these divine qualities.[45] Because Christ in his divine
love is compared with fire, he is able to unite the human soul with
God through charity and peace.[46] His eternal generation from the
Father is a mystery as well as his generation from a virgin mother.[47]

In sermon eight John explains, in his own way, the mystery of
the **incarnation** by which the Son of God became son of man and true man.
First he insists on the origin of the humanity of Christ through his
birth from a virgin, then on the role of the soul of Christ, the human
soul in the mystery of the **incarnation**. A summary of this doctrine
is given in the following text:

> Let us see now of what sort is the brilliance and
> the modesty of the Beloved, in the glory of his
> assumed humanity. As to the admirable beauty of
> his brilliance, four points come to mind at the
> moment. Each of them surpasses the understanding
> of any human or angelic mind. First: complete
> innocence and perfect holiness of his most sacred
> flesh. Second: his super-excelling wisdom and
> perfect justice. Third: his glorious assuming,
> as God, of human nature. Fourth: to balance the
> weight of glory, his marvellous humility.[48]

Then he explains how Christ in his humanity, or, rather, how the

human soul of Christ, received its holiness through the Virgin Mary
from the Holy Spirit. This statement did not please all his monks;
he says that Christ received from his Mother a complete holiness.
Eve transmitted to the whole human family necessario cupidity, so could
Mary, through the grace of the Holy Spirit, transmit to her Son the
liberty from any sin, the complete holiness iure hereditario. John
added a special leaf to his text already completed, in which he quotes
Anselm of Canterbury and Guerric of Igny as sources for his opinion.[49]

By the restoration of the original holiness in his human soul,
Christ himself could become source of holiness for all those who believe in Him. In this way John of Ford expresses the sacramental value
of the humanity of Christ and, at the same time, the role of the Virgin
Mary who, by conceiving Christ through the Holy Spirit, became a new
Eve, mother of redeemed mankind.[50] Another consequence of the mystery
of the incarnation is that the human soul of Christ has two functions;
it is mediator in the hypostatic union itself as media quaedam natura
(by its spiritual nature placed between the divinity of Christ and his
body of human flesh), and it is mediator too in the work of the redemption. The following quotations from sermon eight may illustrate his
doctrine:

> What was that flesh like, how pure, that was born
> of the virgin, conceived by the Holy Spirit? For
> that flesh possessed the glory of holiness as an
> inheritance both from his Mother and from the Holy
> Spirit. As a result it was inviolable for himself

and had power to heal every member of the human
family.[51]

Now what fitting remarks can we make about the
soul of Jesus, which was mediator and special
emissary of that ineffable union--for human
flesh was united with the Word of God. In it
are hidden all the treasures of wisdom and
knowledge (Col. 2:3); in it are preserved all
the riches of God's justice, beyond all calcu-
lation, so that nothing can be added nor taken
away. In his soul the liberty of man's free
will and the dignity of freedom have been restored to their former rightful integrity, not
only fully but also peacefully, to be held
thereafter by perpetual right.[52]

Indeed in all of God's creation nothing is
more like God or can be, than this soul,
nothing equally similar. All who desire to
be restored to that likeness of God, which
was corrupted by the enemy, may follow this
as counsel: in its power is the seal, and
the writer's case is at his waist.[53]

In these texts and in the whole sermon some principal points of

Cistercian spirituality are brought together with the doctrine of in-

carnation. There are in this text some allusions to the doctrine of

image and likeness, consisting in the liberty of the human soul and

in the dignity of human freedom. This liberty is possessed in its

fullness by the soul of Christ. So by his incarnation and redemption,

the soul of Christ becomes the source of a renewed integrity, not only

in itself but for all of mankind. Man who desires to be restored to

that original likeness, lost through sin, has only to look at the soul

of Christ. Paraphrasing an idea of St Paul, John explains this place of the soul of Christ in the human salvation more explicitly:

> The justice of God has become my justice through
> the soul of Christ. In her human existence she
> enjoys peace with all things below her, justice
> in herself, and the glory of God above her.[54]

The way in which the hypostatic union or the mystery of incarnation took place John first explains by quite classic expressions,
giving the generally accepted doctrine of the church. So he speaks
clearly of the incomparable holiness of the humanity (humanitas) of
Christ, which is assumed (assumpta) by the Word in the unity of a
divine person.[55]   Another text is yet more explicit and clear:

> At the same hour and at the same time the majesty
> of God comes down [is condescending] and the hu-
> manity is elevated, and as the only begotten Son
> of God becomes son of man, at the same moment
> too the son of man becomes the only begotten
> Son of God.[56]

In another place John says that God's Wisdom is like a mother for
us, according to the dispensation of the humanity she assumed from us.[57]
The humanity of Christ, his human nature, united to the divine majesty,
is assumed into the unity of a divine person and is enjoying the same
glory. John surely knew and confessed the traditional faith on this
point as it was believed in the whole church and defined in specific
terms by the Council of Chalcedon.

However, in many places he uses another expression for the
humanity of Christ; instead of humanitas assumpta he speaks more
concretely of homo assumptus. This expression was accepted by the

theologians of his time as a possible opinion and only later rejected

by Thomas Aquinas. Someone is assumed into the unity of the Word;

however, he does not understand that this 'someone' really exists

separated from the Word, because such an opinion would be heretical.

But this opinion rather gives a proper existence (esse proprium) to

the man who actually exists united with the divine Word and only

exists actually through this union with the Word.[58]

Some quotations from John of Ford may explain this opinion, for

example:

> ...In the glory of that union, what is greater:
> the dignity of him who was assumed or the dignity
> of him who assumed?[59]

The whole sermon twenty-seven is filled with this kind of expression,

such as: 'The fivefold glory...why this man [homo ille] has been

assumed into the glorious union with the Word.'[60] 'The greatest glory

of Christ and the unthinkable dignity of the Word is, that the Word

united this man with himself through his lovely and almighty strength....

It was impossible, that a man who was glorified in God, could stay for

longer than three days in death.'[61] 'The charity of the Father has

sent his glory [his Son] to unite himself with this man, the son of

the virgin, and to give to Him the nicest covering of the honor of all

his brethren.'[62] 'The son of the virgin has been assumed by the form

of God, the only begotten Son of the Father.'[63]

There can be no doubt that John really knows very well the idea of the homo assumptus. Perhaps he is the only Cistercian who uses

this idea. Can that be explained? This doctrine was widely spread

among the prescholastics of the twelfth century, and it is mentioned

by Peter Lombard and others. Some expressions of Isaac of Stella are

very close to the ideas of John of Ford, but, in the end, Isaac of

Stella is insistent on the traditional doctrine, even when he too

insists upon the importance of the human soul of Christ.

Perhaps we might posit some influence of a contemporary scholar,

John of Cornwall, who lived in the south of England and taught at

Oxford. He clearly admits that this doctrine was acceptable as one

explanation of the mystery of the Incarnation. John of Ford makes

allusions to this same theory, without discussing it more deeply or

in a more theological way.[64]

There is yet another text, in which John makes some allusion to

another theory about the mystery of Incarnation, the habitus theory,

accepted by some theologians of his time. But in speaking of this

theory, John makes at the same time, some necessary corrections to it.

We could find only this one text:

> Thus the holy Mother of God formed a garment in
> her womb for her only beloved son with the cooperation
> of the Holy Spirit. It was a garment [vestis = habitus]
> woven throughout of incomparable splendor, a garment
> never before nor since seen in this earth, a garment
> finally which no stain could defile nor any power
> enfeeble. This is the royal garment with which the
> King of kings was clothed from the moment of his con-
> ception. It bore the following inscription, 'King of

kings and Lord of lords,' an unique privilege for
one born as a human being.[65]

Why did John of Ford speak in this way about the mystery of the

incarnation? Probably it was for him a method to accentuate the

reality of the human nature of Christ, as did the other Cistercian

authors of the twelfth century. Christ was a true man, quite equal

to us in his whole human life; so by extending compassion to us, he

enabled us to enter in the mystery of his redemption, to be redeemed

by this humanity of the Son of God. John's conception of the in-

carnation cannot be understood without the mystery of redemption.

> The flesh of Christ born from the virgin never
> has been soiled by sin; it has been assumed from
> my own flesh, crucified and put to death, buried
> and resuscitated for me; the most innocent human
> nature [flesh] was crucified for me.[66]

So through the reality of his human flesh we are able to see God

in human flesh, and Christ can be in this way a true mediator.[67] Through

his flesh Christ himself participated in the immortality of the Word.

But through his flesh too the Word made flesh participates in all human

infirmities, even in human mortality.[68]

> By the disposition of the Father the Word would
> become flesh and dwell among us, so that by the
> impression [contact] of this flesh and its con-
> formation to us, because it dwelled such a long
> time with us, and finally by the complete expres-
> sion of the flesh in the crucifixion, the charity
> of God should be formed in us.[69]

In explaining further, John of Ford has many texts about the in-

firmities of Christ, assumed for us in his humanity; these are the clothes of Christ in which he appears to us.[70]   In other places he calls

these infirmities the <u>necessitates</u> of Christ, the needs necessarily in-

volved in any human condition.   In this point he has the same doctrine

as St Bernard and he depends directly on him.   These <u>necessitates</u> in-

volve the weakness of the human nature of Christ, infirmities, humility

and humiliation, sufferings and even mortality, but not ignorance and

sin.   The fullness of his knowledge should remove our ignorance and

the fullness of his holiness our sins.   The Lord of liberty accepted

all those necessities, inherent to the human condition.[71]   The faith-

ful have only to make from all these necessities a bouquet of flowers

to put on his breast, so that he may recognize in himself the infirmi-

ties of the Lord.[72]

These seem to be the main ideas of John of Ford about the mystery

of the incarnation, considered in itself and in its immediate conse-

quences for the human existence of Christ.   In this present life only

the human nature of Christ as man can be seen, his life and his death,

but nothing of the light of his eternal existence.[73]   So John insists

on the humiliation of the Word made flesh and the exaltation of the

human nature or rather the human condition of Christ.   Sermon nine

deals more explicitly with this theme of humiliation: exterior hu-

miliation of the Word in the life, the passion and the death of

Christ; humility in his inner dispositions, the humility of the Word

revealed through the humility of a man.   In several sermons too the author speaks on the beauty of Christ, which finds its origin in his

union with the Word of God, in his birth from the virgin and in his

union with the church.   In sermon thirty-five he develops this theme,

but always in the perspective of the mystery of the redemption.

THE DOCTRINE OF THE REDEMPTION.

According to John, redemption was not yet accomplished by the

mystery of the incarnation.   And probably for this reason he speaks

more explicitly about the mystery of redemption in sermon ten, ex-

plaining the motive for the incarnation of the Son of God.   In other

sermons he gives quite different reasons.   If humility is characteris-

tic of the mystery of the incarnation, the charity of Christ, his

divine love, is most clearly revealed in the mystery of the passion,

the death on the cross and the resurrection:

> By your crucifixion and the perforation of your
> side you revealed to us, in an ineffable way, the
> sacrament of your charity and your mercy.   This
> is the victory over the human heart, the effusion
> of your charity.[74]

We may distinguish in John's doctrine on redemption two main lines:

the acceptance of the redemption by the Son of God, explained chiefly

in sermon ten, and the ways this redemption takes shape in the humanity,

in man.

John does not put the question about the motives of the incarna-

tion in an abstract or speculative way, but in a very concrete one:

why did Christ suffer for us, his passion, all his sufferings in body

and spirit, the cross and his death, he who is the flower of all
innocence and holiness?[75] The explanation he gives in sermon ten does
not lack grandeur of imagination. Several biblical themes are mixed
together in a description in which the Son of God is presented being
tried, like Isaac burdened with all the sins of mankind to be sacri-
ficed. The Father calls his Son before the heavenly court, all the
angels surrounding him and waiting for something quite new and admirable. Then there is a vivid dialogue between the Father and the
Son about the redemption of the fallen humanity. The Father imposes
on the Son the great burden of human iniquity, and proposes to him
to leave heaven, to go to the sinners and to himself make satisfaction
for all their sins. The Son accepts this proposal and declares that
he will obey and suffer the fury of his Father, but at this moment
the Son prays to his Father:

> There is only one thing I ask from your kindness,
> that your fury may come on me and not on my people,
> that in my blood there will be reconciliation of
> the whole creation and that my blood will be the
> eternal sign of a new covenant between mankind and
> us.[76]

The Father accepts this willingness of the Son and makes him the
judge of the whole universe. Joy in heaven is immense for several
reasons: for the mercifulness of the Father, for the marvelous obedience of the Son, for the reconciliation of the whole human nature,
and the restoration of the heavenly city.[77]

But, of course, this splendid text is hardly a theological explanation of the mystery of redemption, and the author himself judges
it quite insufficient. He must reconcile the mercy of God, his infinite charity giving his only begotten Son to mankind--even to death
--and, on the other hand, the divine justice: why did Christ suffer
and die in our place, for us sinners, without any merits on our part?
It seems relevant for John's method that before this unfathomable
mystery he sets himself to prayer; he does not try any theological
or speculative answer. But in his prayer he receives a divine answer:
Caritas mea, o homo, hoc est justitia mea ('my love is my justice'),[78]
because God is total justice and total mercy.

The consequences of the redemption for Christ is that he lives
eternally with the Father. There he lives in his origin, and he lives
too in the fruits of the redemption in mankind.

The fruits of redemption are presented by John of Ford in two
ways, and many texts could be quoted for both approaches. The first
is the theme of the imitation of Christ. The main reason why Christ
has taken on himself all the sufferings and the necessities of life,
passion, and death, is that we might follow his example and be able
to accept the comparatively negligible adversities of our present
life.[79] John gives some other fruits of the redemption: death to
crimes, forgiveness of faults in the tears of the penitent, in the
memory and the desires of those who love. Christ is living in the

constancy of the martyrs, in the life of the righteous and yet more

in their death.[80] But the most excellent fruit of the redemption is

the Church, the kingdom of God preached in the whole earth. Here we

might speak about the ecclesiology of John of Ford:

> But who can narrate the novelty of this birth [of
> the Church]? The sword of your own love pierced
> your heart, and your Church, the future mother
> of many kings, was born from the fruitful pleasure
> of your loins and from their pleasurable fertility;
> the Church was formed in the womb of your com-
> passion from your own bone and flesh, and it
> came forth from your side which was the source
> of the marriage bond and of social love.[81]

Another more important topic of John's doctrine is that he uses

the doctrine on image and likeness in a soteriological function.

Christ is the image of the Father in his human existence, or in his

human nature restores the lost original likeness that man had before

the first sin. The image he originally received was a divine seal

of likeness on his soul. Through sin the devil put his own seal of

unlikeness on that divine seal, so that the human soul lost its

divine brilliance and became only darkness. Christ, because he is

the image and likeness of God himself, through his redemption put his

own seal of the real image and likeness of God on human darkness and

restored in this way the original splendor. He did that first through

his example of poverty and obedience; he is able to put his seal or

his own image upon the human soul because he is the seal and the

sealer himself. He is life and source of life; he has conformed himself to the human existence so that the love of God through the

Spirit may be restored in man.[82]

> This is the mercy of God, that as a father he
> restores in us his image and likeness through
> his Son, and that as a mother he is bearing
> us in pain to new spiritual life through Christ
> in his humanity, which he assumed for us.[83]

The conclusion may be that John of Ford was a quite well informed

monk and abbot, but that he was not bound by scholastic or theological

preoccupations. He really knew well the different opinions of the

theologians of his time, he could even mention those in his work, but

along with opposing opinions. He is a classic example of the Cister-

cian school, the center of his doctrine being the doctrine of love:

God's love revealed to us in Christ, becoming also our love for God

through Christ; this was the goal of the mysteries of incarnation and

redemption.

PRAYERS TO CHRIST.

John of Ford is a typical representative of the monastic approach

to revelation through the exercises of monastic life: _lectio_, _medi-_

tatio, _oratio_ and _contemplatio_. Sometimes we can find these four ap-

proaches to divine truth in the same sermon. The sermons are sometimes

prayers, to God, to the Holy Spirit and especially to Christ. It is

impossible to cite all these prayers. But as a conclusion to this

article we give two examples of such prayers:

> O Font of life, Lord Jesus, in the fullness of your
> love you rescue me from so many deaths. You lead me

into that living and life-giving light, not only
by transferring me from death to life but also
from life to life. You have given me such abundant and wonderful proofs of your unequaled love,
as many as the deaths to which I now--how late--
understand I had been subject. For I, once a son
of death, have passed over into the adoption of
your sons. And now, open my mouth to you, so
that I may drink in your living spirit. Even
more, I beg you, enlarge my mouth that I may stand
in wonder before you, O font of life, and ardently
cling to you....[84]

You, O Lord Jesus, are the splendor and image of
the divine majesty; you are the seal of likeness
which no stain of unlikeness can discolor; you
rightly and wholesomely admonish us, that, returning to the seal with which we were sealed
from the beginning, we place it on our heart,
reforming ourselves unto knowledge of you; we
place it also on our arm, renewing your strength
in ourselves. You do well in admonishing us,
provided that afterward you also move us. For
whence can any soul, howsoever dear to you, move
its hand or its finger to such a great work,
unless your hand first come upon it? O you,
who are mighty, the light of whose face is sealed
upon us, imprint it more clearly, imprint it more
brightly, so that the expressed image of your
face may shine forth in us. Do you, I repeat,
put this seal on our heart and on our arm, for
you are both the seal and the keeper of the seal.
For you are the bread of life whom, as you yourself testify, God the Father has sealed, giving
you all the fullness of his divinity, so that
just as he has life in himself, you also may be
with him the source of life and have life in
yourself.[85]

NOTES

1. John of Ford, SC, edd. Edmund Mikkers and Hilary Costello, CC, continuatio medievalis, XVII, XVIII. For a detailed bibliography, see the Introduction, pp. viii–xiv.

2. See Fr. Ohly, Hohelied-Studien: Grundzüge einer Geschichte der Hoheliedauslegung des Abendlandes bis zum 1200. (Wiesbaden, 1958).

3. SC 95, lines 108-110. The sermon number will hereafter be followed by a colon, then the line number.

4. H. Costello, "The Idea of the Church in the Sermons of John of Ford," Cîteaux 21 (1970) 236-64; and the same author's "John of Ford and the Quest for Wisdom," Cîteaux 23 (1972) 141-59.

5. SC 10:250-52; compare SC 7:105-111.

6. SC 59:193.

7. SC 84:114.

8. SC 18:92; 30:58; 31:88, 98; 51:265-66.

9. SC 6:43; 13:252; 104:106.

10. SC 102:116, 178.

11. SC 9:230; 29:91; 62:26.

12. SC 2:86; 12:61, 190; 13:7; 28:196; 34:39; 73:7; 110:294; 112:3.

13. SC 67:63, 75.

14. SC 7:119; 31:75; 43:172; etc.

15. SC 16:47-48.

16. SC 103:141; 104:39.

17. SC 41:184; 104:53.

18. SC 8:195; 11:222, 257, 260, 270; 12:21; 21:13; 28:123; 51:169; 60:60; 67:7, 73, 140, 183, 193; 103:151.

19. SC 7:157, 194; 20:214; 25:173; 105:142, 150.

20. SC 8:63.

21. SC 102:37.

22. SC 86:113.

23. Caprea, SC 72:74; lavacrum, 3:258; lignum, 119:238; lilium, 119:234; cedrus odorifera, 114:225, 241; 115:216.

24. SC 26:218.

25. SC 29:82.

26. SC, passim, especially 100:233-34.

27. SC 50:68.

28. SC 25:82.

29. Caput ecclesiae, SC, passim; caput martyrum, 15:84, 123, 126, 131.

30. Executor divinae voluntatis, SC 76:198.

31. Corona pugnantium, SC 83:12.

32. Principium reparationis, SC 36:171.

33. Sacramentum salutis, SC 69:52-53.

34. SC 103:141. Compare the use of signaculum similitudinis, SC 104 passim.

35. *Initium*, *progressus*, *finis laudum nostrarum*, SC 52:214-15.

36. SC prol.:59; 9:165; 18:104-107.

37. *Amicus unigenitus Patris*, SC 39:126; *amicus amicissimus*, 118:144.

38. *Summa desiderii nostri*, SC 18:294.

39. *Patientia unica patientium*, SC 53:124.

40. *Solitudo amoenissima*, SC 100:86.

41. See the words *Christus*, *Jesus*, *Filius*, *Sponsus*, *Verbum*, *Unigenitus*.

42. SC 120:195.

43. SC 7:40-52.

44. SC 7:111-14, 122-25: '...Essentia una et eadem atque indiscreta...
    non tamen usque ad unitatem naturae...sed usque ad individuam
    adhaesionem atque indissolubilem nexum unionis.'

45. See SC 16:37-40; 37:99-102; 60:248-51; 96:163-64.

46. SC 7:105-107.

47. SC 67:168-71.

48. SC 8:67-75.

49. SC 8:127. In this text John refers to Anselm's *Cur Deus homo*,
    II, 16; PL 158:416-19; and his *De conceptu virginali*, 20; PL 158:
    452. He also refers to Guerric 'igniacenses vir catholicus et
    utique eruditissimus'; SC 8:128-29. See the *Sermo in Annunciatione
    beatae Mariae*, II, 1; PL 185:120A-C.

50. SC 37:99; 92:180.

51. SC 8:79-83.

52. SC 8:153-61.

53. SC 8:167-72.

54. SC 8:197-201.

55. SC 25:121-23.

56. SC 27:125-28.

57. See SC 8:67-68; 20:66-68; 35:105-107; 36:176-79; 60:248-51, etc.

58. Bibliography on this subject can be found in L. Ott, "Chalcedon
    in der Frühscholastik," in Das Konzil ven Chalcedon (Würzburg,
    1953) II, 912-16; A. Landgraf, Dogmengeschichte der Frühscholastik
    (Regensburg, 8 vols., 1952-1956) II, 116f.; H. E. Oberman, The
    Harvest of Medieval Theology (Cambridge, Massachusetts, 1963)
    pp. 251-54. For the opinions of some of the theologians who were
    John's contemporaries, see W. H. Principe, Theology of the Hypo-
    static Union in the Early Thirteenth Century, I, William of Auxerre
    (Toronto, 1963) 77; II, Alexander of Hales (Toronto, 1967) 107
    and 204-208; III, Hugh of St. Cher (Toronto, 1970) 59 and 65. For
    the opinion of Thomas Aquinas, see Sent. III, 6, q. 1, a. 1. Compare, t
    Sermones inediti b. Aelredi abbatis Rievallensis (ed. C. H. Talbot; Rome
    1952) introduction, pp. 20-22.

59. SC 8:203-204.

60. SC 27:91.

61. SC 27:79-81, 100 (hominem in Deo clarificatum), 130-33.

62. SC 35:64-69.

63. SC 36:176; compare 37:92-94; 56:270-71.

64. See N. M. Häring, "The Eulogium ad Alexandrum Papam tertium of

John of Cornwall," Mediaeval Studies 13 (1951) 253-300.

65. SC 8:132-39.

66. See SC 96:241f.

67. See SC 37:90f.

68. SC 92:180.

69. SC 104:63-67.

70. SC 6:227-30.

71. SC 6:249; 25:224; 83 passim.

72. SC 83:89-98.

73. SC 31:219-21.

74. SC 84:149-55; see 30:120f.

75. SC 10:72.

76. SC 10:119-26.

77. SC 10:169-76.

78. SC 10:222-23.

79. SC 109:27-34.

80. SC 26:224-27.

81. SC 32:156-62.

82. SC 104:63-66.

83. SC 28:48-50.

84. SC 105:142-52.

85. SC 104:39-57. Other prayers to Christ as the eternal light, SC
    38, cap. 5; to the 'sweet' Jesus 20, cap. 7: suavitatas nectarea,

aromatica dulcedo, totius suavitatis fons. Other prayers speak
of Christ as the Son of God who forgives sins, 22, cap. 8-10;
as living in others, 26, cap. 9.

THE CISTERCIAN FATHERS, HEIRS TO A TRADITION

John Morson
Mount Saint Bernard Abbey, England

Orpheus, the most renowned of harpers and singers, made his way
up from the underworld, where he had charmed its gods.

> On the top of a certain hill was a level stretch
> of open ground, covered with green turf. There
> was no shelter from the sun, but when the divine-
> ly born poet seated himself there and struck his
> melodious strings, shady trees moved to the spot....
> Such was the grove which Orpheus had drawn round him,
> and now he sat in the midst of a gathering of wild
> creatures and a host of birds. He tested the chords
> of his lyre, striking them with his thumb, till his
> ear was satisfied that the notes they played, though
> different, were all in tune. Then he began to sing.[1]

This theme of Orpheus was so persistent in pagan art that it had
to be baptized by Christians of the early centuries. Here was a type,
outside the chosen people, of the Good Shepherd who would gather a new
flock around him. The evidence is found in several frescoes which have
survived in the Christian catacombs at Rome.[2] We could pursue the
theme in patristic texts. What is to our purpose now is that one of
the most eloquent testimonies comes, as late as the twelfth century,
from the pen of the Cistercian, Amedeus of Lausanne.

> God's Son became the Son of Man, so as in oneness
> of Person to be God and Man: before the worlds
> God begotten of his Father's substance, of the
> substance of his Mother born a man in the world.
> He exulted, danced, that giant of twofold nature,
> singing with melodious voice and playing sweetly

> upon his harp, I mean our body. He used the well-
> built organ of our flesh to give out the most
> lovely sound, and sent forth echoes of unutterable
> harmony. So well did he ply his art that he raised
> up stones, set trees in movement, drew the wild
> beasts after him, led men from flesh to the height
> of heaven. What does this mean? With the sweet-
> ness of his wondrous song he raised from the stones
> children to Abraham. He moved the trees of the
> wood--that is, the hearts of the peoples--to faith
> in him. The wild beasts are the ferocious passions
> and untamed barbarism, which he converted to right
> behaviour, the men whom he led forth from men to
> give them their place among the gods.[3]

Is this talk of the divine Orpheus a phantasy, an entertainment,
or is it an instance of profound theology? Is what we have found in
Amedeus a particular instance of something which recurs all through
the theological reflection of the pre-scholastic centuries?

The answer may be found in a treatise of Isaac of Stella, given
in the form of nine sermons assigned to Sexagesima Sunday. The author
becomes aware of the difficulty of predicating anything, even wisdom
or justice, of God.

> I think we do better if we call him 'supersapientia,'
> 'superiustitia,' and so on, just as we call him
> 'supersubstantia.'...We speak more accurately if
> we deny all things of him than if we affirm any one
> of them.

Isaac then distinguishes two kinds of theology. In the light of
the 'divine theology' God neither is nor has substance or wisdom. But
we have a 'rational theology,' poor and confined, by which we say that
God is indeed both the one thing and the other. However, we are not

restricted to choosing between these two. There is another: a 'sym-

bolic theology,' which may even be called sensual. God is called

'heaven and earth, sun, fire, lion, ox, wood, stone, gold.'

> There is a likeness in the nature, function or
> use, so that those things are said of God with
> all the less restraint, in that none of them is
> said of him in its strict and proper sense....
> Wanting to speak of the unspeakable, of whom
> nothing can be said with literal accuracy, we
> say what we can. We have no option but to keep
> silence or to use words that are borrowed.[4]

Isaac's distinctions were not original. There was of course a

tradition, centuries old already, which relied largely upon the symbol,

and took symbolic theology for granted.[5] Also, Isaac was one of the

few in his time—surprisingly almost alone among the Cistercians—who

was familiar with the idea from the Celestial Hierarchy of Denys the

Areopagite.

> There are those [says Denys] who hymn the blessed-
> ness of the superessential Godhead as Word, Wisdom,
> Essence, thus manifesting the Divine Reason and
> Wisdom, that very Existence which is the true
> cause of existence for all things that are, fash-
> ioning it for us as Light, giving it the name of
> Life.[6]

So far so good, Denys then seems to say, provided that we acknow-

ledge that this venerable terminology falls infinitely short of the

Reality to which we want to give expression. So he prefers a supra-

mundane ('hyper-cosmic' is his word) expression of what God is—or

more properly, expression of what he is not. The inspired writers

speak better of God, when they say that he is invisible, unlimited,
infinite.[7]

But neither does Denys leave us with the choice between predicating of God something which is immeasurably inadequate, as 'Wisdom,' or
on the other hand of saying only what God is not: 'infinite,' that is,
without limits. So we arrive at the principle of symbolic theology.

If the symbol which we use to express what is divine, or nearest
to God, be of the noblest order, there is the danger that some will be
deceived and think that they have succeeded in conceiving and expressing
the reality. The further the symbol be removed from this reality, the
less the danger of deception. In the highest order of image we hear of
the Sun of Justice, Morning Star and unveiled Light. In the lowest we
have animal imagery: the Lion, Panther, Leopard, the Bear rushing upon
its prey. It is interesting to remember that Denys would have been
acquainted with the ancient Physiologus, the precursor of the twelfth-
century Bestiary, known and used by the Cistercians, at least in England.[8]

There are also the images called intermediate: as Fire which does
not consume, and Water which brings fullness of Life. The Sweet Oint-
ment and Corner-Stone are left with the animals in the lowest order.[9]

Our Cistercian Fathers, then elaborated a treatment which Isaac
recognized as a true theology, as Denys had seven centuries before him.

This was only because the Cistercians had their roots in Scripture
and Tradition. Denys had done no more than give a systematic account
of a way of knowing God and speaking about him which had been prac-
tised for centuries even before his time. It would be taken for granted long afterwards, until that other theology, called by Denys 'philosophical and demonstrative' would so prevail that what he seemed to
regard as the nobler kind, 'symbolic, initiating into mysteries,'
would come to be held of little account.[10]

We have grown up--at least the older among us--surrounded by a
mentality which has cast such a theology aside as childish phantasy.
At the moment we are concerned not directly or precisely with the
much discussed 'senses' of Scripture, but rather with different kinds
of theology, a symbolic as opposed to a rational. Scripture itself
uses the symbolic language, or else we borrow the persons and events
of the scriptural narrative to express profound truths. Whether or
not we are thereby laying ourselves open to the charge of free accommo-
dation, we are nonetheless following an age-long tradition. There are
indeed signs that in our own day the somewhat exclusively rational approach has brought disappointment, and the symbolic is coming back
into its own.[11]

If the greatest of the Cistercians are strangely unfamiliar with
Denys,[12] they know well one who made constant and striking use of the

symbolic way: St Gregory the Great. Whether or not they have taken
his tomes from their library shelves, they know him through their
liturgy.[13] It is from the readings in choir that they know of Christ
as the Axe, held by the wooden handle of his Manhood, striking with the
iron of his Godhead;[14] the Fish, upon whose broiled flesh they feed at
the lake-side;[15] Honey, for the honey saturating the wax is the godhead in the manhood;[16] the Sun reflected in the Moon which is the
Church.[17]

   So Aelred of Rievaulx is using a traditional idiom when he writes
a sermon On the Three Coats of Joseph, and, in the youth arrayed in
the coat of many colours which his Father has made for him, sees God
the Son made Man in Mary's womb.[18] For Guerric of Igny, Christ growing
in us is Bud, Flower and Fruit;[19] the Love which has been born in Mary,
but always abiding in her is spread abroad, is the Fountain sealed in
the garden of chastity, but pouring out its waters for those who thirst
in the streets and squares of the city.[20]

   Two instincts are basic in man, or rather they form one root from
which all the others grow. He must keep alive, so he must eat and
drink. Since he will some day die, he must have successors if human
life is to continue upon earth. So the attraction of man to woman, a
good certainly in its own right, is still ordered to the propagation
of the species.

The monks for whom our Cistercian Fathers wrote could not deny
hemselves food and drink, but they were at pains to restrict it, even
egarding their eating and drinking as a regrettable necessity.   The
leasure of conjugal union they renounced absolutely.   Yet even those
piritual teachers who were hardest on the flesh were too good psycho-
ogists to think that rigorous inhibition was the final solution of
he problem.   Knowing that the desires and instincts were there, they
ere also conscious that spiritual interest could accrue to this capi-
al.

It can be noted that we are now leaving aside christological
ymbolism as such and are concerned with means to be used for the at-
ainment of our end.   The means however--to have recourse to another
ymbol--is a way to be travelled, and in fact no other than Christ
imself.

Bernard tells us that he has needed to have at his command spir-
tual food, a kitchen and a fire, that he has spent a whole night pre-
aring the banquet.   He must now give out to us what he has prepared,
it he is only the refectory servant.   He has had to beg from our Lord
d Father; it is the Father who now feeds us with the living bread
rom heaven.   This food is doing the Father's will, as Christ said to
is disciples; every word that comes from the mouth of God, as he an-
ered the Tempter; the consummation of this, as he promised, the

sacrament of his Body and Blood on the table of the Altar.[21]

A Cistercian of a later generation, Baldwin, abbot of the English monastery of Ford and archbishop of Canterbury, wrote one of the early treatises on the Eucharist. His De sacramento altaris is a developed commentary upon a series of scriptural texts, and it is only to be expected that the theme throughout should be that of food and drink. If any creature is living--even fire, he says--that is because there is a food to sustain its life. All the bodily senses, even the higher faculties of memory, understanding and will, seek what will nourish and delight them. The apostate angels hunger for lost souls; their victims tear and devour one another. The good angels feed upon the sight, praise and love of God. The just in this life hunger and thirst after justice, above all after the one who is the author of all justice and has said to them: 'I am the living bread.' This is by way of introduction to a commentary on St John's record of the eucharistic discourse,[22] and leads up to Christ's insistence that we must eat his Flesh and drink his Blood. It is done in two ways: first by our faith in his mysteries--'believe and you have eaten,' in the words of St Augustine;[23] secondly by the sacramental eating and drinking of his Body and Blood.[24]

When St Bernard turned his attention to the Song of Songs, he was of course in a tradition hallowed by many centuries. He knew in particu lar the small part of Origen's homilies and commentary which had sur-

vived, and whatever had come to him under the name of St Gregory the

Great.   Of Bernard's early sermons, all of them given by way of intro-

duction to that parable of divine and human love, the seventh is spe-

cially to our purpose.   He is still commenting on the text: 'Let him

kiss me with the kiss of his mouth.'

> Never have been found names so tender as these for
> describing exchanges of love between the Word and
> the Soul; never names so tender as these of Bride
> and Bridegroom.   With them all things are in
> common, nothing withheld by one from the other.
> The two have a single heritage, one table, house
> and bed, even one flesh....She loves who asks for
> the kiss--not freedom, temporal gain, right of
> inheritance, not even doctrine--it is the kiss
> she asks, speaking as a Bride who has kept chas-
> tity inviolate, whose every breath is holy love,
> who cannot keep hidden the flame which devours
> her....Without introduction or craving a benev-
> olent hearing, from the fulness of her heart with
> boldness undisguised, she breaks into that cry:
> 'Let him kiss me with the kiss of his mouth.'
> She loves chastely who seeks no other gift from
> him, but him alone whom she loves.   That is a
> holy love, which comes not from lust of the
> flesh, but from purity of spirit.[25]

This imagery is to be carried to its conclusion.   The union of

man and wife must be fruitful, and the offspring be nourished at the

breasts of the Spouse.   John, another abbot of Ford, gives us perhaps

the fullest and most explicit development of the theme.   The Spouse

has no breasts, until she has been privileged to conceive from the

embrace of Christ, her lawful husband.   But the day awaited comes:

> The Soul, then, happily married to the Word of
> God, has conceived by the Holy Spirit. Made
> fruitful by that seed of divine offspring which
> is charity, she cherishes it in the womb of
> loving desire. At once, that she may give
> nourishment to the life begun within her, her
> breasts are filled by the same Spirit, for he
> who has given her a child will take care of
> its growth. What are those two breasts, at
> which the sacred offspring of divine love is
> weaned and raised to manhood, but frequent med-
> itation on the God to be loved, prayer raised
> up to him watchful and unremitting? The bosom
> of any who loves must grow heavy with these
> breasts, that love may trust and may find there
> its nourishment.[26]

What is this offspring, nourished at the breasts of the Spouse?

It may be undoubtedly the souls committed to the preacher's care.[27]

But, in the thought of John of Ford, it is not necessary that the

fruitful Spouse should be exercising this pastoral office. The Infant

conceived in her womb is in the first place Divine Love (divini amoris

sacer fetus); the milk from those breasts is for the nourishment of

Charity (affluit lacte in alimoniam caritatis).[28]

The imagery of food and drink, then of the loving embrace, has

brought us back to Christ: to that love which is perfectly realized

between God and Man only in the sending of his Son.[29] But the sending

and receiving cannot remain something external. That to which we are

to give birth is Christ himself. It is the thought of Saint Paul and

of Saint Augustine, expanded by Guerric of Igny: we are to share the

motherhood of Mary, give birth to Christ and foster his life within ourselves.[30]   Thus begotten by us, and at the same time imparting to

us his life, he brings us now to a glimpse of that Vision which will

leave no room for speculation; fullness of Reality such that the Symbol

will have done its work and can be laid aside.

NOTES

1. The passage in its entirety is Ovid, Metamorphoses X, 1-85. The
    two short excerpts given here are taken from the translation by
    Mary M. Innes, in Penguin series (1955). All other translations
    are my own.

2. Leclercq, Henri, "Orphée," in Dictionnaire d'Archéologie chrétienne
    et de Liturgie 12/2, 2735-55.

3. Amedeus of Lausanne, De laudibus B. Mariae, hom. 4; SC 72:110-12.
    It remains true that the allegorization of pagan myths is one thing;
    the recognition of types in the inspired Scriptures is another. In
    a short study of the kind presented here, we need to guard against
    the gross over-simplification discussed by Henri de Lubac in
    Exégèse médiévale II, 2, ch. 8/1: Allégorie et allégorie, pp.
    125-49.

4. Isaac of Stella, Sermo 22; PL 194:1762.

5. John Scotus Eriugena, two centuries earlier, had given a very
    clear account of the theologies which Isaac called 'divine' and
    'rational.' Scotus had called them 'affirmative' and 'negative,'
    using the Greek words Kataphatikē and apophatikē; De divisione
    naturae (Periphyseôn) I; PL 122:458. In this place he did not
    make a clear distinction between the 'divine' theology and the
    'symbolic.' This is not to say that he was unaware of the

distinction; he had of course both translated and commented upon
Denys' De hierarchia coelesti. For the possible influence of
Eriugena on William of St Thierry, more evidently upon Isaac,
see the unpublished paper presented to the Cistercian-Orthodox
Symposium of 1973 by I. P. Sheldon-Williams: "Eriugena and Cîteaux."

6. Denys the Areopagite, Hierarchia coelestis II, 3; SC 58:78.

7. It is interesting to find that 'infinite,' 'without limits' (apeiros,
achōrētos) are classed by Denys as negative and apophatic
predications. A limit is itself a negation. If the negation is
denied, we have something positive, so that 'infinite' conveys to
us the idea of 'fullness of Being.' But that is precisely the point
of apophatic theology. Anything that we predicate of God positively (essence, being), taken as it is from our experience, falls
immeasurably short of what God is. By then proceeding to deny it
of him, we come nearer to the Fullness of Reality.

8. See Hosea 5:14; 13:7, 8. I have given some account both of the
ancient Physiologus and of the medieval development in a study:
"The English Cistercians and the Bestiary," Bulletin of the John
Rylands Library 39 (September 1956) 146-70.

9. Denys, Hierarchia coelestis II, 2-5; SC 58:75-85.

10. Denys, Letter 9, to Titus; PG 3:1103-114. Denys seems to speak
in the opening lines of a work which he has entitled Symbolic

Theology. If it ever existed, it has not survived.

11. Indeed it may be an understatement to say that 'there are signs,'
     when we have before us the volumes of de Lubac's Exégèse médiévale,
     to which reference has been made already (two volumes in four,
     1959-1964). The author seemed conscious, in the Preface to his
     first volume, that he was undertaking to build up the waste places.
     Father (now Cardinal) Daniélou some years earlier had significantly
     begun the series Sources chrétiennes with the Life of Moses by
     Gregory of Nyssa (editions in 1942 and 1955).

12. As for the extent of their familiarity, one could hardly do better
     than refer to Bernard McGinn, "Pseudo-Dionysius and the Early
     Cistercians," in One Yet Two: Monastic Tradition East and West,
     ed. M. Basil Pennington, CS 29 (Kalamazoo, Michigan, 1976) 200-41.

13. This is clear from the "St Stephen's Breviary." See ASOC, 2
     (1946) 146-47; Coll. 20 (1958) 80. I understand that the text
     will be edited by ASOC. Meanwhile it has been possible to study
     the Breviary in microfilm. Most of the gospel homilies are drawn
     from Gregory or Bede. For anything that I know about the ancient
     lectionaries I am indebted to the good services of Father Chrysogon
     Waddell of Gethsemani Abbey, Kentucky. We hope that we shall not
     have to wait too long until the fruit of his researches is availabl
     in print.

14. Gregory, _Homiliae in Evangelia_ 20, n. 10; PL 76:1164C. Such
     symbols referred to the twofold nature of Christ are to be used
     with caution. They easily make a Nestorian impression upon the
     Oriental Orthodox (that is, the non-Chalcedonians, sometimes
     called Monophysites). This is clear from many interventions
     published as a supplementary issue of _Wort und Wahrheit: Non-
     official Ecumenical Consultation between Theologians of the
     Oriental Orthodox Churches and the Roman Catholic Church_ (Vienna,
     1972).

15. Gregory, _Homiliae in Evangelia_ 24, n. 5; PL 76:1187A.

16. _Ibid._

17. _Ibid._, 30, n. 10; 1227A.

18. Aelred, _Sermo in annuntiatione de tribus tunicis Ioseph_ in _Ser-
     mones inediti beati Aelredi_ (ed. C. H. Talbot, 1952), pp. 83-89.

19. Guerric, Ann 2, n. 3; SC 202:134-36.

20. Guerric, Asspt 1, 3; SC 202:420. We cannot be sure whether
     Guerric knew the eloquent use of this fountain symbol made al-
     ready by Rupert of Deutz: _In Cantica Canticorum_, lib. 4; PL 168:
     899.

21. Bernard, OS, 1, 3; Op. S. Bern., 5:329.

22. Baldwin of Ford, _De sacramento altaris_; SC 93:238-44.

23. Augustine, _In Iohannis evangelium_, tr. 25, n. 12; CC 36:254.

24. Baldwin of Ford, De sacramento altaris; SC 93:272.

25. Bernard; SC, 7, 2.3; Op. S. Bern. 1:31-32.

26. John of Ford, SC, 111, n. 7; CC, continuatio medievalis 18:754.
     Hilary Costello (co-editor of the text with Edmund Mikkers) has
     commented on this and several texts of the kind ('copula amoris,'
     'copula coniugalis [nuptialis],' '...de legitimi viri amplexu con-
     cipere meruit'), in his article: "John of Ford and the Quest for
     Wisdom," Cîteaux, 23 (1972), 141-59 (see p. 150).

27. This obvious interpretation is clearly taken for granted by
     Bernard: SC, 9, 6; 10, 1.2; Op. S. Bern. 1:46, 48-49. See also
     in John of Ford the passionate and beautiful appeal of the children
     to the Mother who has given them birth: SC, 40, 4; CC, continuatio
     medievalis 17:296-97.

28. John of Ford, SC, 111, 7.8; CC, continuatio medievalis 18:754.
     Costello unites the two: 'This motherhood consists first of all
     in bringing the word to birth within her own soul by meditation
     and contemplation. At the same time it also consists in forming
     souls to Christ, since the true spiritual mother is anxious to gain
     souls and make them grow in their love of Christ.' Loc. cit.

29. 1 John 4:19.

30. Gal. 4:19. Places are cited from Origen, Augustine and Bede, in
     our Introduction to Guerric: SC, 166, 40, n. 4 (CF

8, p. xxxvii, no. 171). Guerric, Nat 3, 5; Ann 2, 4-5; SC 166:198; 202:138-42.

GUNTHER OF PAIRIS AND THE MAN OF GOD

Richard Spence
Syracuse University

The splendor, color, and violence of the crusades have intrigued

historians for centuries. Indeed, no other series of events in the

Middle Ages provides as much excitement, tragedy, and moral turpitude--

the crusades have something for every taste. Historians have depended

on the crusading chronicles to understand the individual crusades, but

these chronicles can tell us much more than just the flow of events.

In writing about the crusades, the chroniclers also reveal their atti-

tudes, prejudices and, most importantly, their world views.

One of the most important focal points for the historian to

consider when he works with crusade literature is the chronicler's

attitudes toward God and particularly God's role in human affairs.

One hitherto ignored chronicler, a Cistercian named Gunther of Pairis,

is an example of an early thirteenth-century author who vividly depicts

God's participation in human events. Gunther is important for this and

two other reasons: he was well-educated and in touch with the intellec-

tual innovations of his time, and he wrote a history of the Fourth Cru-

sade, the Historia Constanopolitana.[1] In his chronicle, Gunther tells

us not only about the events of the Fourth Crusade, but also he reveals

his spiritual values as he follows the actions of his abbot, Martin,

through the course of the crusade. We will concern ourselves with these

values to illuminate the metamorphosis of God's role in human affairs
and not with the events themselves.

The chroniclers, whether of the eleventh or the thirteenth centuries, saw the hand of God behind their efforts. The attempt to
understand human history in the light of God's plan and divine behavior
appeared as a continuing theme in the chronicles. But alterations occurred from chronicle to chronicle as new factors were introduced into
the crusading ideology of Urban II, who saw the crusade as a redemptive
holy war undertaken by the chosen people of God to aid their Christian
brethren in the East. Future alterations did not change the conception
that the crusade was an armed pilgrimage, but men's role in this divinely guided effort underwent a metamorphosis of interpretation in the
crusading chronicles. This change in emphasis is precisely what makes
the Historia important. For in Gunther's work the thirteenth-century
world view is spelled out in great detail.

Before detailing aspects of Gunther's contributions to crusade
ideology, we should be aware of the climate in which he composed his
work. In general, the cultural life of the twelfth and thirteenth
centuries was connected with theological developments in the growing
urban centers of France, although their influence manifested itself
in all parts of Europe. The central aspect of the ferment revolved
around dramatic changes in forms and expressions of Christian piety.

These were voiced as men discovered new modes of religious discussion and organization.[2] Some of the more notable aspects of this period of religious transformation were: the creation of a number of reform religious orders, most significant of which were the Carthusians and the Cistercians;[3] the application of dialectic to theological discussion and organization;[4] the compilations of canon law;[5] and a renewed interest in mystical theology, especially among the Cistercians.[6]

It is not our purpose to address ourselves to the ultimate meaning of the ferment of the twelfth and thirteenth centuries, but to a limited manifestation of these larger changes. Richard Southern, in his work Medieval Humanism and Other Studies, showed how man grew conscious of his own importance in the Christian cosmology, that is, man became the link between the finite world and its divine creator.[7] This process Southern termed 'medieval humanism,' a label which fits Gunther's description of the acts of Abbot Martin, who, as we shall soon see, consciously explored his relationship with the deity. The flowering of medieval humanism is indicative of a parallel shift in emphasis in medieval Christianity, which still retained the idea of divine judgment, but at the same time stressed God as the savior of mankind through the intercession of Jesus and Mary.[8]

The tradition of the earlier chronicles, typified by the Joshua and Judges concept of God as the inscrutable leader and chastiser of

his people as a collective body, showed a shift in emphasis,[9] and
in Gunther we see clearly a different interpretation of the deity's
role in human affairs. Indeed, the Historia demonstrates that man
can play a part in his own salvation. Gunther states this in his
first chapter when he said that he composed his history to show that
God desired Martin to bring the relics of the Pantocrater back to
Pairis.[10] Gunther also contends Martin knew that God had selected
him for his mission. As the army started out from Basel, Gunther
states that Martin was aware that he was the instrument of God, and
it is through this conscious appreciation of the divine plan that
Gunther demonstrates the impact of the twelfth- and thirteenth-century
milieu on his chronicle.[11] Gunther further defends Martin's motives
and states that one cannot judge that all of these deeds came about
accidently unless the great deeds of God in their splendor would be
disparaged by calumny.[12]

The idea of Gunther participating in his own salvation seems to
parallel the same conception in contemporary literature. Wolfram von
Eschenbach's Parzival illustrated this point. As the reader may re-
call, Parzival's rigid adherence to a mistaken notion of chivalry led
him to not ask his host in a strange castle after his health, a breach
which had long term consequences. The stranger, his uncle Anfortas,
king of the Grail, was doomed to suffer until his nephew asked him

what ailed him. Parzival's actions resulted in God's ordaining Parzival
to toil and struggle for five years before he met Anfortas' brother, a
hermit, who gradually unveiled Parzival's sins and misunderstandings.
Parzival confessed, was given absolution, and was able to go to the
Grail castle and ask his question. It is clear in Parzival that God
led him to the hermit because Parzival had earned grace by the tena-
cious conquest of doubt and despair.[13] Further, Parzival was aware
of this honor.

Gunther reflected similar thinking in the crusade chronicles, and
he often stresses the fact that Martin is earning grace by his acts.
On one such occasion, Gunther states that no believer should permit the
slightest doubt that God's grace was involved when so many great and
celebrated relics, despite countless hindrances, were brought to Pairis.
He contends that Martin's humble demeanor was a key factor: '...This
certainly was no coincidence, but was of divine origin.'[14]

Thus, in Gunther's work, we can discern elements of the new theological view of the relationship of man and God found elsewhere in the
thirteenth century. Specifically, the Historia depicts the mentioned
reciprocal dialogue between man and his creator, a dialogue which always existed but one in which the earlier chronicles did not always
recognize the human element. Gunther's chronicle probed Martin's relationship with God, and as a result the protagonist of his chronicle

emerged as more than an individual working under divine guidance.

We do not claim that Gunther is one of the intellectual giants
of the period in which he lived. Hence we are not concerned here with
an innovator such as St Bernard, but with the thoughts of a man who
probably, like Wolfram, represented the popularization of the ideas
of his milieu. For Gunther was not writing about speculative theology,
although he probably had some acquaintanceship with it as he was well-
educated,[15] but with the more mundane task of recording the spiritual
progress of the armed pilgrimage, especially the deeds of Martin. It
might seem that since Gunther wrote the Historia at Martin's behest,
we must be aware of a bias of patronage. Admittedly, his work reveals
such a bias, but what is more important for us is that Gunther also
illustrated the mores of his society, which in turn, although perhaps
indirectly, displayed the theological innovations of his epoch.

Gunther defined human-divine relationships of two sorts.[16] First,
there were men of pride used by God to accomplish his purpose, but who
did not possess the pious humility to be men of God. Therefore, although a man of pride might enact the divine will, he was not aware of
this fact as would be a man of God. The man of God, like Abbot Martin
of Pairis, was blessed with the task of revealing, through his deeds,
aspects of the divine plan. The man of pride, apparently, was never cog-
nizant of the Deity's intentions or that he was being used to further

God's design.[17]

    We do not intend to give the impression that Gunther's work did
not include traditional interpretations as well as innovations. While
preaching the cross at Basel, Martin presented himself as the mouth-
piece of Christ (as did Urban II in 1095). He spoke to the assembled
throng saying:

> Listen to me, my lords and brothers. Listen
> to me for the words are not mine but Christ's.
> He is the origin of these words and I am but
> his fragile instrument. Today Christ speaks
> to you through my mouth and bemoans his
> injuries.[18]

Here Martin pleaded Christ's cause and, in this respect, was a means
to further the divine plan. At the same time, because he was aware of
this role, Martin was also a man of God.[19] When Martin was ordained
to bring relics out of the corrupt city of Constantinople, he might
have been merely a vehicle for enhancing the divine will. But Martin,
according to Gunther, due to his pious and humble personality, possessed the mark of a man of God.[20] Martin's foreordained actions,
perpetrated on behalf of the City of God, not only enhanced the divine
plan, but his deeds also augmented his own salvation.[21] This would
not have occurred if he merely had been a man of pride, and God showed
his favor by entrusting the relics of the Pantocrater to the abbot of
Pairis.

    In the Second Crusade, the Emperor Manual, who many Latins felt

was perfidious as a Christian and as an ally, was seen as God's instrument when he despoiled the city of Adalia for its gold and silver,
which that city had extorted from pilgrims in exchange for ships and
a market. Odo of Deuil stated: 'Thus, God and he [Manual] held opposite opinions, but both punished the city.'[22] In the Third Crusade,
Saladin was also an instrument of God, not unlike the Philistines,
Assyrians, or Neo-Babylonians of the Old Testament, in punishing those
Christians in the Holy Land who departed from His teachings.[23] During
the Fourth Crusade, Boniface de Montferrat, the leader of the crusade
and perhaps the instigator of its diversions,[24] served God's purpose
in a two-fold fashion: first by conquering Constantinople so that
Martin could obtain the relics and, secondly, by punishing the Greeks
for their heresy and pride. However, Saladin, Manual, and Boniface
were men of pride and belonged to the City of Man by virtue of their
arrogance. They were not men of God. Gunther specifically states in
the opening passage of the Historia that great and arduous deeds are
to be cherished, especially those which God reveals through humble
persons, both through men who are in themselves deeply humble and also
through others who are less humble but who are destined for great things.[25]

Martin, because of his piety, was singled out as an individual and
presented a contrast to the central characters in other chronicles, as
most other crusading chronicles centered around a king or a mass of

pilgrims under the direction of God. Although Gunther did portray Martin as the leader of the German contingent and one of the five envoys to Innocent III after the sack of Zara, Martin was actually a man of minor position in the Fourth Crusade and became the center of attention only in Gunther's work as he participated in his own salvation under the guidance and protection of God. Gunther's chronicle was singular in that it made no attempt to fill in the gaps left in the narrative caused by Martin's departure from the body of the crusade. This left the impression that the performance of God's will by Martin was more important than the chronology of events performed by God's army.

In addition to the above observations, Martin was shown as a man, having the faults of mortal men. His eagerness for relics seems to annoy Gunther.[26] Yet, one of the most interesting portions of the chronicle relates Martin's hunger for relics. Gunther states that the gates of Constantinople lay open and

> Now the victors sacked the city, which they,
> under the law of war, considered as their right
> to freely plunder. Abbot Martin also began to
> think of spoils and decided not to leave empty
> handed when all the others became enriched. His
> hands stretched out after consecrated plunder as
> he thought it unworthy that such hands should
> take common worldly spoils to rest upon. There-
> fore, he planned to bring together a part of the
> holy relics, which he thought were in the city
> in great numbers.[27]

Gunther gives us a picture of Martin arriving at the Pantocrater, out of breath, but still eager. After frightening a priest into revealing the location of relics, Gunther relates:

> When he now (if I am permitted to say), stuffed each person [his chaplains], he hurried to the ships. He saw friends and acquaintances, who had just run from the ships to get booty, and they asked him jokingly whether he had plundered something himself and with what kind of things he burdened himself. But, he said, with his customary hearty manner, the friendly words, 'It goes well with us...'[28]

and hurried to his ship.

Gunther's attitude toward Martin indicated an individualized personality, not unlike Joinville's description of St Louis, although Joinville's biography at times reads like a hagiography. Geoffrey de Vinsauf, a chronicler of the Third Crusade, pictures Richard of England as a one-dimensional implement of God, because of his efficient slaughtering of heathens, but unfortunately Richard never went beyond that stage in his salvation. This was sufficient to the mind of Chanson de Geste Christianity.[29] It was hardly edifying from the view of the twelfth and thirteenth centuries, which stressed the individual and his works in relation to the divine.

Abbot Martin of Pairis was a man destined to illuminate God's purpose on earth while earning his salvation. The distinction between the man of pride and the man of God is a useful one to use when read-

ing the chronicles. Furthermore, the uniting of the man of God with
the man of pride was the link between the older and newer concept of
man in the chronicles. God's inscrutable judgment is a focal point
in the earlier crusading works. God tried men's souls, testing his
army collectively through tribulation and in doing so purified it.
This is the approach of Raymond d'Agulers, the Gesta, Fulcher of
Chartres, and Richard Devizes. The role of God received a different
connotation in the chronicles of Robert of Clari, Geoffrey Villehar-
douin, and Geoffrey de Joinville. In the later chronicles, those who
are saved are often judged worthy directly by Christ or even Mary,
which illustrates a change of ideology at least indirectly affected
by the theological innovations of Gunther's era. This change in emphasis, clearly depicted by Gunther, evolved from the twelfth and thirteenth centuries' probing of man's relationship to God and is indicative
of a new emphasis in Christianity. Gunther's chronicle thus evidenced
a contemporary view of the role of God in his relationship with individual men.

In Martin's pursuit of divine objectives, God appears less inscrutable than in earlier chronicles,[30] for we know that Martin, as a
man of God, is on a divinely ordained mission. It was Gunther's intention to justify the taking of relics from Constantinople, but the
Historia is also an example of the new emphasis in Christianity in which

man and God worked together to effect Martin's salvation. Finally, it

was Gunther's aim that Martin's deeds be recorded so that, when the

faithful heard his story and saw his relics at Pairis, they might recog-

nize that Abbot Martin took part in an aspect of the divine plan.

NOTES

1. Gunther of Pairis, Historia Constantinopolitana, seu de expugna-
    tione urbis Constantinopolitianae, unde inter alias reliquias,
    magna pars sancte crucis in Alemanniam est alata, in Paul Riant,
    Exuviae Sacrae Constantinopoltanae (Geneva, 1870-1878) I, 57-
    126. About his education, Gunther states: 'Scripsit autem hanc
    historiam Magister Guntherus quidam, tunc monachus, prius autem
    scholasticus, vir admodum liberaliter eruditus...,' Historia, p.
    125.

2. Bede Lackner, The Eleventh-Century Background of Cîteaux
    Washington, D.C., 1972).

3. Christopher Brooke, The Twelfth Century Renaissance (Norwich,
    England, 1969).

4. Etienne Gilson, Reason and Revelation in the Middle Ages (New
    York, 1938).

5. Steven Kuttner, Harmony from Dissonance: An Interpretation of
    Medieval Canon Law. (Latrobe, Pennsylvania, 1960).

6. Amedée Hallier, The Monastic Theology of Aelred of Rievaulx
    (Spencer, Massachusetts, 1969).

7. Richard W. Southern, Medieval Humanism and Other Studies (New
    York, 1970) p. 50.

8. For an analysis of this topic see Henry Adams, Mont-Saint-Michel

and Chartres (Garden City, New York, 1933).

9. According to the chronicles of the First Crusade, Christians had
    little to say about their ultimate salvation or damnation, as
    their fate was already known to God. Fulcher of Chartres, A
    History of the Expedition to Jerusalem, ed. Harold S. Fink
    (Knoxville, 1969) p. 97; Gesta Francorum et aliorum hierosoli-
    mitanorum, ed. Rosalind Hill (New York, 1962) pp. 41, 74; Raymond
    d'Aguilers, Historia Francorum qui ceperunt Iherusalem, edd. John
    and Laurita Hill (Philadelphia, 1968) p. 40. This does not imply
    predestination since men were still depicted as being capable of
    making choices--usually the wrong ones. Unless the crusaders re-
    mained mindful of God's aid, punishment was swift. Raymond d'Agui-
    lers notes that the crusaders were unmindful of God's blessing
    which had allowed them to take Antioch, and thus they were besieged
    by the Turks as punishment. Raymond, Historia, p. 48; similar
    sentiments are found in the Gesta, p. 34; William of Tyre, Godeffroy
    of Bologne (London, 1893) p. 149.

10. Gunther, Historia: '...Neque tamen omnino poterimus reticere, ne
    Deo, quo auctore hec gesta sunt, qui suos humiles exaltare consue-
    vit, evidentem faciamus iniuriam. Quapropter ita inter utrumque
    calamum temperare curabimus, ut et Dei magnalia, que per eum gesta
    sunt, non lateant et ipse in sua humilitate inoffensus permaneat'
    (p. 58).

11. Gunther, _Historia_: 'Postea valedicens clero et populo eiusdem
     civitatis, a quibus plurimum diligebatur, leto vultu & mente
     impavida, sancte profectionis laborem cum sociis aggressus est:
     qua ex re illud coniicere possumus, hominem Dei nescio quid magni
     iam tunc in animo concepisse, et que Deus per ipsum facturas erat,
     certo iam mentu augurio, presagire' (p. 67).

12. Gunther, _Historia_: 'Nullus ergo, ut alia multa, ita hoc fortuito
     estimet evenisse; quod utique nil aliud esset, nisi magnis Dei
     operibus debitum splendorem calumniando detrahere' (p. 123).

13. Wolfram von Eschenbach, _Parzival_ (New York, 1961) p. 268;
     Brooke, _Renaissance_, pp. 181-82.

14. Gunther, _Historia_: 'Nemo igitur fidelis aliud, vel credere
     debet, vel etiam opinari, quam hoc actum esse divine gratie
     respectu, ut tot et tante, tam celebres reliquie, per hominem,
     seipsum in tanta humilitate conservantem, inter tot rerum im-
     pedimenta, ad nostram pervenirent ecclesiam....Hec omnia rofecto
     non esse casus fortuitos, sed muneris divini...' (p. 123).

15. See n. 1 above.

16. Gunther, _Historia_: 'Specialiter tamen ea mirari consuevimus,
     que magna et ardua per humiles personas, illorum scilicet hominum
     qui, et apud seipsos per humilitatem in imo sunt, et apud alios
     tantis rebus minus putantur ydonei, eadem virtus divina dignatur

ostendere' (p. 57); 'Inveniet siquidem ibi res magnas et celebres

et que, nisi divino issu, nullantenus vel fieri, vel accidere po-

tuerunt...' (p. 59).

17. See nn. 11, 14 above, especially n. 11 where Martin seems aware of his role.

18. Gunther, Historia: Verbum mihi ad vos, domini mei et fratres mei,

verbum mihi ad vos! non meum utique, sed Christi. Christus ipse

verborum auctor est; ego fragile instrumentum; Christus vos hodie

per os meum suis alloquitur verbis, suas vobis deplorat iniurias'

(p. 62).

19. Gunther, Historia: '...Qua ex re illud coniicere possumus, homi-

nem Dei nescio quid magni iam tunc in animo concepisse, et que

Deus per ipsum facturus erat, certo iam mentis augurio, presagire'

(p. 67).

20. Ibid.

21. Gunther, Historia: 'De his autem ipsis celestis gratie donis,

que Dominus iam sepissime dominico famulo suo, abbati Martino,

et per ipsum ecclesie Parisiensi contulerat...' (p. 125). This

stress on Martin's role as an individual is comparable to Joinville's

treatment of Louis IX and contrasts the role of individuals in most

earlier chronicles. This is particularly apparent in the role of

miracles and relics. In the chronicles of the First and Third Cru-

sades (Odo of Deuil states that he omits them because he does not

wish to distract the reader from his narrative), relics and miracles occurred to demonstrate the efficacy of the Christian cause
and benefited the army as a whole. The Historia depicts several
miracles through which God showed his protection of Martin and
his relics, thus he showed his favor to the individual, the man
of God. Even Gunther's portrayal of Martin stealing relics is
viewed as a demonstration of Martin's piety rather than the army's
spiritual worthiness.

22. Odo of Deuil, The Journey of Louis VII to the East, ed. Virginia
     Berry (New York, 1948) p. 143.

23. Geofrey Vinsauf, Chronicles of the Crusades (London, 1871) pp.
     69-70.

24. Donald Queller, The Latin Conquest of Constantinople (New York
     1971); Paul Riant, "Le Changement de Direction de la IVe Croisade,"
     Revue des Questions Historiques XVII (1877) 321-74, discusses the
     culpability of Boniface and other related issues.

25. See n. 16 above.

26. Gunther, Historia, pp. 104-107; A. J. Andrea, "Abbot Martin
     and the Fourth Crusade," a paper presented at the Sixth Conference
     of Medieval Studies, Kalamazoo, Michigan, 1971.

27. Gunther, Historia, pp. 104-107.

28. Ibid.

29. By <u>Chanson de Geste</u> Christianity we refer to the view of religious
     faith put forth in the early chronicles. Their structure and theme,
     which was the simple narration of the war of Christians against pa-
     gans as a depiction of the struggle between good and evil, is close-
     ly modeled (in the case of Raymond d'Aguilers copied), after the
     literary genre of the <u>Chanson de Geste</u>. In formal Christian ex-
     pression, such as that expressed by the Cluniacs, monasticism of
     the pre-twelfth century also displayed a similar preoccupation with
     saints who defended the Christian faith. This was a militant
     Christianity.

30. See n. 21 above.

THE FOUNDATION AND EARLY HISTORY OF THE MONASTERY

OF SILVANÈS: THE ECONOMIC REALITY

Constance H. Berman
The University of Wisconsin, Madison

In 1132 a group of pious men founded a hermitage in the valley of
Silvanès.[1] This valley lay in the southern hills of the French province
of the Rouergue, halfway between the coastal plain of Languedoc and the
high plateau of central France. Several years after coming to that place
these holy men sought to affiliate their house with a religious order
and applied to the nearest Cistercian abbey, Mazan, to the east in the
Vivarais. They completed a year of novitiate there at Mazan before
they returned to found the abbey of Silvanès in 1136. Silvanès' early
years were auspicious, but the house never became large or powerful.
Twenty years after its foundation its inhabitants numbered only twenty
or twenty-one religious and between forty-five and fifty lay brethren
(conversi).[2] Silvanès' growth within the Rouergue was soon limited by
the foundation of the Cistercian houses of Bonneval in 1157 and Bonnecombe
in 1166, which came to share predominance in the central parts of the
Rouergue.[3] More immediate competition came from the military-religious
orders, especially those on the Causse de Larzac.[4] Finally, Silvanès
was perhaps unfortunate in its political ties with the Trencavel family
of Béziers rather than with the more powerful counts of Toulouse or those
of Rodez.[5]

Although outstripped in growth by other Cistercian houses of

southern France, Silvanès interests the economic historian because administrative documents have survived which illuminate the abbey's foundation as well as its early economy. These were edited and published
in 1910 by the local historian P.-A. Verlaguet. Most important are the
nearly five hundred charters dating from the twelfth century which have
survived in the copies included in a cartulary redacted by the monks of
Silvanès shortly after the transactions occurred.[6] In addition there
are charters from various local notarial cartularies and charters which
were copied by a seventeenth-century royal commission. Among the latter
was a chronicle recounting the foundation of Silvanès.[7] Although the
original of the chronicle has not been found, correspondence between
the author, a monk named Hugh Francigena, and the bishop of Lodève suggests that this is an authentic narrative record from the third quarter
of the twelfth century.[8]

    The Latin chronicle relates the conversion of a knight from the
region of Lodève, Pons de Léras, and details his subsequent foundation
of Silvanès. Its composition between 1161 and 1171 by Hugh Francigena
under the direction of the abbot Pons I, followed close upon the events
themselves; nevertheless it is not wholly reliable.[9] The author asserts
that he recounts only what he had heard of the foundation from the abbot
or the participants, but his work is predominately literary, permeated
with biblical allusions and the typical elements of medieval prose.
The narrative elaborately compares Silvanès to a tree in the forest

growing strong in the care of the "heavenly gardener."[10] The conversion

of the knight Pons de Léras parallels the life and passion of Jesus

Christ as well as encompassing many of the obligatory signs and miracles

of the typical saint's life.[11] Its literary devices prove that this is

not a totally factual document. Its content suggests that it is a tract

written for the promotion of Pons de Léras to sainthood. The chronicle's

stress on his poverty, saintliness and adherence to Cistercian virtues

was not without effect, for Pons de Léras was elevated to the rank of

beatus among the Cistercians, and his feast was celebrated in Lodève.[12]

Although such a propagandistic piece probably contains an element of

truth, it must be used with care.

The administrative documents for Silvanès are more reliable. The

cartulary, containing 462 charters for the years 1132 to 1169, appears

from internal evidence to be a virtually complete record of the land

transactions of the abbey in that period. The cartulary was compiled

in the third quarter of the twelfth century and was the working record

of the abbey in its land acquisitions.[13] In the original, charters were

organized by grange and cross-referenced for ease in upholding claims

and determining rights. In their careful compilation of records of the

abbey's land conveyances, the monks of Silvanès unintentionally provided

the historian with a more valuable and more objective source for their

early history than the chronicle which they wrote describing their foun-

dation. In some cases the cartulary provides evidence in direct contradiction to the chronicle, particularly on the question of whether clearance and settlement in the region had preceded the Cistercian arrival. The record of the chronicle must be supplemented and qualified by the less biased evidence of the cartulary.

The Cistercian statutes specify a monastic site, "in civitatibus castellis, villis, nulla nostra construenda sunt coenobia, sed in locis a conversatione hominum remotis."[14] The chronicle of Silvanès presents a similar picture of that abbey's location. According to the chronicle, after the conversion of Pons de Léras, he gathered a band of followers who went on pilgrimages with him before seeking a deserted site where they could serve God and support themselves by manual labor. They refused revenues from the estates and churches offered by many admirers, choosing instead to follow a simple life in the wilderness. Receiving permission from the bishop of Rodez to settle somewhere in his diocese, they eventually found the valley of Silvanès in the region of Camarès. There they were granted a site by the nobleman Arnaud de Ponte, who had lordship over the area, and there they built their first dwellings in the mansus of Teron.[15] The chronicle suggests that this was a wild and dangerous place where their only neighbors were wild animals. It was a place

> In quo casulas propriis manibus fabricantes man-
> serunt, bestiis sociati, quotidiano tamen labori
> insistentes, dumeta falcibus resecantes, terram
> ligonibus proscindentes, locum habitabilem ex
> inhabitabili reddiderunt.16

Such a place coincides with the ideal presented in the Cistercian

statutes, but it is a misleading picture of the valley of Silvanès in

1132.[17]

The cartulary of Silvanès proves beyond doubt that the valley of

Silvanès and the sites of most of the granges acquired by the abbey

were not wilderness areas when Pons de Léras and his followers arrived

there to pursue their religious lives. Personal names and place names,

the existence of churches, the legal terminology describing land units

and rights over land, the existence of political and ecclesiastical

taxes, all predicate the existence of lords and peasants in the region

for a number of generations before the Cistercians arrived. Thus, in

the southern Rouergue where Silvanès was founded, the Cistercians were

not primarily engaged in the opening of new lands by clearance and re-

clamation on what one historian has labeled an 'internal frontier.'[18]

The charters make it clear that the Cistercians of Silvanès had been

preceded in the activities of défrichement by anonymous lords and pea-

sants.[19] Solitude, if they found it, was the creation of their own

efforts to create large, compact, isolated holdings, and if they had no

neighbors in the area it was because they had successfully bought out

other landholders Such are the conclusions which must be drawn from

the cartulary evidence, despite the considerable obfuscation of its

legal terminology. In those documents there is extensive evidence of

previous settlement and cultivation in the valley of Silvanès and its
environs; this paper will cite only a few examples.

As the French geographer Charles Higounet has pointed out, the
Rouergue had been more thoroughly influenced by Carolingian institutions
than most of the rest of southwestern France.[20] Because of this, by the
eleventh century a full-fledged variety of seigneurialism not unlike
that of northern France had developed there.[21] Documents from the monastery of Vabres in Camarès make it clear that this seigneurialism existed even in the southern reaches of the province and in the vicinity
where the abbey of Silvanès and its granges were founded in the mid-
twelfth century.[22] Documents from the cartulary of Silvanès, as well
as charters from other Cistercian houses in the Rouergue, suggest that
by the mid-twelfth century this seigneurialism had begun to break down.
This is documented in the fragmentation of both lordship and usufruct
and in the scattering of rights among many individuals.[23] Silvanès'
charters also show that prior to the Cistercian arrival in the area,
an expansion of the previous bounds of settlement into adjacent forest
and wastelands had taken place. Such expansion is demonstrated by the
presence of land units such as the appendaria. As far as the documents
show, the appendaria was a land unit similar to the mansus or caputmansus; the later provenance of this addition to the arable or assart
is suggested by the term itself.[24] Other smaller land units, mostly

plots for vines and gardens, also seem to have been brought under cultivation sometime after the establishment of the seigneurial system but before Cistercian acquisition.[25] Increasing fragmentation by the processes of inheritance coupled with expansion that may have been linked to population growth caused the usages of tenurial terms to become altered from their original meanings by the twelfth century. A confusion of rights is reflected in a confusion in the tenurial terminology which had come to describe landholders' rights by combinations of legal terminology which in an earlier century would have been absurd.[26] The usage and context of such terms must be carefully studied to determine the meanings. Seigneurialism had reached a state of crisis caused by a long history of settlement and change within the area before Silvanès was founded; this can be inferred from such unexpected usages.

Despite problems of terminology, there are many clear indications of circumstances in the area. The abbey of Silvanès was built in a place known as the mansus de Terundo. The chronicle implies that this was a deserted area until the monks arrived. The charters reveal that it was a land-holding once occupied by a family whose members, still bearing that name, resided in the immediate vicinity: a charter for 1164 has 'Bernardus de Terundo, capellanus de Senomes,' as witness.[27] Similarly the grange of Promillac, not far from the abbey, had also been previously occupied, for there are several men who bear the name 'de Promillac' among both donors and witnesses to the charters. Most

interesting of these are Déodat de Promillac and Hugh de Promillac,
brothers who gave Silvanès in 1162 all their rights in Promillac
and in return entered Silvanès as <u>conversi</u> laborers.[28]   (Their status
as <u>conversi is clear</u> in later charters.) That they should have accepted such a status in the monastery suggests that they were from the
peasant class. Their disposal of land rights at Promillac shows them
to have been free men with legal rights over the land they had tilled.
Yet they were <u>not the only owners of that land</u>, for Arnaud de Ponte,
lord of the castle of that name, and the knights of the castle of Brusque
all gave rights over the allod of Promillac to Silvanès.[29] There are
numerous cases in the charters of such men who had agnomens associating
them with a <u>mansus</u> or other piece of land which became monastic property. It is obvious that they or their predecessors had had some connection with the land in question. Thus, men's names alone reveal that
this land had been settled before the Cistercian arrival.

The existence of castles in the area, such as that of Arnaud de
Ponte are also indications that this was a settled area. Arnaud de
Ponte was not a frontier lord, but controlled an area where he had banal
and allodial rights.[30] His wife Bouissone and five sons Bertran,
Guillaume, Aimeric, Bérengar and Arnaud were donors with him in the many
gifts he made to the monks of Silvanès. After Arnaud entered Silvanès
as a monk, his sons acted as co-lords in confirming his donations and
in making their own.[31] Such a division of lordship among five sons is

more suggestive of an overcrowded area than of a frontier where each
son might have built his own castle.

Political rights and taxes such as the vicaria and sirventage
were well established in the area. The holding of fragments of such
rights by several individuals and their transformation into regularized
exactions indicates that these had existed in the area for some time.
Vicaria had originally been a right over justice under the Carolingians,
exercised by the vicarius. By the twelfth century it had become an
annual tax.[32] The less fragmented and less widespread tax levied on
both land and tithes, sirventage, appears to have been a more recently
introduced levy, probably associated with military service or the growth
of the power of castles in the region.[33] Both the existence and subsequent transformation of such rights into regular taxes suggests the
lengthy history of settlement and cultivation in the region which excluded the possibility of Cistercian reclamation at the time of the
foundation of Silvanès.

Transactions involving tithes and parish churches also indicate
previous settlement of the lands which Silvanès acquired. While in
theory Silvanès, like all Cistercian houses, had been exempted by papal
privilege from paying tithes on the lands which its members cultivated,
in practice this exemption was exercised only after the abbey had purchased the various portions of the tithes from their previous holders.[34]
That these were not tithes on noval lands is clear from the facts that

they were fragmented into many parts, that they had fallen under lay
control in many cases, and because these owners gave up those tithes
only when compensated.[35] If these had been noval tithes the number of
transactions to acquire them would have been limited and the amount of
fragmentation extremely small. In fact, transactions involving tithes
account for more than ten percent of the total transactions in the cartulary of Silvanès and in many cases these tithes are clearly fragmented.[36] If such claims had not been revenue-producing, they would have
been of little interest to layholders and would not have needed to be
redeemed for cash. The charters show many instances of titheholders
receiving gifts of cash de caritate from the monks in return for their
donations of tithes. Only well established tithes producing revenues
from the agricultural and pastoral activities of the area would have
required such attentions.[37] These agricultural and pastoral activities
were carried on by the inhabitants who had lived there with their fami-
lies and divided land rights with the passing of each generation.

Controversy over tithes existed not only with layholders, but in
some cases with Silvanès' ecclesiastical neighbors as well. A dispute
over the tithes of the parish of Prugnes with the Hospitallers is a good
example of how the area's monastic corporations attempted to establish
spheres of influence in which they were sole authorities, as well as
showing how difficult it was for Silvanès to exercise its papal exemption
from tithes.[38] In 1154 arbitrars were chosen by the two sides to resolve

the dispute. Silvanès claimed exemption from tithes on its lands in
the parish of Prugnes by authority of papal privilege. The Hospitallers
claimed rights to collect tithes throughout the parish by their control
of the parish church of Prugnes. The dispute was pacified by an agreement in which Silvanès gave up one tenth of the lands which it then
held in the parish of Prugnes, and agreed to give up in the future one
ninth of any additional lands acquired there, to the Hospitallers. They
in turn gave up their claims to the tithes of Silvanès' remaining lands
in the parish.[39]

Like those of the Hospitallers', Silvanès' property acquisitions
included parish churches. The bishop of Rodez granted the monks of
Silvanès in 1164 the churches of Sainte-Croix de Sarrus and Saint-Amans
de Cénomes and confirmed the earlier donation of Saint-Jean de Gissac.[40]
In these parish churches, Silvanés would henceforth have the sole right
to appoint the parish priest and in these parishes Silvanès' exemption
from tithes was confirmed. All three churches were located in the immediate vicinity of granges belonging to Silvanès. The existence of
churches there is further proof that such areas had been populated before Cistercian acquisition.[41]

Like terminology and the existence of taxes, the descriptions of
land units and rights over land which are included in the cartulary are
also indices of previous cultivation and settlement. Although the duration of previous settlement cannot be determined by the evidence of the

charters, the fact that land units and tenures were fragmented, as well
as the existence of such land units as the appendariae which document
expansion, both suggest that this area had been populated for much longer
than a single generation previous to the Cistercian arrival there. There
are many indications of lordship and allodial ownership of these lands,
but the cultivators were free men with legal rights to alienate their
landrights. A certain confusion of tenures makes it difficult to identify individuals as lords or peasants, but all were free and serfs did
not exist there at that time.[42]

Land units were frequently those associated with the villa, although the term villa itself is rarely mentioned, usually being replaced
by less distinctive terms such as territorium or honorem.[43] The most
frequently occurring land units in the charters are those associated
with the seigneurial regime or its expansions: mansus, caputmansus and
appendaria. Half of the charters in the cartulary mention one of these
three land units.[44] In most cases such land units are identified by
traditional names, the mansus of Teron and so on, rather than by contiguous owners or natural boundaries of a mansus in question. There
are some cases when land is identified by a place name or by the name of
its tenant.[45] Although in a few places mansi appear to have been
isolated farmsteads which show up as place-names on modern maps, often the
mansi were parts of larger units. For instance, a gift might
be made of the mansus of a certain tenant in Cabriac; another gift might

include two <u>mansi</u> in that place, or parts of a third.[46] Such terminology implies that Cabriac was, if not a villa, at least a center in
which a number of <u>mansi</u> were located.

All three land units, <u>mansus</u>, <u>caputmansus</u> and <u>appendaria</u>, are
treated as virtual equivalents in the terminology of the charters. All
are land units including the formulaic descriptions of 'all rights in
cultivated and uncultivated land, in woods, meadows, pasture and water.'[47]
Such descriptions are not applied to other land units, and, although the
description appears formulaic, it does describe the rights in common
lands which a peasant tenure would have commanded. The <u>mansus</u> has generally been considered to be the farmstead of a single family.[48] Obviously such a definition covers a variety of local types, but the evidence
of the charters upholds this interpretation for the region of Silvanès.
There are occasionally <u>mansi</u> which had been divided into halves and
quarters, but they are rare in these charters.[49] The <u>appendaria</u> is
quite obviously a later assart, but there is no clear distinction in
the charters between <u>caputmansus</u> and <u>mansus</u>. The <u>caputmansus</u> appears
much less frequently than the <u>mansus</u>, but since it is described in exactly the same terms as the <u>mansus</u>, it cannot be seen as a particular
fraction of the <u>mansus</u>, or as a <u>mansus</u> that had once been part of the
lord's demesne.[50] A more probable solution is that <u>caputmansus</u> was
used only to distinguish between two <u>mansi</u> that would otherwise bear
the same name and which were probably adjacent to one another. (This

would be a distinction of the same kind as that between major and minor

mansi, as found in the cartulary of Silvanès, or between mansus superior

and mansus inferior, as found in other parts of the Rouergue.[51]) Thus,

the caputmansus of Estorns given in 1166 by Peire de Minèrve and the

mansus of Estorns given in 1171 by Aldiarde and Guillaume de Caylus

are equivalent units.[52] Whatever the precise distinctions in

terminology, the presence of such land units associated with the villa

and with seigneurial agriculture, suggest a period of settlement prior

to the Cistercian foundation.

Silvanès also acquired vines and gardens and minor land units

which must have been intended for gardens and vines, such as the faisca

and versana.[53] There are indications that the vines in question had

been planted by a system of complant or méplant in which the owner con-

tributed land to be planted with vines and a cultivator contributed his

labor until the vines had begun to produce, at which time each party

received all rights to half of the vineyard.[54] Such systems of division

are one explanation for the unusual combinations of rights which developed

on certain lands. Such lands planted with vines and gardens appear to

have been put under cultivation much more recently than the mansi, for

they are less encumbered with multiple owners.

Multiplicity of levels of ownership on many lands which Silvanès

acquired is a final index of previous settlement and cultivation in the

region. Almost all land was held by both an allodial owner and an owner of benefice or fief.[55] However, a certain confusion in the terminology

reflects a disorder among the actual rights. In many cases one owner

would claim rights to both allod and benefice, another might have rights

to benefice and fief, and so on.[56] In the case of vines in particular,

a single owner was often found claiming rights not only to the allod

but 'all rights, allod, benefice and fief.'[57]   Allod seems to have

come to mean only a part of the total rights to a piece of land; an

owner of all rights had to include benefice and fief in his list of

rights along with allod in order to express his exclusive ownership.

Tenurial rights of allod, benefice and fief, were, like the land

units themselves, fragmented among various holders. Not only could

several individuals hold the allod of a piece of land, but one indivi-

dual might hold half of the fief of a single mansus while another man

held the other half share of the fief.[58] Such fragmentation of tenurial

rights, like the existence of half and quarter mansi is an indication of

a long history of settlement, but it also suggests economic problems

such as overpopulation and the associated underemployment and diminishir

returns.   The mansus appears to have been occupied by multiple househol

and seigneurial agriculture in the region to have reached crisis condi-

tions.[59]

Only in those granges located farthest from the monastic center

where animal husbandry was more important than cereal production was

there an exception to this pattern of fragmentation and confusion among

the land units which Silvanès was acquiring. In those granges of Sols,
Margnes, Lassouts and Silvaplana, the number of land units associated
with seigneurialism was much smaller and fragmentation less apparent.
In those areas, however, the abbey generally acquired only pasture
rights. In large expanses of waste suitable only for grazing, boundaries were indicated by hills, streams and topography.[60] Even in these
areas, the monks had been preceded by peasant pastoralists whose livelihood was protected by limits on the numbers of animals which Silvanès
might keep.[61] These granges, although extremely important in Silvanès'
economy, accounted for only a small part of the total arable land which
Silvanès acquired. Even if the soil had not been too poor for cultivation, there is no indication that Silvanès had any rights to carry out
clearance in these less-settled areas.[62] There are none of the indications of clearance, allowing either _exheremare_ or _extirpare_ or _renovatio_,
which are found in donations to Cistercians in other areas, like Gascony
and the region of Toulouse.[63] The only charters which suggest a possibility of clearance are those mentioning increased hearths on the Causse
de Larzac, but those charters specifically forbade Silvanès to cut or
burn trees and, in the event of future colonization, limit the abbey's
rights to pasture in the area.[64]

The examples discussed make it clear that Silvanès was creating
its granges and building its church on lands which had been previously
settled and cultivated. Such acquisition of previously settled land

does not in itself rule out major contributions to clearance and reclamation as well, but there are simply no indications of such activities by the monks of Silvanès. A quantitative survey of the charters
for Silvanès between 1132 and 1250 suggests that there was no such
clearance, for such a survey shows that a substantial majority of the
transactions involved lands which had undoubtedly been cultivated and
settled before the Cistercian arrival.[65] Only twenty-seven percent of
all the charters do not involve the mansus or its concomitant units of
caputmansus and appendaria; or vineyards and gardens; or houses, churches,
mills, or other buildings; or tithes and privileges. Of the remaining
twenty-seven percent, only a small number could possibly have involved
land intended for clearance; most of the charters in this category are
donations or confirmations by individuals giving up all rights in a
general area, or giving up claims to a gift that a relation had made, or
donating rights to some sort of pasture. These are simply those charters which are not specific enough to immediately exclude clearance and
drainage, yet which in no way specifically suggest it. There are only two
charters which might be considered exceptions; these concern rights to
build mills and permission to 'move water to make meadows.'[66] Both
seem to involve the irrigation of meadows to produce hay. With this
exception, the charters show that virtually all the land the abbey acquired was land which had definitely been settled and cleared before
the monastic foundation. In short, there are no indications in the

charters of clearance or drainage of new arable land by the monks of
Silvanès.

If this abbey was not opening up new lands for agriculture, was
there any significant difference between its agricultural practices and
those of earlier monasteries? Did this Cistercian foundation contribute
in any way to the economic expansion and well-being of the twelfth century? Silvanès certainly did not become totally divorced from old
sources of monastic revenue, for it acquired banal rights over mills
and rights over parish churches.[67] However, the monks of Silvanès did
have significant effects on agriculture by their introduction of the
grange economy following the careful consolidation of land into large,
compact blocks. Unlike earlier monastic orders, the Cistercians advocated active participation in the agricultural process, and at Silvanès
lay brethren and hired laborers replaced the tenant farmer as the primary
labor force in the fields. Direct cultivation meant that the Cistercians
could introduce new, scientific techniques and by careful management undoubtedly increased yields per laborer if not total output. The abbey
could have acquired better draft teams and equipment that would have
been too expensive for an individual tenant, and release from traditional
rents would have allowed more rational planning of land use.

The first major goal in such an effort was the consolidation of
land into large holdings where no outsider had claims. These became
granges after the careful consolidation of all the fragments of rights

which many people had held over the smaller plots of land which made up
the grange. A cartulary was a major tool in such an effort for it allowed the monks to know what land they already owned, what should be
purchased and what individuals had witnessed sales or donations in cases
of claims against the abbey.[68] Once freed from all outside claims and
interference, these large consolidated granges could be cultivated by
the conversi with the newest methods and equipment available. Such
granges soon were among the largest and most prosperous farms in the
Rouergue.[69]

Silvanès' granges could be planted with the cereals and crops
best suited to soil and climate. Their production would be geared to
the needs of the abbey and to meeting the demands of local commerce
rather than according to the dictates of traditional payments which
required certain crops to be grown because those crops must be paid to
lords and tithe-holders. Land not suitable for cultivation, or too
poor to produce well, might be converted to pasture for sheep and
other animals. Surpluses in both cereals and animal products would
have had an increasing value in the region at this time as cities and
urban industries began to grow. Silvanès could adopt the most productive crops for its fields and convert marginal areas to pasture and by
doing so create marketable surpluses. The conversi labor system would
also have tended to create more marketable surpluses than land farmed
by tenants, for celibate conversi members had no unproductive children,

or pregnant wives, or aged parents to feed. More of the products
of their labor could go to markets. Such an advantage would have been
especially great during the first years after the foundation. Obviously
with the aging of members there would have come a time when some must have
been supported without laboring, but in the early years this lack of unproductive mouths was an economic boon.[70] There is no question that
Silvanès was indeed employing the labor of conversi. The charters
not only show men giving donations to the abbey in return for entrance
as conversi, but they also show conversi acting as witnesses to various
acts.[71] The recruitment of these lay brethren seems to have been closely tied to the early expansion and accumulation of land in an area where
these men had previously been making a living as tenant-cultivators.
Giving up rights to a piece of land and entering Silvanès assured them
of a livelihood even if crops failed or they became disabled. Such an
alternative must have been extremely attractive to those whose holdings
were too small to really support them. Recruitment of a labor force in
such a way had an obvious disadvantage, for once the abbey was established
in an area and had attracted the surplus population as its original
labor force there would be problems in replacing that labor force. Unlike the tenant farmer, the celibate conversus did not provide heirs to
take his place when he became too old to work in the fields.[72]

The establishment of grange agriculture based on conversi labor in
an already settled area presents one baffling question. What happened

to those men who had previously tilled the fields which now became part
of Cistercian granges? At Silvanès in some cases, like that of Déodat
de Promillac and Hugh de Promillac, the men who tilled the land became
conversi in the monastic economy.[73] In many cases, however, cultivators
gave up rights to land but did not enter the monastery. In a few cases
a lifetime annuity was established for a donor by the monks in exchange
for land.[74] Such annuities, like admission into the monastery, provided
a measure of security and freedom from fears of crop failure and other
disaster. Such instances were exceptional. In most cases, the payment
for land was simply cash or a cash substitute, like a horse or wool or
a measure of grain.[75] In these cases, what happened to the peasant and
how did he use the cash payment that he had received for land 'donated'?
Because the cartulary only provides information on land which fell into
monastic hands, it is impossible to tell how many of those peasants had
other land in the vicinity. In cases where they had other lands, such
cash would have been useful in purchasing plows, draft animals or making
other improvements. Nonetheless, a number of the alienations must have
been sole holdings of individuals who may then have permanently left
the countryside. Some of the cash must have financed migration to the
growing urban centers of the Rouergue and Languedoc. It appears that
cash paid was not generally reinvested in local property, for a simpler
negotiation than two sales would have been an exchange of land; the cartulary shows only one percent of the conveyances were exchanges.[76]

Thus, it seems that peasants in the vicinity of Silvanès experienced some dislocations as a result of the monastic activity in land acquisition. However, the relatively small numbers of land claims and controversies suggest that there was no general dissatisfaction with monastic handling of that acquisition.[77]

More rational use of land resources by the monks of Silvanès is not just suggested by the apparent consolidation of land into granges and the use of _conversi_ labor. There are also evidences of capital investment, of unmistakable emphasis on land rather than labor, intensive animal raising and a concern for acquiring privileges in commercial centers. Capital investment in agricultural equipment and draft animals is difficult to demonstrate, but evidences of other capital investment suggest that it took place. The most conspicuous investment was for watermills and waterworks. Silvanès developed mills and milling rights in three major centers. In the valley of Silvanès itself the abbey acquired several _paxeriae_ or mill dams, with permission to repair them, to build mills and fishponds and to divert water for meadows.[78] On the Graxou River Silvanès also acquired several pre-existing mills for its grange there.[79] Finally, in the grange of Promillac on the Dourdou River, Silvanès acquired mill dams and sites on which to build fishponds and meadows and to build two mills under one roof, one for grinding and one for fulling cloth.[80] Rational economic policies in introducing and controlling not only grinding but industrial mills which could have tied

into Silvanès' own wool production and to the growing woolen industry
of the area make it obvious that Silvanès must have invested capital
for other uses which have not left such records.[81]

The extensive pasture rights which Silvanès gained in the second
half of the twelfth century reveal the abbey's growing emphasis on animal husbandry. The commercial privileges which the monks gained indicate that commercial production of animal products in particular was
intended. Meat, cheese, wool and leather would have been easily trans-
ported and were profitable commodities in the markets of urban centers
in the region.

Silvanès gained extensive grazing privileges and grass for its
animals, especially in those four distant granges already mentioned
where topography was especially suited to pasture but soil and climate
not suited to cereal production. The grange of Sols near La Couvertoirad
on the Causse de Larzac was located in an area still famous today for
raising sheep and producing the cheese which is aged in the famous caves
of Roquefort.[82] Margnes, given by the viscounts of Béziers, and Lassouts
both to the southwest of Silvanès in the Monts de Lacaune, were also located in areas too rough for cereals.[83] Silvaplana, near the Languedoc
plain, not only had grazing land, but was close to urban markets and a
convenient terminal for flocks coming from the Rouergue.[84]

Grazing rights were not limited to distant pasture for there were al
extensive donations, particularly of general rights to pasture of 'omnes

herbas' or 'pascuas in omni terra nostra,' in the vicinity of the abbey
itself.[85] Near the abbey these were not just grazing areas but enclosed
cattle parks and glandage for pigs in the woods.[86] The most important
pasture in the immediate vicinity was Mont Tenez, an estival pasture or
montagne, as such areas are called in northern Rouergue and Aubrac where
such lands are used exclusively for summer pasture of transhumant flocks.[87]
Mont Tenez was an important piece of property for which the monks paid
four marks of silver:

> ...Totum montem qui vocatur Mons Tenez, quicquid
> in eo habemus et possidemus, et Collem Frigidum,
> et omnes colles ad ipsum montem pertinentes et
> quidquid ibi aliqua personna de nobis habet.[88]

There are only a few indications of the precise number of animals
which Silvanès must have owned. In the area of Calmels on the Causse
de Larzac limits were established. Silvanès might pasture there one
flock of sheep, four pairs of oxen, thirty horses and their young, and
twelve cows and their young.[89] At Laurat, no new animals were to be
introduced except in the areas of poorest soil, but this gives no indication of numbers.[90] The only specific figure for sheep comes from
near Silvanès, in the region of Sarrus where Arnaud de Ponte limited
the number of sheep that Silvanès might keep in the parish to one flock
of one thousand.[91] This number alone could have provided for the internal needs of a much larger establishment. Moreover, this was only one
parish where Silvanès had pasture rights. Without doubt Silvanès had

substantial flocks producing considerable amounts of wool, cheese,
meat and other animal products for local markets.

The conclusion that Silvanès produced meat and animal products
as well as agricultural produce for local and regional markets is sub-
stantiated by the monastery's accumulation of market privileges in many
of these centers. These privileges, exemptions from market taxes called
leddae and from the passage toll of peage, gave the monks of Silvanès a
competitive advantage in marketing their goods. Like exemptions from
tithes, such privileges allowed Cistercian abbeys to accumulate cash for
land purchases and capital expenditure. Liberties were granged primarily by the great lords of the region. In Languedoc, Silvanès received
safe passage and exemption from the ledda in the region of Narbonne
from the Viscountess Ermengarde and similar privileges in the city of
Narbonne itself from the archbishop, Berengar.[92] The Trencavels, viscounts of Béziers, granted exemption from the ledda first in the city of
Béziers and later through all their territory.[93] In the region of
Montpellier, Silvanès enjoyed an exemption from ledda in the lands of
the Benedictine house of Villemagne; it also shared with Valmagne's monks
control of a house in Montpellier for the use of the monks of both abbeys
and their agents coming to that city, presumably for business.[94] It is
also noteworthy that in the Languedoc Silvanès received rights to salt,
which would have been necessary for the abbey's flocks.[95]

In the Rouergue an exemption from the ledda of the market of

Laucune near the granges of Margnes and Lassouts was given by the three
owners of the market.[96] In Millau, Silvanès had an exemption from
market taxes as well as freedom from tolls on the bridge over the Tarn
River which controlled access to Millau and to the Roman road that led
into central Rouergue and Rodez.[97] In a vernacular charter, the count
of Rodez granted Silvanès exemption from peage throughout his lands.[98]
Such commercial rights and privileges were gained in those cities most
likely to have been outlets for Silvanès' produce, and these cities
were developing woolen and leather industries in the twelfth century
which would have needed the kinds of raw materials which Silvanès was
producing.[99]

The cartulary shows that the Cistercians of Silvanès were involving
themselves in the growing commerce of the high middle ages. The evidence
suggests that they attempted to market surpluses and increased agricultural production through rational economic planning. Their clear efforts
to consolidate land into large granges free from the subsistence demands of traditional agriculture not only increased their own productivity but freed capital to lords and peasants who could in turn improve
their own land. Displacements may have occurred which pushed some peasants to urban centers, but the total production of the region probably
improved as a result, since underemployed laborers were pushed from
farms into urban industry and commerce. Silvanès' pastoral efforts
supplied raw materials for the wool industry developing in the region,

and Silvanès' introduction of the fulling mill to the area also was
geared to the production of that incipient woolen industry.[100] Any
such activities would have increased economic prosperity in the region.

The economy of Silvanès in this early period was neither the
traditional monastic economy based on ownership of estates tilled by
dependent peasant laborers, nor was it an economy of land clearance
and reclamation such as that so often associated with the abbeys of
the Cistercian reform. Instead, an economy in which managerial efforts
increased productivity and commercial incentives favored exchange with
urban centers is revealed in Silvanès' charters. Other local studies,
particularly the studies of Cistercian economies in England, have made
it clear that similar trends existed for other Cistercian abbeys of
the twelfth century.[101] It is becoming rapidly apparent that the
Cistercian abbey had a range of local variations in its economic practices. Other Cistercian abbeys in the Rouergue show a similar pattern
to Silvanès, but it remains to be seen just how far this pattern fits
the economies of Cistercian houses in the rest of southern France.

NOTES

1. This paper is part of research done for an M.A. thesis under the
    direction of David J. Herlihy and Barbara M. Kreutz at the University
    of Wisconsin. The results concerning Silvanès are part of a larger
    study of Cistercian economies in southern France in the twelfth and
    thirteenth centuries being prepared for the Ph.D. dissertation.

2. P.-A. Verlaguet, Cartulaire de l'Abbaye de Silvanès, Archives
    Historiques du Rouergue, I,(Rodez, 1910). Verlaguet's charter numbers
    are referred to throughout; the cartulary is hereafter referred to as
    Silvanès.

    There are no exact figures for the population of Silvanès
    in the twelfth century. For the number of monks, reliance must
    be placed on a charter from 1153 (Silvanès, no. 70) which appears
    to list all the religious members of the community. When abbot,
    prior, presbyter and scribe are included, they number twenty-one.
    For conversi, we can only estimate their proportion to the number
    of monks by comparing the number of donations which include a
    clause allowing entrance into the monastery as conversus to the
    number allowing entrance as monks. In twenty-seven cases, en-
    trance as conversus is allowed (Silvanès, nos. 81 [two], 98

[two], 103, 104, 119, 126, 138 [two], 139 [two], 140 [three], 173, 179, 202, 220 [two], 224, 263, 311, 319 [two], 333, 339). In twelve instances we find men entering as monks (Silvanès, nos. 25, 49, 77, 107, 202, 245, 277, 292, 375 [two], 401, 453). These instances with a precise stipulation of status provide a ratio of twelve monks to twenty-seven conversi, or roughly four monks for nine conversi. This ratio, given twenty-one monks in 1153, would mean about forty-seven conversi.

3. P.-A. Verlaguet, Cartulaire de l'Abbaye de Bonnecombe, I [only volume published so far], Archives Historiques du Rouergue, V (Rodez, 1918-1925) pp. xvi-xvi. P.-A. Verlaguet, Cartulaire de l'Abbaye de Bonnev en Rouergue, with introduction, appendices, and tables by J.-L. Rigal Archives Historiques du Rouergue, XIV (Rodez, 1938) pp. xii-xvii.

   The land acquisitions of Bonnecombe and Bonneval are included in the author's continuing research on Cistercian economies. Bonnecombe and Bonneval will be discussed in a subsequent publication.

4. On the competition for land with other Cistercian abbeys and with the military-religious orders on the Causse de Larzac, see the similar problems of Nonenque, the convent founded by Silvanès in the mid-twelfth century in a valley not far from the valley of Silvanès, as discussed by G. Bourgeois, "Les Granges et l'Economie de l'Abbaye de Nonenque au Moyen Age," Cîteaux, XXIV, (1973) 140-141.

5. Silvanès, nos. 425, 426, 459, 460-76, 477, 483.

6. Silvanès, intro., pp. xvii-xix.

7. Silvanès, intro., pp. xii, xiii.

8. Silvanès, intro., p. xii, n. 2.

9. Silvanès, intro., p. xii; chron., pp. 371-73.

10. Silvanès, chron., p. 371; 'abinitio Celestis Agricole manus.'

11. Silvanès, chron., pp. 373-81.

12. Silvanès, intro., p. xvii.

13. Silvanès, intro., pp. xx-xxi.

14. J.-M. Canivez, Statuta Capitulorum Generalium Ordinis Cisterciensis ab anno 1116 ad annum 1786 (Louvain, 1933) I, 13.

15. Silvanès, no. 8: 'ecclesie beate Marie, que in manso Terundi fundata est, et habitationibus ejusdem loci.'

16. Silvanès, chron., p. 382.

17. See Verlaguet's similar conclusions. Silvanès, intro., p. xxviii.

18. Archibald R. Lewis, "The Closing of the Mediaeval Frontier, 1250-1350," Speculum, XXXIII (1958) 476.

19. Such conclusions have been reached wherever local research has been done; see Georges Duby, Rural Economy and Country Life in the Medieval West, trans. Cynthia Postan (1968) 78.

20. Ch. Higounet, "Observations sur la seigneurie rurale et l'habitat en Rouergue de IXe au XIVe siècle," Annales du Midi, LXII (1950) 121.

21. Higounet, "Observations," pp. 122-23.

22. Higounet, "Observations," pp. 121-22.

23. Higounet, "Observations," pp. 126-28, notices this 'désagrégation.'
    Examples will be cited from the cartulary of Silvanès, but they can
    be found in other twelfth-century charters as well, for instance, in
    the cartulary of Bonnecombe.

24. Higounet finds this term, used as a separate holding, from the tenth
    century on. "Observations," p. 129.

25. Their situation outside the seigneurial regime is clear from
    Silvanès' charters, for vines and other small holdings are not
    described with the formulaic descriptions attached to the mansus.
    Higounet notes that once such separate entities appear the vines
    attached to a mansus are more specifically designated in the char-
    ters; see "Observations," pp. 128-29.

26. For example, 'unum vinaletum in Promillac, videlicet alodium,
    fevum, benefitium.' Silvanès, no. 205.

27. Silvanès, no. 353.

28. Silvanès, nos. 98, 106, 205, 217, 220, 240, 489; especially 220.

29. Silvanès, nos. 146, 184, 185, 189.

30. Silvanès, nos. 9, 10, 44, 145, etc.

31. Silvanès, nos. 145, 146.

32. For the Carolingian vicaria or vigueries, see Edouard Perroy,
    "Carolingian Administration," in Early Medieval Society, ed. Sylvia

L. Thrupp (New York, 1967) pp. 142-43.

33. Sirventage or sirventatgue seems to be related to military service,
    perhaps similar to northern French sergeantry. It appears more
    recent because it is less fragmented and less widely distributed than
    vicaria. DuCange identifies this only as a political right similar
    to vicaria; Glossarium mediae et infimae latinitatis, ed. Favre (1937-
    1938) VI, 208.

34. For examples, see Silvanès, nos. 34, 51, 55, 68, 82, 88, 386, 390, 411,
    etc. Not all decimae are ecclesiastical revenues; they can also be
    rent-payments of tenths.

35. For example, Deodat Guifre and his family give Silvanès in 1164,
    'duas partes tocius decime, quas habemus in tribus mansis in
    Cantalops' with the confirmation of their relatives. The donors
    were compensated for this: 'Pro hac donatione et laudatione de-
    distis nobis de caritate CC solidos Melgorienses ut firma et
    stabilis omni tempore permaneat.' Silvanès, no. 99.

36. See note 65. The ten percent included in that table does not in-
    clude tithes which may have been given in donations mentioning
    mansi, etc., which would have given a much higher number of trans-
    actions in tithes.

37. Silvanès purchased exemptions from tithes on the 'food for its
    animals' as well as on the produce of its labor; see Silvanès,
    no. 411.

38. For the papal privileges see Silvanès, nos. 1, 2 and 6.

39. Silvanès, nos. 170, 171, 174 (1154-1165).

40. Silvanès, no. 231.

41. The lay population of these parishes must have been considerably
     diminished by Cistercian acquisitions. There is no indication that
     the monks were interested in acquiring parishes in which they would
     be involved in the care of souls.

42. Nowhere in the cartulary is Silvanès ever found acquiring serfs or
     rights over peasants attached to the land. Men and women are never
     included in donations of land, nor are there enfranchisements.

43. See Silvanès, nos. 129, 151, 196.

44. See note 65.

45. For example, 'in manso Terundi et in appendaria de Gallac,'
     Silvanès, no. 73, or 'illam faissam, quam habeo inter terras
     vestras in Marcillon.' Silvanès, no. 74.

46. Silvanès, nos. 110, 111.

47. 'Terras cultus et incultus, nemora, prata pascuas, aquas, cursus
     aquarum, et recursus, introitibus et exitibus et quicquid in manso est
     mansus pertinet.' Silvanès, no. 244.

48. March Bloch, Feudal Society (Chicago, 1966) p. 243; Duby, Rural
     Economy, p. 28.

49. See Silvanès, nos. 269, 291.

50. In nearly five hundred charters, caputmansus is mentioned only

twenty-one times and <u>appendaria</u> only eighteen times.

51. <u>Silvanès</u>, nos. 159, 161, show a **masmajeur**; <u>Bonnecombe</u>, no. 222,
    has 'in mansis d'Orssalessas et de Soyri lo major, el menor.'
    <u>Bonnecombe</u>, no. 251, shows a use of <u>caputmansus</u> which would
    accord with this interpretation, 'et in manso de Costa, et in
    capmas cum omnibus pertinentiis suis.'

52. <u>Silvanès</u>, nos. 234, 475.

53. <u>Silvanès</u>, nos. 74, 209.

54. Because the names of contiguous owners are included in descriptions
    of these pieces of land, it is possible to see that in several in-
    stances the pieces fit together into a larger unit. For a descrip-
    tion of <u>méplant</u> or <u>complant</u>, see Duby, <u>Rural Economy</u>, p. 139.

55. Nowhere in the cartulary are allod, benefice and fief held by
    three distinct individuals. <u>Fevum</u> is not necessarily a military
    tenure in southern French contractual practice. Unless vassalage
    or homage are explicitly mentioned (and they are not in the charters
    for Silvanès) this word simply means a conveyance of land rights for
    a certain sum and often an annual rent. See H. Richardot, "Le fief
    routurier a Toulouse," <u>Revue Historique de Droit</u>, 4th series, 40th
    year, 1935, 307-359. Thus my translation of the word <u>fevum</u> as <u>fief</u>
    in this paper implies only this limited sense.

56. Allod held alone, thirty-seven times; benefice alone, forty times;
    fief alone, sixty-six times; allod and benefice in same hands,

sixteen times; allod and fief in same hands, six times; benefice

and fief in same hands, nine times; allod, benefice and fief held

by one person, sixty-two times.

57. Silvanès, no. 205.

58. Silvanès, no. 117.

59. Higounet, "Observations," p. 128, also sees a fragmentation of the
mansus in the Rouergue.

60. Silvanès, nos. 382, 381, 419.

61. Silvanès, nos. 381, 448.

62. Indeed, in many of the places where Silvanès had extensive pasture
rights there were also prohibitions against harming the crops of
peasants, or against allowing agriculturalists to practice agriculture, but no permission for Silvanès to do likewise. See, for
example, Silvanès, no. 429.

63. For example, see the first two charters of A. Clergeac, Cartulaire
de l'abbaye de Gimont, Archives historiques de Gascogne (Paris, Auch
1905), nos. 1 and 2.

64. Silvanès, no. 381.

65. Land descriptions in transactions by Silvanès can be tabulated by
counting numbers of charters mentioning key words.*

Privileges:	28	6%	Vineyards, vines:	24	5%
Mansus, caput-mansus and appendaria	249	50%	Buildings, mills, etc.	8	2%
			Tithes	48	10%
Pasture rights	16	3%	Other	133	24%
			Totals:	506	100%

N.B.* Because certain categories overlap, those categories latest
in the table may actually be larger because tithes or pasture
rights, for example, may be donated in charters which mention mansi.
This does not affect the 'other' category.

66. Silvanès, nos. 59, 210

67. Silvanès, nos. 145, 231.

68. Silvanès, intro., p. xviii.

69. Such granges are still among the largest in the Rouergue. Such
Cistercian granges were still intact at the time of the French
Revolution and in the national sales of confiscated goods brought
higher prices than any other farms in the region. See P. A. Verlaguet, Vente des biens nationaux du département de l'Aveyron (Millau,
1931-33) passim.

70. For an economist's view of the problem, see Richard Roehl, "Plan
and Reality in a Medieval Monastic Economy: The Cistercians,"
Studies in Medieval and Renaissance History, IX (Lincoln, Nebraska,
1972) 81-113.

71. Silvanès, nos. 70 or 481, for example.

72. The problem of replacement of conversi became drastic by the mid-
thirteenth century for many Cistercian houses, and more and more
problems of discipline appeared. Might not such problems be seen
as inherent in the growth cycle of the Cistercian abbey, as results
of an end to expansion rather than as a result of such nebulous

316   Ideals and Reality

causes as a failure of enthusiasm?

73. See Silvanès, nos. 42, 81, 98, 103, 104, 119, 126, 138, 139, 140.

74. Silvanès, nos. 81, 107, 124, 230, 258, 292 (some for children).

75. For example, Silvanès, no. 225.

76. There are six in the 462 charters concerning Silvanès; see
     Silvanès, nos. 44, 68, 69, 102, 153.

77. There are few cases in which arbitrars must be called in to settle
     claims such as those between Silvanès and the Hospitallers, Silvanès,
     nos. 170, 171, etc.

78. Silvanès, nos. 9, 43, 59, 94, 89, 108.

79. Silvanès, nos. 145, 253, 282, 267.

80. Silvanès, nos. 145, 176, 184, 210, 192, 227.

81. Robert-Henri Bautier, The Economic Development of Medieval Europe
     (London, 1971) pp. 117, 118, discusses the wool industry of the area.

82. Parish of Saint-Christophe of La Couvertoirade.

83. Commune of Margnes-de-Brassac (Tarn).

84. Commune of Laurens (Herault).

85. For example, see Silvanès, nos. 89, 173.

86. Silvanès, nos. 9, 28, 38, 141, 155, 375.

87. In the region of Aubrac in northern Rouergue, famous for its trans-
     humance, a montagne is a unit of pasture, as it has been since the
     medieval period. At that time the exploitation of Aubrac was shared
     between the Cistercians of Bonneval and the independent military-

religious order of Aubrac. During the late middle ages animals
were brought from Quercy to Aubrac by regular transhumance routes
across central Rouergue. See Jacques Bousquet, "Les Origines de
la transhumance en Rouergue," in L'Aubrac: Etude Ethnologique,
Linguistique, Agronomique, et Economique d'un Etablissement Humain
(Paris, 1971) II, 217-55.

The elevation of the highest hills in the vicinity of Silvanès
is about 700 meters compared to the 1400 meter elevation of Aubrac.

88. Silvanès, no. 10.

89. Silvanès, no. 381.

90. Silvanès, no. 429.

91. Silvanès, no. 70.

92. Silvanès, nos. 396, 400.

93. Silvanès, nos. 459, 460.

94. Silvanès, nos. 461 for Villemagne, 462-63 for Valmagne.

95. Silvanès, no. 403.

96. Silvanès, nos. 407-409.

97. Silvanès, no. 457.

98. Silvanès, no. 458.

99. For the growth of new towns in the region, see Henri Enjalbert,
    Rouergue/Quercy (Paris, 1971) p. 45 ff.

100. This appears to have been the earliest mill of its type in southern
     France; see Anne-Marie Bautier, "Les Plus Anciennes Mentions de

moulins hydrauliques, industriels, et de moulins à vent," <u>Bulletin</u>
<u>Philologique et Historique (jusqu'au 1610) du Comité des Travaux</u>
<u>Historiques et Scientifiques</u> (1960) I, 583.

101. See the many articles on the subject of Cistercian economic practices in England by R. A. Donkin; for example: "Settlement and
Depopulation on Cistercian Estates during the Twelfth and Thirteenth Centuries, especially in Yorkshire," **<u>Bulletin of the Insti-</u>**
<u>tute of Historical Research</u>, XXXIII, 88 **(November, 1960)** 141-57.
Donkin has published the most complete bibliography of Cistercian
economic history to date. See R. A. Donkin, "Cistercian Bibliography," <u>Documentation Cistercienne</u>, II (1969).

For a more recent article which shows interesting cross-Pyrenean
parallels to the present author's current research on Cistercian
economies in southwestern France, see L. J. McCrank, "The Frontier
of the Spanish Reconquist and the Land Acquisitions of the Cisterci
of Poblet, 1150-1276," ASOC XXIV (1973) 57-78.

THE ARCHITECTURAL AND PHYSICAL FEATURES OF AN

ENGLISH CISTERCIAN NUNNERY*

John A. Nichols
Slippery Rock State College

While the establishment of the institutional nature of a Cistercian
nunnery is most important, it is also instructive to reconstruct, when
circumstances permit, the physical features of a medieval monastery.
In the process of researching the history of the Cistercian nuns of
Marham Abbey, England, it became apparent that not only were there extensive documents about this convent's history but also sufficient evidence to permit an assessment of the architectural and physical characteristics of the monastery. Armed with this evidence, I made a personal
tour in July 1972, to photograph and measure the nunnery's physical
remains. The following is the results of my inspection.

Marham Abbey was founded by Isabel of Aubigny, countess of Arundel,
on January 27, 1249, in the village of Marham, Norfolk. The village,
as it probably appeared <u>circa</u> 1300, had these characteristics: the
natural geographic formations of the Nar River to the north; Marham Fen
or Marsh with peat bogs and meadows to the northeast; and the cultural
geographic features of the roads, arable fields, and pasture land which
extended to the boundaries of the parish, a water mill on the river; and
buildings of the tenants' tofts, windmill, castle, Saint Andrew church,
Holy Trinity church and the buildings in the Marham Abbey courtyard in
the center of the village.

The convent was opposite Holy Trinity church and bound by Northgate and Eastgate roads. The site was enclosed behind a wall which set
the nunnery apart from the village proper. Although this wall was in
existence as late as 1627,[1] no trace of its features can be seen today.
In addition to the main buildings of the cloister and church, which
stood 200 feet from Eastgate and 250 feet from Northgate, there are
mounds (fig. 1)--which measured 3 to 4 feet in height--of four buildings
that must have been the outer houses of the convent. When the nunnery
was suppressed in 1536, the suppression commissioners took an inventory
of the site which included their description of the contents found in a
bake-house and barn.[2] Although the locations in the courtyard were not
given, two of the four buildings can be at least identified; as a result
it seems probable that the two other buildings were the guest house and
the infirmary.[3] The size of the buildings, as measured from the mounds,
allows the following description of their dimensions and locations in
the convent courtyard (fig. 2).

The largest of the outer structures was the guest house. It was
141 feet north of the main buildings and measured 36 feet in width and
141 feet in length. Its unusual length for a single dwelling would mean
that it contained a number of chambers which could be utilized for the
convent's special needs. In a straight row, 255 feet north of the
cloister, were the other buildings of the courtyard. The first, in a
line parallel with the guest house, was the convent's infirmary, 24 feet
wide and 60 feet long. The last two buildings lying 117 feet northeast

of the infirmary and in close proximity to one another were the bake-house and barn. Both buildings were at right angles to the guest house and measured 21 feet in width. The bake-house was 63 feet long, while the barn, 48 feet away, was 75 feet long. In respect to these last three buildings, a mound was situated in the exact middle of the outer mounds which suggests the buildings were divided into two major parts.

The main buildings of the convent can be reconstructed with very little difficulty because all monasteries have common physical plant characteristics which makes their remains identifiable; also there is some documentary evidence which refers to the major features of Marham Abbey's buildings. The earliest source for the composition of the major chambers in the convent comes from the suppression commission's inventory of the site in 1536.[4] The first reference to the dimensions and windows of the church was by the prominent and prolific historian of Norfolk, Francis Blomefield, when he specified the ruins of the abbey in the early eighteenth century.[5] The last mention of the remains comes from an archaeological tour made in the summer of 1932 which published a scaled diagram of the cloister and outer parlor.[6]

The only section of the convent church now standing is the south wall (fig. 3). This wall built, in the thirteenth century, of clunch or hard chalk stone, is 66 feet in length, 4 feet in width and 30 feet in height.[7] Blomefield observed that there were originally four oval windows but only two were still intact in his time. These two center windows are of a quatrefoil and sexfoil design. The quatrefoil window

(fig. 4) was a style common in thirteenth-century monastic buildings.
The feature can be seen in the remains of the famous Cistercian abbey
of Rievaulx, Yorkshire, and the gate house of Bury St. Edmunds Abbey in
nearby Suffolk county. The sexfoil window (fig. 5) was yet another
thirteenth-century type of design and its quotation can be seen at
Binham Priory, Norfolk, and in the remains of Tintern Abbey, a distin-
guished Cistercian monastery in Monmouthshire.[8] Blomefield recorded that
the window next to the transept was of a quatrefoil pattern and one may
assume, although Blomefield did not confirm it, that the destroyed window
towards the rear of the Church, was of a sexfoil design to balance the
arrangement.[9] Windows of this style were common in medieval England
and their numerical symbolism was well known. The number six denoted
'...the attributes of the Deity, that is, Power, Majesty, Wisdom, Love,
Mercy, and Justice'; whereas, the number '...four and the quadrifoil
[sic] were held as sacred to the Supreme Spirit as was the number three,'
since the quatrefoil illustrated perfection and divinity.[10]

The only other standing remains of the convent is the outer parlor
which was on the west range of the cloister (fig. 6). It measured 31
feet in length and 18 feet in width with its north wall forming an end to
the convent's church. The interior has three bases (figs. 7, 8, 9) for
the ribbed vault supports and of the two remaining corbels, one has a
grotesque human shape and the other has an ornamental animal design. The
chamber was built in the fourteenth century of a flint stone material.
'The flints are dressed, or "knapped" as it is called, and laid with

relatively little mortar, and some very fine craftsmanship is the result.
A speciality of East Anglia, rarely to be met with elsewhere, is the combination of knapped flint and squared freestone that has been developed
since the fourteenth century. This chequework is seen at its best in
Norfolk, where the small flint blocks [fig. 10], usually about four
inches square...are weathered to a darkish grey, giving the houses and
churches a distinctive regional flavour.'[11]

        To the south of the outer parlor and the church wall are mounds
that have already been described. With these mounds as a guide and
with collaborative documentary evidence, it is possible to advance some
conclusions about the arrangement of the buildings of the convent (fig.
11). The nunnery was constructed along lines which were standard for
English monasteries in general and Cistercian houses in particular. The
center of the convent was the cloister with the main buildings adjacent
to it. Therefore, with the cloister garth as the focal point, it is
possible to discuss the major components of the nunnery in a clockwise
manner.

        The church was built to the north of the cloister with the cloister
roof attached to the wall of the chapel. The exterior and interior of
the church, made of chalk stone, is not distinctive. Blomefield wrote
that there was a bell tower on the church but no other mention of it
was made, and it should be pointed out that the Cistercians had opposed
the construction of towers on their unpretentious churches. The church
was built in the traditional west to east direction in a simple cruciform

design with north and south transepts. The presbytery of the church
was probably square-ended, since the Cistercians opposed the fashionable
apsidal east-end design. The interior of the church, said to be aisle-
less, may have had its nave separated from the choir by a stone screen.
If the austerity of the Cistercians were maintained, the interior would
be quite simple. What light that did penetrate through its plain glass
windows must have come from larger, more lofty windows in its now completely vanished north wall. The overall dimensions of the church were
probably 194 feet in length and 30 feet in width.[12]

Moving from the north to the east side of the cloister, one finds
immediately after the south transept the sacristy chamber where the
sacred utensils and vestments were kept. This chamber adjoined the
nunnery's chapter house which measured 55 feet in length and 40 feet in
width. This building was second in importance only to the church of
the convent and in it was conducted the daily business. The remainder
of the east range was dominated by the dorter, or sleeping compartments
of the nuns, and the rere dorter. The south range of buildings would
have first, the warming house, so named since it contained the only fire-
place in the nunnery, next, the refectory or frater, the convent's
dining room, and finally, the kitchen. The refectory was constructed at
a right angle to the cloister which was customary in Cistercian houses.
This chamber was unusually large, being 72 feet in length and 50 feet
in width. The western side of the convent contained three chambers that
could be used for storage, but in 1536 the suppression commission found

featherbeds in these rooms which indicated that they were being used,
at least on that date, as sleeping quarters. The last building of the
west range was the outer parlor which was the only area in the cloister
where business between the nuns and the outside world was transacted.[13]

This attempted reconstruction of Marham Abbey's physical plant
accomplishes a number of objectives. For the art historian, the analysis
of the architectural and physical features of this English nunnery is
a complete study in and of itself. For the Cistercian studies special-
ist, the remains of this convent are a medieval monument to the spirituality of the order. For the historian, the knowledge of the abbey's
buildings is an added dimension for the history of the nunnery. For
example, the bailiff account rolls of the abbey imply that no extensive
building program was undertaken by the nuns in the fourteenth and fifteenth centuries, and an analysis of the ruins confirms this impression.
In writing the history of a monastery the material remains must be explored and analyzed. To ignore the architectural and physical features
is to ignore a major element in the recovery of the past.

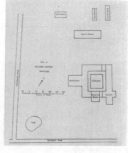

FIG. 1. CLOISTER MOUNDS LOOKING SOUTHEAST   FIG. 2. ENCLOSED CONVENT COURTYARD

FIG. 3. INTERIOR SOUTH CHURCH WALL

FIG. 4. EXTERIOR EAST QUATREFOIL WINDOW

FIG. 5. EXTERIOR WEST SEXFOIL WINDOW

FIG. 6. INTERIOR OUTER PARLOR

FIG. 7. OUTER PARLOR RIBBED VAULT BASE

FIG. 8. OUTER PARLOR HUMAN CORBEL

FIG. 9. OUTER PARLOR ANIMAL CORBEL

FIG. 10. CLOSEUP OF 'KNAPPED' FLINT WALL

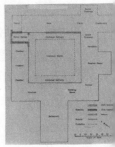

FIG. 11. CONVENT GROUND PLAN

Notes

* The author would like to thank Professor Coburn V. Graves, under whose direction this study was begun, and Kent State University for its Supplemental Graduate Award which helped defray the expense of this research.

1. From an indenture grant made in 31 July 3 Charles I (1627), the following appeared: 'All that this site of the Abbey and Manor of Newhall in Marham in ye County above said with all ye houses, buildings, barnes, stables, and edifices whatsoever actuale standing and being within ye walls of the abbey yards of the laste dissolved nunnery of Marham above said and also all those pastures and meadowes and marshes grounds lyeing and being within the walles of yardes of said Abbey....' Norwich, Norfolk Record Office, Hare 2277/195X5.

2. London, Public Record Office, Church Goods, King's Remembrance, E 117^{11}/7, fo. 2^r.

3. Given the traditional features of a monastery's physical plant, the possibilities as to what else these building might have been is limited. See, for example, Olive Cook, English Abbeys and Priories (London, 1960) plates 2, 5.

4. London, Public Record Office, Church Goods, King's Remembrance E 117^{11}/7, fos. 1^r-2^r.

5. Francis Blomefield, An Essay toward the Topographical History of the County of Norfolk (London, 11 vols., 1805-1810) VII, 392-93.

6. "Summer Meeting at King's Lynn, 1932, Marham Abbey," Royal Arch-
    aeological Institute, 36 (1933) 328-29.

7. For the dating of this wall, see the diagram in Ibid.

8. Cook, English Abbeys and Priories, plates 58, 62, 77, 81. Windows
    of this style were usually constructed in the thirteenth century;
    see Margaret Wood, The English Mediaeval House (London, 1965) p. 348.

9. Blomefield, History of Norfolk, VII, 392 and plate I, fig. 15.

10. Harold Bayley, The Lost Language of Symbolism (London, 2 vols.,
    1912) I, 79-80, 210.

11. F. R. Banks, English Villages (London, 1963) p. 95.

12. For the specifics Ibid. and Blomefield, History of Norfolk, VII,
    392-93. For the general diagram and Cistercian features see Cook,
    English Abbeys and Priories, pp. 14-22, and Louis J. Lekai, The
    White Monks: A History of the Cistercian Order (Okauchee, Wisconsin,
    1953) p. 193.

13. Ibid. and London, Public Record Office, Church Goods, King's Remem-
    brance, E $117^{11}/7$, fo. 1^{v}.

ST BERNARD AND POPE EUGENIUS IV (1431-1447)

Charles L. Stinger
State University of New York at Buffalo

Recent scholarship has drawn attention to the extensive popularity of St Bernard's writings in the fourteenth and fifteenth centuries. His affective mysticism, his devotion to the humanity of Christ, his concentration on inner spiritual development, the figural and metaphoric richness of the biblical imagery in his works, the union of contemplation and action in his own life, the spiritual authority he commanded in his lifetime--all were part of his compelling appeal to such late medieval devotional mevements as the devotio moderna.[1] But Bernard was deeply admired by the Italian Renaissance as well. His Sermons on the Canticles were the source of key figural images in Dante's Commedia,[2] and of course it is Bernard who is the final guide to Dante's beatific vision in Paradiso.[3] Petrarch included an admiring sketch of Bernard in his De vita solitaria,[4] cited Bernard's admonition to monks in his De otio religioso,[5] and seems to have possessed the De consideratione.[6] Salutati, the Florentine Chancellor, regarded Bernard as one of the Fathers, for in joining wisdom (sapientia) and eloquence (eloquentia) he followed the tradition of Hilary, Jerome and Augustine.[7] For Quattrocento humanists, then, Bernard stood out as a last representative of the patristic tradition of learned piety before the barbarous, disputatious, obfuscatory, inelegant, and irrelevant theology of the schoolmen. Shortly before 1420, Bernard's Sermons on the Canticles were translated into Italian by the Florentine Camaldulensian monk Giovanni da Sanminiato (1360-1428), and they, along with Italian translations of Gregory the Great's _Moralia_ and Petrarch's _De remediis utriusque fortunae_, were prominent works in the lay piety promoted by the humanists.[8]

Northern humanism also regarded Bernard as one of the _patres antiqui_. The circle of Lefèvre d'Etaples, for instance, promoted the study and publication of his works, and praised his emphasis on scriptural exegesis as the heart of theology.[9] Luther, in his admonition to Pope Leo X which prefaces his _Freedom of a Christian_, writes, "...I am following the example of Saint Bernard in his book, _On Consideration_, to Pope Eugenius, a book every pope should know from memory."[10] For Luther, Bernard alone of all the medieval theologians was worthy of the name "Father," though what he admired in Bernard was not the union of _doctrin_ and _pietas_ but rather his christocentric theology of grace.[11]

It is the purpose of this paper to examine one episode in the Italian humanist concern for Bernard's life and works.

On 3 March 1431, Gabriele Condulmaro was elected pope, choosing the name Eugenius IV. Born in 1383 of a prominent Venetian patrician family, Condulmaro as a youth had embraced the religious life. He coll. orated in founding a chapter of reformed canons at S. Giorgio d'Alga, and he gave his entire personal fortune of 20,000 ducats to the poor. After serving a year as bishop of Siena, he was named Cardinal in 1408 by Pope Gregory XII, the uncle of his close friend Antonio Correr. For the following two decades Condulmaro was a prominent papal administrator, holding the governorships of Ancona and Bologna. He served often as well on papal embassies. Yet in this career as ecclesiastical statesman he preserved his initial interest in monastic reform. He became Cardinal Protector of the Camaldulensian Order, and in 1430 he convened a General Chapter to work for Observant reform of the Order.[12]

Among those who staunchly supported Condulmaro's work of reform was Ambrogio Traversari (1386-1439), Florentine Camaldulensian monk, humanist, Greek scholar and leading proponent of the humanist revival of patristic theology. To this end he sought manuscripts of the Latin Fathers, studied the history of the Early Church, and translated some two dozen homiletical, devotional and ethical works of Chrysostom, Basil, Gregory Nazianzen and other Greek Fathers into humanistic Latin.[13] Among these was a translation of Pseudo-Basil's *De vera integritate virginitatis*, dedicated to Condulmaro in 1424.[14]

When Traversari learned of Condulmaro's election, he was elated. 'I was marvelously moved,' he wrote to the Venetian humanist Leonardo Giustiniani, 'when I heard the joyous news that your fellow citizen Gabriele had become Roman Pontiff. Great hope has arisen that not only Italy, long agitated by war, will enjoy repose, but also that all things will turn for the better, and the whole world return to ancient holiness.'[15]

To Niccolò Niccoli, his closest friend among the Florentine humanists,
Traversari was even more exultant, 'Our city manifests the greatest delight. A new dawn seems to shine forth.'[16]

On 10 March, a week after Eugenius' election, Traversari wrote a
long letter to the new pope, elaborating a vast program of reform intended to regenerate the spiritual fervor of the apostolic and patristic
church. He exhorted Eugenius to give particular attention to reform of
the regular and secular clergy, to reconciliation with the 'schismatics'
(that is, the Greek Orthodox and other Eastern Chrisitans) and to the
conversion of the 'heathen' (Islam). In this task of reform and renewal Eugenius' essential task was prayer and a resolute trust in the
power of God's will. So that the new pope might know clearly what was
proper to the high office of the papacy, he intended to send him Saint
Bernard's De consideratione.[17]

A month later Traversari fulfilled his intention.

> Behold! As I promised you, I am sending those books
> On Consideration which Saint Bernard sent to his
> Eugenius [III], a quite modest gift which testifies to
> to my poverty, but a gift not to be regarded with
> indifference by you. Rather you should receive it
> with the greatest avidity, for you will discover in
> this work the most diligent rule for living and for
> administering rightly the pontificate.

Traversari observes further that Bernard's work was as appropriately
addressed to Eugenius IV as to his twelfth-century predecessor Eugenius
III. Just as Eugenius III, a devoted monastic disciple of Bernard and

a Cistercian abbot when elected pope, was elevated to the apex of the
papacy after early training in the monastery, so Eugenius IV had received
the first rudiments of spiritual training in the monastery, nor had his
mode of life been other than that of a monk.

> I would steadfastly assert that the saintly author
> of this most noble work, were he presently alive in
> the flesh, would have written the whole of this work
> no less to you than to him....His ardent soul prompts
> you primarily to the restitution or restoration of
> ancient sanctity and decorum to the body of the Church
> ...I pray and beseech you blessed Eugenius, to read
> and reread this work, and that the desire for piety
> imparted to your holy breast be kindled into deeds.[18]

Traversari's esteem for the De consideratione and for Bernard's
spiritual authority is obvious. It is all the more noteworthy, moreover, in that it was in Bernard alone of all the medieval Doctors of
the Church that the patristic scholar Traversari manifested any interest.
Like his fellow humanists Traversari dismissed the whole of the scholastic theological tradition as puffed-up knowledge (inflata scientia)
unrelated to the pressing spiritual needs of personal moral regenera-
tion and the resuscitation of charismatic ecclesiastical leadership.[19]
In Bernard's asceticism Traversari saw the ardent power of the spirit
which had inflamed the Desert Fathers, Basil, Benedict, Romuald and
other founders of the religious life.[20] Equally important, he admired
Bernard as spiritual counsellor. Indeed he ranked Bernard's Sermons
on the Canticles with Augustine's Confessions and Jerome's Letters for
their power of exhortation to faith.[21] Moreover Traversari's own

stress on **meditation** in spiritual life, and his account of grace as the
coming of Christ to the soul, seem to owe much to Bernard's christocentric affective mysticism.[22]

What impact did the De consideratione have on Eugenius IV? When
the pope wrote that he had received with delight Bernard's work, Traversari replied that this was a clear sign of the pope's will, devotion
and desire, that he was hastening with all his powers to follow what
Bernard had expressed so aptly and salubriously.[23] At later points
Traversari continued to hold up the De consideratione as a model for
Eugenius' conduct and policy. In 1438, admonishing Eugenius to bend
all efforts to restoration of the Church, he reminded him that Bernard
had taught that unless within his inner-most heart he was rightly dis-
posed to God he could not deal properly with those things extra te vel
circa te.[24]

Eugenius IV did in fact make substantial efforts to reform abuses
in the Church. He intervened in the Curia to curtail fiscal malpractices
regarding the collation of benefices, and he worked to eradicate expec-
tative favors. The Roman secular clergy, which was directly under his
authority, also received his reforming attention. In February 1432,
for instance, he issued a long instruction governing their conduct. He
continued as well to promote the Observant Reform movement among the monastic orders. Indeed, in the Fall of 1431 he secured Traversari's election as a reforming General of the Camaldulensians. In his personal life

Eugenius practiced an ascetic decorum in stark contrast to the cultivated magnificence of later Renaissance popes. Like his twelfth-century
predecessor he remained abstemious in diet and drink. He also recited
daily the monastic office, had devotional and theological works read
to him nightly and impressed observors with his saintly carriage and
dignity.[25] That Eugenius IV was consciously emulating his predecessor
is strongly suggested by Vespasiano's report that as death approached,
the Pope went into Saint Peter's, and at the entrance to the third door
saw a marble tombstone inscribed 'Pope Eugenius III.' Turning to his
entourage, he remarked, 'I wish my tomb to be next to his, with a stone
which says '"Eugenius IV."'[26]

Other parallels in the two pontificates are striking. Just as
Eugenius III promoted personally the Second Crusade, so Eugenius IV
organized a crusade against the Turks. And both ended in disaster, the
Second Crusade before the walls of Damascus in 1248, while the 1444 cam-
paign headed by the Cardinal Legate Cesarini reached only the shores
of the Black Sea at Varna before being routed by Turkish forces.[27]

Both popes also promoted efforts at reconciliation with the Greek
Orthodox Church and other Eastern Christians. Eugenius III supported
the theological discussions between Greek and Latin theologians at Con-
staninople, and read attentively the proceedings. He also received with
favor the overtures of the Armenians who were seeking reconciliation with

the See of St Peter.[28] Eugenius IV sought an end to the schism with
the Greeks, an ecumenical policy which found fruition, though only ephem-
erally, in the Council of Ferrara-Florence of 1438-1439 His pontificate
also saw ecumenical overtures to the Coptic and Syriac Churches, as well as
to more distant Eastern Christians.[29]

Further, both popes patronized the translation of Greek patristic
theology into Latin. Eugenius III commissioned Burgundio of Pisa, one
of the participants in the theological disputations at Constantinople,
to translate John of Damascus' De fide orthodoxa. The translation, completed in 1148, had an immediate and lasting impact on Latin medieval
theology, for it formed the model and basis for Peter Lombard's
Sentences.[30]   In 1151 Eugenius also commissioned Burgundio to translate
the whole of John Chrysostom's Homilies on Matthew--only the first twenty-
five of the ninety homilies were extant in an old Latin translation.
Burgundio's literal Lation translation was not widely diffused, but Thomas
Aquinas was said to have made so much of Chrysostom's Homilies on Matthew,
in Burgundio's translation, that he would not have exchanged it for the
whole city of Paris.[31] Eugenius IV not only encouraged Traversari's
translations of the Greek Fathers, but it was precisely a new humanistic
Latin translation of Chrysostom's Homilies on Matthew which he commissioned
Traversari agreed to the task, and made preliminary arrangements

to undertake the work, but his scholarly activity for the Council of
Ferrara-Florence delayed the project, then death intervened in November
1439.[33] The Greek emigré scholar, George of Trebizond, eventually made
a new translation of the Homilies for Pope Nicholas V, in the 1450s.[34]

Such parallels are perhaps more striking than substantive. The
fifteenth-century papacy was obviously very different from that of the
twelfth century. The Avignon papacy had created a monarchical Church
far beyond what Bernard had warned against in the 1140s. Then the Great
Schism had eroded papal spiritual authority and prestige. When Martin
V returned to Rome in 1420, he returned not only to a depopulated city
filled with decaying basilicas, but also to a papacy whose fiscal resources from the Church at large had virtually dried up. Martin succeeded in recovering the Papal States for the Church, but in the process
laid the foundations for the papacy as an Italian Renaissance state.[35]
Eugenius IV had the misfortune to see his rancorous conflict with the
Colonna end in yet another revolt of the Roman populace, and he was forced
to flee, disguised as a monk, down the Tiber in a rowboat. He was res-
cued by Florentines at Civitavecchia, and brought with great pomp to
Florence in June 1434. But for the next decade he was largely subser-
vient to Florentine diplomatic and political interests. And again papal
independence was preserved only with the reconquest of Rome and the Papal
States, an accomplishment attained through Eugenius countenancing the

savage depradations of the condottiere, Cardinal Vittelleschi. Prompted
by the same political and military considerations, Eugenius imposed a
harsh regime on recalcitrant Bologna, the largest city in the Papal
States. This policy, adopted despite Traversari's vehement objections
that the Angel of Peace ought not be the fomenter of war,[36] led inevitably to revolt. In short, Eugenius IV, despite his personal sanctity
and his beginning efforts at Church reform, found his energies absorbed
by the political and military exigencies of the Papal States.

In his sharp attack on the avarice of the Roman curia, Bernard warned
Eugenius III that the popes had become successors not to Peter but to
Constantine.[37] If Eugenius IV emerges as a reluctant warrior, within
sixty years of his death the See of St Peter would be held by a pope--
Julius II--who would glory in military victories and celebrate triumphs
emulating those of the Caesars. From this perspective Traversari's eloquent appeal for the restoration of apostolic spiritual charisma at the
head of the Church appears sadly naïve. But his vision of the Church
reformed through the inspired spiritual leadership of the successor to
St Peter was a noble one, and testimony to the enduring impact of
Bernard's life and thought.

NOTES

1. Giles Constable, "The Popularity of Twelfth-Century Spiritual Writers in the Late Middle Ages," in <u>Renaissance</u> Studies in Honor of Hans <u>Baron</u>, edd. Anthony Molho and John A. Tedeschi (Dekalb, Illinois, 1971) pp. 3-28.

2. Erich Auerbach, "Figurative Texts Illustrating Certain Passages of Dante's <u>Commedia</u>," <u>Speculum</u>, XXI (1946) 474-89.

3. Cantos XXXI-XXXIII.

4. <u>The Life of Solitude by Francis Petrarch</u>, trans. Jacob Zeitlin (Champagne, Illinois, 1924) pp. 223-25.

5. Charles Trinkaus, <u>In Our Image and Likeness: Humanity and Divinity in Italian Humanist Thought</u> (Chicago, 1970) I, 655.

6. Pierre de Nolhac, <u>Petrarque et l'humanisme</u>, 2nd ed. (Paris, 1965) II, 224-25.

7. <u>Epistolario di Coluccio Salutati</u>, ed. Francesco Novati (Roma, 1891-1911) III, 82-84; IV, 140-41.

8. Georg Dufner, <u>Die 'Moralia' Gregors des Grossen in ihren Italienisches Volgarizzamenti</u> (Padova, 1958) pp. 49-80.

9. Eugene F. Rice, Jr., "Jacques Lefèvre d'Etaples and the Medieval Christian Mystics," in <u>Florilegium Historiale: Essays Presented to W. K. Ferguson</u>, edd. J. Rowe and W. Stockdale (Toronto, 1971) pp. 89-124; <u>id</u>., <u>The Prefatory Epistles of Jacques Lefèvre d'Etaples</u>

and Related Texts (New York, 1972) pp. 180-81.

10. Martin Luther: Selections from his Writings, ed. John Dillenberger
    (New York, 1961) p. 51.

11. Carl Volz, "Martin Luther's Attitude toward Bernard of Clairvaux,"
    in Studies in Medieval Cistercian History Presented to Jeremiah F.
    O'Sullivan (Spencer, Massachusetts, 1971) pp. 186-204.

12. Joseph Gill, S.J., Eugenius IV: Pope of Christian Union (Westminster,
    1971).

13. See my Humanism and the Church Fathers: Ambrogio Traversari (1386-14
    and Christian Antiquity in the Italian Renaissance (Albany, New York,

14. Laurentius Mehus, Ambrosii Traversarii...latinae epistolae (Floren-
    tiae, 1759) II, Ep. XXIII:4.

15. 'Laetissimo nuntio adfecti mirifice sumus, quo civem vestrum summae
    reverentiae virum Gabrielem adsumptum Pontificem Romanum percepimus.
    Magnaque suborta spes est, fore ut non modo Italia a bellis, quibus
    iamdiu vexatur, conquiescat; verum omnia vertantur in melius, et in
    antiquam sanctitatem redeant universa.' Mehus, VI:36 (36, 10 March
    1431). N.B.: For the dating and chronological rearrangement of
    Traversari's correspondence, see F. P. Luiso, Riordinamento dell'
    epistolario di A. Traversari con lettere inedite e note storico-
    cronologiche (Firenze, 3 vols., 1898-1903).

16. 'Maximam civitas nostra laetitiam ostendit, novaque sibi lux oriri

visa est.' VIII: 36 (36, March 1431).

17. I: 1 (1, 10 March 1431).

18. 'En, ut tibi pollicitus sum, libellos Sancti Bernardi de Consideratione ad Eugenium suum ad te mittimus, exile quidem munusculum,
et quod tenuitatem adtestetur nostram, sed tamen abs te non tenu-
iter amandum, et maxima aviditate subscripiendum: quippe in quibus
vendi, Pontificatusque rectissime administrandi diligentissimam
reperies normam....Ego id pro constanti adseveraverim sanctum
illum nobilissimi Auctorem operis ea omnia, si adviveret in carne,
non minus ad te scripturum, quam ad illum....Ardet animus pleraque
subgerere Sanctitati tuae de restitutione, seu reparatione veteris
sanctitatis, antiquique decoris in Ecclesiae corpore....Te oro
aque obsecro, Eugeni Beatissime, id opusculum relegas, inditumque
sacro pectori pietatis adfectum in opus apertae actionis exsuscites.'
I: 2 (2, 7 April 1431). For the circumstances of Bernard's composition of the De consideratione, see Jean Leclercq, Recueil d'études
sur saint Bernard et ses écrits (Roma, 1969) III, 117-35; and Elizabeth
Kennan, "The 'De consideratione' of Saint Bernard of Clairvaux and
the Papacy in the Mid-Twelfth Century: A Review of Scholarship,"
Traditio, XXIII (1967) 73-115.

19. II: 41 (2, April? 1426).

20. XVIII: 3 (12, 26 March 1433).

21. XIII: 23 (5, 11 October 1432); V: 12 (31, 1436?); V: 31 [c. 1424:
     see, Remigio Sabbadini, Storia e critica di testi latini, 2nd ed.
     (Padova, 1971) pp. 313-29; and VIII: 9 (11, 21 June 1424)].

22. XIII: 32 (16, 22 December 1435).

23. I: 3 (3, 1 May 1431).

24. I: 32 (32, 19 July 1438).

25. Gill, Eugenius IV, pp. 184-86.

26. Vespasiano da Bisticci, Vite di uomini illustri del secolo XV, edd.
     Paolo d'Ancona and Erhard Aeschlimann (Milano, 1951) p. 21.

27. Horace Mann, The Lives of the Popes in the Middle Ages, 2nd ed.
     (London, 1925) IX, 183-90; Ludwig Pastor, The History of the Popes
     from the Close of the Middle Ages, 6th ed. (St. Louis, 1938) I, 324-
     28.

28. Mann, IX, 138-42.

29. Joseph Gill, S. J., The Council of Florence (Cambridge, England,
     1959).

30. J. de Ghellinck, Le mouvement théologique du XIIe siècle, 2nd ed.
     (Bruges, 1948) pp. 221-49.

31. Mario Flecchia, "La traduzione di Burgundio Pisano delle Omelie di
     S. Giovanni Grisostomo sopra Matteo," Aevum, 26 (1952) 113-30.

32. VII: 9 (8, 27 November 1436).

33. XIII: 9 (10, 8 January 1437), IV: 29 (31, 11 January 1437), XIII:

17 (29, 7 April 1438), I: 31 (31, 13 April 1438).

34. Angelo Maria Bandini, Catalogus codicum latinorum Bibliothecae
     Mediceae Laurentianae (Florentiae, 1774-1777) IV, cols. 439-41.

35. Peter Partner, The Papal States under Martin V: The Administration
     and Government of the Temporal Power in the Early Fifteenth Century
     (London, 1958).

36. I: 7 (7, 14 August 1434).

37. Csi IV, 3.

A FIFTEENTH-CENTURY CISTERCIAN PROCESSIONAL

Sister Jane Patricia Freeland, CSJB

I am a second-hand scholar, dependent on others. When a medieval manuscript came my way, I said, 'How interesting!' and sent it back. Later, when I was working with medieval French, I remembered it and asked to see it again. Then I was immersed in it.

The owner was an old friend whose brother came back from England in 1936 with the book in his trunk, but he died before he explained it. Recognizing the abbreviations of medieval Latin, I began transcribing it for my own interest, and I found that the French used the same abbreviations. When it began to take form, I wrote the paleographic department of the Abbey of Saint Pierre at Solesmes, and it is they, with Dom Pierre Combe at their head, who have given me all the information for it. In 1968, I was able to take the book to them and leave it for twenty-four hours for their examination; whereupon they asked for the text. It was finally in shape for publication in their Etudes Grégoriennes of 1971.

The pages of the book are leather and measure 7 by 4 3/4 inches, with a leathered wooden cover only slightly larger, on the inside of which are pages of some older manuscript with versicles and psalms in a smaller hand than the rest of the book. One hundred of the 180 pages are given to the processional antiphons.

The monks of Saint Pierre have set the date as about 1450 because of the calligraphy--just the time of the wealth of tapestries from France displayed recently by the Metropolitan Museum. The house was a convent of nuns because of the mention of 'labbesse,' 'deux religieuses,' 'la malade'; the order Cistercian since the processional antiphons are those in many other Cistercian books, and Saint Benedict and Saint Bernard are invoked twice in the litany; and the place near Lyon because of the names of Saint Irenaeus and Saint Lambert.

Following the Cistercian custom, the feasts of Holy Week, Ascension and Corpus Christi, with five feasts of Our Lady, are allowed processions, and the chants are the expected ones. Dom Pierre Combe himself in an interview at Solesmes emphasized the remarkable uniformity of these chants throughout Europe for some four centuries. Exceptions are one for the Visitation:

> Magnificat dominum totum genus fidelium; concrepet
> armonica laude cohors angelica in marie gaudia.

For the Annunciation:

> Hec est dies quam fecit dominus; hodie dominus
> afflictionem populi sui respexit et redemptionem
> misit; hodie mortem quam femina intulit femina
> fugavit; hodie deus homo factus id quod fuit
> permansit et quod non erat assumpsit; ergo
> exordium nostre redemptionis devote recolamus
> et exultemus dicentes gloria tibi domine.

And three for the feast of Corpus Christi:

> Ave verum corpus cristi, qui nos tuo redemisti
> preciose sanguine.

> O sacramentum pietatis, o signum unitatis, o vinculum

caritatis, nos in via reficiens sub aliena specie.
Post presentis vite cursum refice nos in patria iam
revelata facie sine spetie media.

O panis vite, natus de virgine, qui te pura mente
sumentibus vitam gratie donas in via, da nobis in
patria vitam glorie sempiterne.

These are unique to this book.

The monks at Saint Pierre at first thought the book to come from
the sixteenth-century because of its good preservation. Many of the
chants begin with illuminated letters; others alternate red and blue
initials, as some of the contemporary tapestries at the Metropolitan
alternate red and blue backgrounds. The words are in black in a clear
hand, and the music is in black notes on four red lines of staff. All
rubrics are in red and written in French.

After the processional comes the ceremonial for the dying and the
dead. Directions are written in French, but the liturgical texts are
in Latin. Text and music are of the Cistercian ceremonial, but the rubrics show some variations. The patience of the assistants and of the
dying nun has caught the attention of my friends. After prayers and
the Creed, the rubric says, 'If she is still alive...' they are to say
a litany of sixty-three saints: Our Lady, angels, apostles, martyrs,
monks, holy virgins; the rubric repeats, 'If after this she is still
alive...' they are to say the seven penitential psalms. Again, 'If
after the psalms she is still alive...' they all go out.

Then comes what is definitely unique, and to my untutored mind the most interesting part. It is a long prayer in French in the first person, called a 'protestation' to be made at the death bed. 'Lord God Almighty, I have great joy in that I have been called to the Christian and Catholic faith. And I praise you for that you caused me to be born therein. Lord, I know that I have never employed my time in serving and honoring you as I ought, neither for my own profit nor for that of my neighbor, nor for my fulfilment, as I could have done, and of that I am displeased and repent....Lord, I put all my trust and hope in this holy and piteous death and passion which you paid as a most glorious offering for me. For which offering I beseech with all my power that you grant me grace to receive death joyfully, and joyfully to go to you.' There follows a passage of typical medieval penitence, and then comes the 'protestation': 'Lord God, I here and now declare for all time, past, present and to come, that I bear witness against anything that might come into my heart or into my thought, intending to keep myself from it and to preserve myself against all occasions which might happen to me in time and place if they should confront me. Firstly, to take heed of being in the power of sins that are not the truth, and renounce all justification of any sin whatsoever...)' After this is elaborated she says:

Secondly, Lord, I bear witness for all time, past,

present, and to come, against what might cause
me to presume that you, Lord, might owe me any
debt or have ever owed me anything, instead of
all the grace that you have done to me in time
past and do and still will do, from your kindness. And likewise I also bear witness against
all evil thoughts by which I might think that
you, Lord, were doing me wrong or acting for my
pleasure. Thirdly, Lord, I declare here and
now, for all time, past, present, and to come,
that I renounce all claim to any of my works,
however worthy or virtuous or fruitful on my
part....And fourthly I do now bear witness in
my common sense, memory, and understanding to
all the time which seems to be lost...because
of variability of the heart, illusion, dreaming,
lack of good sense, or because of illness or
emptiness of the head or of some other thing,
if I deviated in some way from the holy belief
and true faith in God and the holy church in
any manner contained in the articles of our
credence, especially in that which I had in
the convent or from the holy font of baptism
when I was baptized, when godfathers and god-
mothers answered for me saying credo. Which
response I accepted and in faith undertook....
Fifthly I further bear witness, Lord, if any
human creature acted against me or I against
him...that whatever right I may or might have,
I fully and wholly give into your hand, Lord,
to whom I owe so much...what I must surely
submit to you who have supported me so many
times through my wrongdoing and still do.
Sixthly, I affirm to you, Lord, who are my
only God, that I renounce all prayer I ever
made, make, or shall make, in which I demanded
or seemed to demand anything which was, is, or
will be displeasing to you....And in remembering
all that I have done wrongly or may do, as
said above, from this, Lord, be pleased to
guard me. And in submitting myself completely
to the holy phrases of the Pater Noster, be-
seeching you humbly with all my heart to unite
me with you in your holy will. And with these

> six protestations I wish to finish and to live,
> which thing, Lord, be pleased to grant me, and
> your grace at all times to love, serve, and
> honor you. Amen.

A friend who has spent her life on translations writes, 'I find this "declaration" or "affirmation" (or probably in older English quite correctly "protestation") touching, interesting, true. Surely it must originally have been the recorded saying of a saintly religious on her own death bed? And then used perhaps as what another would have wished to formulate but was unable? There is a sort of incoherence which does not entirely depend on pre-punctuation writing and only adds to the authenticity.'

There are still other devotions which seem to be original to the manuscript. The words of Saint Anselm in French for her who is going to die are in a catechetical form. 'O created soul, you who are going to die, are you joyful that you die in the Christian faith? And she should reply, Yes. Do you realize that you have never lived as you should? Yes. Are you repentant? Have you the will to amend if God gives you space of life? Do you believe that Jesus Christ, the son of God, suffered death for you?' etc., ending with a prayer offering the blessed passion of Christ to stand between herself and the wrath of God.

The rest are in Latin. One called 'Another devout prayer' begins with various psalm verses, then turns to Saint Mary and to the passion and blood of Christ. One called 'A very devout prayer to Our Lady'

begins with her titles, 'Ave, Maria, stella dei, mater alma, atque
semper virgo, felix celi porta....May you take that AVE as you took
it long ago from the mouth of Gabriel, bedewing us with peace, changing
the name of Eva....' It asks her prayers for the soul in necessity
at the hour of death, so that she may be taken up by the angels of light
and placed among the saints and elect of God, and that she may enjoy the
beatific vision without end. Then comes one named only 'Another prayer,'
addressed to the Blessed Virgin, mother of pity and grace; and another
to Our Lady. Then follows one to Saint Michael begging his powerful
defence from the infernal dragon. The final prayer is a triple one
to be used with three Pater Nosters and three Ave Marias with the note
that it is instituted by the pope. A few prayers follow in a later hand
which are of little interest to the paleographers.

My co-translator adds: 'How close all these things are in experi-
ence--math, language, logic, art, philosophy. Lord! Let me not get los
in the branches! I have a job to do.'

This Cistercian nun who so movingly makes her protestation for all
time, past, present, and to come, and looks joyfully toward her death,
was using the book in the yearly round of processions some five hundred
years ago, singing the chants whose music her careful hand has recorded
here. Someone has said, 'The difficulty of singing Gregorian music well
is a spiritual rather than a material one. Alongside the slow, labori-

ous work of mastering the chants, there goes the slow, laborious work of grace.'

Child
Desolate